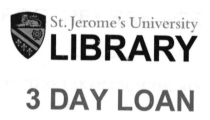

JOHN STEINBECK:

A Dictionary of his
Fictional Characters

edited by

Tetsumaro Hayashi

The Scarecrow Press, Inc.

Metuchen, N.J.   1976

Library of Congress Cataloging in Publication Data

Hayashi, Tetsumaro.
    John Steinbeck, a dictionary of his fictional
characters.

    Bibliography: p.
    1. Steinbeck, John, 1902-1968--Characters.
2. Steinbeck, John, 1902-1968--Dictionaries,
indexes, etc. I. Title.
PS3537.T3234Z7137   813'.5'2   76-14803
ISBN 0-8108-0948-6

Copyright © 1976 by Tetsumaro Hayashi

Printed in the United States of America

TO
WARREN FRENCH
AND
RELOY GARCIA,
WHO HAVE BEEN MY SCHOLARLY CONSCIENCE,
AS A TOKEN OF MY PROFOUND GRATITUDE

CONTENTS

ACKNOWLEDGMENTS

I am grateful to Miss Elizabeth R. Otis, McIntosh and Otis, for granting us permission to quote Steinbeck in this book; I also gratefully acknowledge The Viking Press for granting us permission to quote Steinbeck from the Viking editions of Steinbeck's 17 novels which are listed in Appendix I.

PREFACE

by Tetsumaro Hayashi

John Steinbeck knew, like Aristotle, that character is one of the essential elements of the drama of life and of the life of fiction. Certainly his memorable characters have assumed not only their own immortality, but that of their creator as well. They remain as appealing today--perhaps more so--as when his pen gave them birth. As a group, they comprise a unique and one of the most extensive galleries in American letters. Such characters as Doc (in Cannery Row and Sweet Thursday), Ma Joad, Tom Joad, and Jim Casy (in The Grapes of Wrath), Danny and his boys (in Tortilla Flat), Adam Trask, Cathy, Samuel Hamilton, and Lee (in East of Eden), and many others walk in their own literary cosmos. Against the dome of this cosmos Steinbeck has furnished his image of man, and within this world of the imagination the creative tensions of his fiction interplay: the theme of free will and the claims of fate, Steinbeck's holistic view of the world, his group-man concept, and the countless adventures for truth that have enticed readers for a good part of this century. Steinbeck's people are not only fictional characters, but unforgettable individuals and types, embodying extraordinary ideas and ideals, and defending with ruthless energy those values they embrace and honor. In a sense, they allow us to view ourselves, only one step removed from Steinbeck's metaphorical mirror, for the house of fiction has a real foundation.

Yet, although more than twenty book-length studies have been published on Steinbeck to date--most of them discussing Steinbeck's people--there is no dictionary of his characters. In contrast, at least three such dictionaries have been prepared on William Faulkner's characters: Harry Runyan's A Faulkner Glossary (1964); Margaret P. Ford's Who's Who in Faulkner (1963); and Robert W. Kirk's and Marvin's Faulkner's People: A Complete Guide and Index to Characters in the Fiction of William Faulkner (1963). The lack of comparable attention to Steinbeck, a Nobel prize laureate, first impelled me to prepare John Steinbeck: A Dictionary of His Fictional Characters and to serve as editor and project director. Mr. Robert Franklin, Executive Editor of Scarecrow Press, encouraged me and my colleagues, Professors Astro, Benton, Court, Morsberger, Peterson, and Slate, to complete this project.

A remarkably versatile artist, Steinbeck has created a variety of memorable fictional characters: good and evil; naive and cunning; brilliant and stupid; trustful and distrustful; righteous and wicked; talkative and shy; deceitful and realistic; and pleasant and obnoxious. No adjectives seem sufficient to categorize Steinbeck's creatures, so extraordinary is his capacity to create such diversified characters.

Thus, this dictionary attempts to provide Steinbeck readers an opportunity: 1) to see all of those interesting fictional characters; 2) to understand the nature of his characters and his characterizations; 3) to grasp the way in which these characters differ and yet to see how they are unified by a common bond of humanity. An attempt has been made to integrate all of the major and minor characters under one roof in what we hope will serve as a useful reference guide. This guide not only catalogs Steinbeck's characters but allows its users to determine, for example, how many "Elizabeths" appear in Cup of Gold; or refreshes the reader's memory on favorite characters whom he may remember only vaguely; or helps the reader track down and confirm those characters he wishes to quote in his lecture, sermon, or essay. The book, furthermore, attempts to aid the reader in determining names with different titles or ranks as well as the names of those belonging to a family or a clan; and, finally, the book can assist the reader in comparing a character in two works, such as Doc in Cannery Row and Doc in Sweet Thursday.

As editor/project director of this dictionary, I have encouraged each contributor to use his discretion concerning the treatment of those characters in his charge. The user of this dictionary will find, therefore, that character identifications vary, sometimes consisting of a serious literary discussion, sometimes merely telling what each character does or determining what his function is in the novel, etc. I believe that the dictionary itself thus allows us to grasp the dimension of Steinbeck's art. His characters are bound to speak the artist's mind, to suggest his preoccupations, and to represent his values and his prophetic vision.

In order to enhance the reference value of his dictionary, I have included Richard Astro's "John Steinbeck: A Biographical Perspective." Since biographical data are in great demand today among Steinbeck students, teachers, and reference librarians, and since current and dependable biographical data may not always be readily available until the publishing, in a few years, of Professor Jackson Benson's authorized biography of John Steinbeck, Astro's biography will serve as the key to essential biographical data. Because each fictional character is arranged in a dictionary form, I have provided "see references" for the reader's convenience. I have also added an up-to-date "Selected Bibliography" to inform students, teachers, and reference librarians of the scope of Steinbeck's published works and recent secondary sources. For greatest efficiency, the user of this dictionary should check the "Key to Abbreviations" before consulting the book.

Steinbeck's reputation now places him among the literary masters of modern literature, as the increased scholarly and popular attention proves. Conferences and seminars are being held regularly; for instance, the annual Steinbeck seminars and meetings which have been conducted in the United States, Japan, and elsewhere. Similarly, weekend seminars, such as that at the University of California at Berkeley in September 1974 as well as that at Oregon State University in May 1974, are held with increasing regularity. The biases against Steinbeck, held not so long ago in many universities, are quickly eroding (Harvard now accepts senior honors papers on Steinbeck, for instance), and there is every evidence that a reference work such as this can be an indispensable research and teaching tool for serious students, teachers, and reference librarians everywhere. Since Steinbeck's reputation depends in large part on his ability to create impressionable characters, the publication of this work fills a bothersome gap in Steinbeck studies.

Tetsumaro Hayashi
Ball State University
Muncie, Indiana
October 25, 1975

JOHN STEINBECK: A BIOGRAPHICAL PORTRAIT

by Richard Astro

John Ernst Steinbeck was born in Salinas, California,
on February 27, 1902, the son of John Ernst Steinbeck, Sr.
and Olive Hamilton. Certainly, the most important fact
about Steinbeck's early life was that he was born and brought
up in that long, narrow strip of fertile agricultural land called
the Salinas Valley, which is bordered on the east by the Gabilon Mountains and on the west by the Santa Lucia Range and
the Pacific Ocean. As a boy, Steinbeck roamed the valley,
invented names for grasses and secret flowers, smelled the
trees and the seasons, and observed the way the people
"looked and walked and smelled even."[1] He played on the
banks of the Salinas River which winds through the center of
the valley until at last it empties into the sea. Often, he
would travel the seventeen miles west to the great crescent
of Monterey Bay and explore the towns along its shore--
Monterey, Seaside, Pacific Grove and Carmel. On the way,
he would stop at the Corral de Tierra, a wrinkled bowl of
land where there is a special softness to life which surpasses
definition. And he would venture south of Carmel to the Big
Sur with its unending miles of sea-cliffs, its high mountain
peaks and its deep forests blanketed in thick wet fog.

It was in the Salinas Valley and the Corral de Tierra,
and on the Monterey Peninsula and the Big Sur that Steinbeck
found much of the material for his fiction. Of Mice and Men
(1937), In Dubious Battle (1936), and The Grapes of Wrath
(1939) are set in California's central agricultural valleys.
Tortilla Flat (1935), Cannery Row (1945), and Sweet Thursday (1954) take place along that narrow piece of land that
borders Monterey Bay. The Pastures of Heaven is Steinbeck's name for the Corral de Tierra. And the almost mystical quality of such works as To a God Unknown (1933) and
"Flight" reflect the strange, brooding nature of Big Sur.
Novelist Frederick Manfred has said that "it's [a] place that

1

writes your books. "[2] And while Manfred may be overstat-
ing the case, it is certainly true that the Salinas Valley and
the Monterey Peninsula were to Steinbeck what Yoknapatawpha
was to Faulkner. There is an acute consciousness of place
in Steinbeck's California fiction, a way of seeing which informs the design of his most successful fiction.

Steinbeck's father was for many years the Treasurer
of Monterey County and his mother taught school in several
Salinas Valley communities. From his father he won respect for his chosen career as a writer. From his mother
he learned to love books--not only the fiction of such current favorites as Donn Byrne and James Branch Cabell, but
also such classics as Dostoevski's Crime and Punishment,
Flaubert's Madame Bovary, Milton's Paradise Lost, and
Hardy's The Return of the Native. He also read the "great
books," the Bible and Apocrypha, the Greek and Roman his-
torians (especially Herodotus, Thucydides, and Julius Caesar) and Malory's Morte d'Arthur. As a man, he read less
fiction than he did as a boy, but his interests expanded to
include works of philosophy, anthropology, and psychology.

Though he was well read by the time he entered high
school, he was in every way a rounded student. He contributed to El Gabilon, the school paper, joined the track and
basketball teams, and served as president of the senior
class. His career as an undergraduate at Stanford University was less distinguished. He attended that university
intermittently for six years and never earned a degree.
Perhaps the most important thing that happened to him at
Stanford was the excellent instruction he received in short
story writing from Edith Ronald Mirrielees. She taught the
aspiring writer that the story writer's medium was the spot
light, not the search light. This point Steinbeck never for-
got, and it is his use of the "spot light" which accounts for
his ability to write from a distance where things are as they
are, because they must be. Steinbeck contributed stories
and poems to Stanford literary publications, none of which
intimates even a hint of the greatness he would later achieve.
But they do reflect his decision, as early as 1923, to become a writer.

When Steinbeck wasn't writing or attending classes at
Stanford, he labored at a variety of manual jobs, including
rancher, hod carrier, and cotton picker. He even worked
as a bench chemist in a Salinas Valley sugar factory. During the summer of 1923, he took courses at the Hopkins

Marine Station (the oceanographic research facility of Stanford University) in Pacific Grove. In a basic zoology class he was exposed to the ideas of William Emerson Ritter, whose biological theories were currently in vogue among West Coast scientists and naturalists. Ritter's organismal conception of life, the idea that wholes are greater than the sums of their parts, and that wholes work purposively on their parts, made a deep and lasting impression on Steinbeck and, when reinforced years later in his conversations with professional marine scientists, served as the philosophical basis of much of his fiction.

Sometime in late 1926, Steinbeck left California and went to New York to become a writer. By his own account, he spent the year doing various odd jobs (including a short stint as a reporter for the New York American) while he tried unsuccessfully to publish some stories. Within a year he retreated to California as a deck-hand on a ship via the Panama Canal.

Steinbeck's trip through the Canal did provide him with the setting for his first novel, Cup of Gold, which was published in 1929 by Robert M. McBride and Company. He had worked on it for two years. (Part of that time he spent as the caretaker of a Lake Tahoe resort which was owned by the mother of Webster F. Street, a Stanford friend.) The novel, which tells the story of the famous eighteenth-century buccaneer, Henry Morgan, failed to sell. And Steinbeck himself admitted that he wasn't proud of the book. "Outside of a certain lyric quality," he wrote, "there isn't much to it. I rather wish it had never been published."[3]

II

Nineteen-thirty was a watershed year in Steinbeck's development as a writer, though nothing more of his was published until 1932. For one thing, 1930 was the year when Steinbeck began his long association with Elizabeth Otis of the literary agency of McIntosh and Otis. More than his agent, Elizabeth Otis was Steinbeck's close friend. Most importantly, she believed in him and was certain that he would become a greater writer; she labored unceasingly to get his work published. Indeed, as Lewis Gannett notes, there were times when Steinbeck had more faith in his agents than he had in himself.[4] And Steinbeck's many letters to Elizabeth Otis in which he expresses his hopes, as well as his fears and anxieties, form what may be the best portrait of the artist on record.

Nineteen-thirty was also the year in which Steinbeck married Carol Henning of San Jose, a bright, free-wheeling, aggressive girl who was to exert a tremendous effect on his greatest fiction. Most importantly, it was in 1930 that Steinbeck met Edward F. Ricketts, the marine biologist who owned and operated the Pacific Biological Laboratory on the Monterey waterfront (a few blocks from the small cottage on 11th Street in Pacific Grove, which Steinbeck's father had provided for the newlyweds), and who was to become the novelist's closest personal and intellectual companion during the two decades of Steinbeck's greatest work. It was Ricketts who provided much of the matter which went to make up Steinbeck's mature view of man and the world. It was Ricketts who was to serve as the source of the personae in at least six of Steinbeck's novels (In Dubious Battle, The Grapes of Wrath, Cannery Row, Sweet Thursday, The Moon Is Down, and Burning Bright). And it was Ricketts who collaborated on Sea of Cortez (1941), which is one of the most important of Steinbeck's works.

Steinbeck's second novel, To a God Unknown (1933), grew from an unfinished play by Webster F. Street, who, after leaving Stanford, earned a law degree and joined a Monterey legal firm. Street's play, entitled "The Green Lady," was about a man who fell in love with a forest which he somehow identified in his mind with his daughter, and who killed himself when he walked into that forest when it was ablaze. Street's play contains troublesome hints of incest and a good many structural flaws which the author could not work out. And so he gave the manuscript to Steinbeck, telling him to do whatever he wished with it. Steinbeck had been at work on a 30,000-word manuscript entitled "Dissonant Symphony" and a cheap thriller called "Murder at Full Moon," neither of which interested him very much. He eagerly took Street's play, which he felt might be turned into a worthwhile novel. Steinbeck worked on it for several years (taking time off to write The Pastures of Heaven, which appeared in the fall of 1932), and the book was finally published by Robert Ballou in 1933.

To a God Unknown is Steinbeck's most unconventional novel, a fact which explains its poor critical reception and accounts for the fact that its sales, like those of Cup of Gold, were poor. Even Steinbeck recognized that the novel, which chronicles the life of Joseph Wayne--a visionary hero of god-like stature whose perceptions of universal wholeness enable him to redeem the land--might fare poorly. "It will probably be a hard book to sell," he wrote his agents. "Its characters are not 'home folks.' They make no more attempt at being human than the characters in the Iliad. Boileau insisted that only gods, kings, and heroes are worth writing about. I firmly believe that."[5]

There are passages in To a God Unknown describing the California landscape which can please almost every reader. But the novel's chief importance lies in Steinbeck's presentation of his developing holistic world-view (gleaned largely through conversations with Ed Ricketts) and his statement of his belief in man's ability to "break through" to an understanding of wholeness, and apply the knowledge of his vision to benefit the natural order. It is little wonder that the novel was five years in the writing. For by expanding Street's unfinished play about a man's strange fascination with a forest into an elaborate morphology of "breaking through," supported by a comprehensive structure of myth and symbol, Steinbeck outlined the thematic base of much of his future writing. To a God Unknown is not a flawless novel, but it greatly surpasses Cup of Gold in characterization, invention, and sweep of imagination.

Much has been said about the impact of Rickett's ideas on Steinbeck's most important novels and short stories; critics have pointed to how Ricketts' ideas about "breaking through," his gospel of what he called "non-teleological thinking," and his ecological view of life form the philosophical substructure of Steinbeck's mature fiction. Indeed, I have written a book on the subject in which I conclude that Steinbeck combined Ricketts' broad-visioned and compelling metaphysic with a personal belief in the value of social action, and so fused part and ethics, science and philosophy to define and portray the uniquely complex nature of the contemporary human experience.

At the same time, it must be pointed out that there were other forces at work on Steinbeck's developing philosophical and social consciousness during the early 1930s. The Monterey Peninsula--often called the Seacoast of Bohemia-- was a haven for intellectual types during those years, and Steinbeck learned much from many of these people. Evelyn Reynolds Ott, a psychiatrist and former student of Carl Jung, established a practice in Carmel and became friendly with the

novelist. From Dr. Ott, Steinbeck learned the principles of
Jungian psychology which he used to advantage in a number
of novels and short stories. Joseph Campbell, the famous
comparative mythologist whose theory of "the hero with a
thousand faces" explains many of the behavior patterns of
Joseph Wayne in To a God Unknown, was a close friend of
Steinbeck during the early 1930s. Indeed, Campbell read an
early version of To a God Unknown and cautioned Steinbeck
against excessive philosophical speculation unclothed with a
believable story line.[6] From Richard Albee, a former student of philosopher John Elof Boodin at UCLA, Steinbeck
learned the current trends in American philosophical thought
--and there are echoes of Boodin's philosophy in such Steinbeck works as In Dubious Battle and The Grapes of Wrath.
And at Tor House, near Carmel, Robinson Jeffers had written his famous poem, "Roan Stallion," in which he defines
the idea of "breaking through" which, of course, underscores
the action in To a God Unknown.

The stories in The Pastures of Heaven (1932) grew
from tales told to Steinbeck about the follies of the people of
the Corral de Tierra by Beth Ingels, a Monterey newspaper-
woman and a long-time resident of that valley. Actually,
while The Pastures of Heaven sold poorly, it was Steinbeck's
first novel that was accorded a favorable critical reception.
For in this collection of stories about human fallibility--
about how man's illusions can turn the pastures of heaven into the pastures of self-deception--Steinbeck's writing is simple
and moving, and his characterization is superb.

The same is true of many of the short stories Steinbeck wrote during the early 1930s which were later collected
and published in The Long Valley (1938). Except for the four
sections of The Red Pony, there is no unifying thematic
thread or story line which connects the eleven stories in The
Long Valley. Rather, what unifies the volume is Steinbeck's
ability to communicate to his readers a genuine sense of life
lived beyond the confines of their own experience. And in
stories such as "Flight," "Johnny Bear," "The Harness,"
"The Chrysanthemums," and "The White Quail," Steinbeck
examines the hopes, dreams, and fears of simple people with
a unique sensitivity toward the human condition.

Actually Steinbeck's first notable success as a writer
was Tortilla Flat (1935), on which he began work in early
1933 after returning to the Monterey Peninsula from a brief
sojourn in the Eagle Rock section of Los Angeles, where he

had tried without success to write a series of articles of local interest. The publishing history of Tortilla Flat is well known: publisher Pascal Covici visited a bookstore in Chicago owned by Ben Abramson who pressed him to read To a God Unknown and The Pastures of Heaven. Covici liked what he read and contacted Steinbeck's agents in New York whom he knew were trying to sell a new novel by the Californian. Tortilla Flat, which had been turned down by a number of publishers, was finally issued by Covici-Friede in 1935, nearly two years after Steinbeck finished work on it. Covici and Steinbeck became close friends, and when Covici joined the editorial office of the Viking Press in 1938, he took Steinbeck's work with him. Steinbeck never had another publisher.

Steinbeck's stories about the paisanos of Tortilla Flat made so much money (by comparison with his earlier books) and received such favorable praise, that the book's success surprised even Steinbeck. At the same time, the novelist was puzzled (before and after publication) by the inability of readers and critics to identify the novel's theme. Steinbeck told his agents in 1934:

> The book has a very definite theme. I thought it was clear enough. I had expected that the plan of the Arthurian cycle would be recognized. Even the incident of the Sangreal in the search of the forest is not clear enough, I guess. The form is that of the Malory version--the coming of Arthur, and the mystic quality of owning a house, the forming of the Round Table, the adventures of the knights and finally, the mystic translation of Danny. The main issue was to present a little known and to me delightful people. Is not this cycle or story or theme enough? Perhaps it is not enough because I have not made it clear enough. Then I must make it clearer. What do you think of putting in an interlocutor, who between each incident interprets the incident, morally, aesthetically, historically, but in the manner of the paisanos themselves? This would give the book much the appeal of the Gesta Romanorum, those outrageous tales with monkish morale appended, or of the Song of Solomon in the King James Version, with the delightful chapter headings which go to prove that the Shulamite is in reality Christ's Church. It would not be as sharp as this, of course. But the little dialogue would at least make clear the form of the book, its tragi-comic

theme, and the strong but different philosophic-
moral system of these people. [7]

Fortunately, as Lewis Gannett suggests, Steinbeck decided against using an interlocutor. [8] And the public loved
the stories about Danny and his paisanos (most of which were
told to Steinbeck by schoolteacher Susan Gregory or inspired
by the antics of a famous Monterey dropout, a picaresque
remittance man on whom one of the leading characters is
based) whether or not they recognized the Arthurian cycle
which carries the message of the feeble talisman of escape:
that there is nothing in the "philosophic-moral system" of the
paisanos that will enable them to survive.

III

In contrast to Steinbeck's earliest fictional efforts,
The Pastures of Heaven and Tortilla Flat contain the elements
which pinpoint Steinbeck's greatest achievement as a writer:
his ability to portray human aspiration alongside of human
fallibility; his rendering of the idea that we all long to, yet
somehow cannot live in "the pastures of heaven." More and
more, Steinbeck was becoming aware of what he would later
call "the tragic miracle of consciousness,"[9] the realization
that man is not always able to attain the object of his heart's
desire. And while, when writing To a God Unknown, Steinbeck may have believed Boileau's thesis that only gods, kings,
and heroes are worth writing about, he was beginning to realize that "present day kings aren't very inspiring, the gods
are on a vacation, and about the only heroes left are the scientists and the poor."[10]

It is the scientists and the poor who are the heroes of
Steinbeck's most important fiction. First in Of Mice and
Men (1936), that memorable parable about man's voluntary
acceptance of responsibility for his fellow man--his realization that man owes something to man--Steinbeck's heroes are
two itinerant ranch hands who demonstrate the frail nature of
primeval innocence as they attempt to transform an impossible dream into reality. This small book, which was a Book-
of-the-Month-Club selection and made the novelist a national
figure, is one of Steinbeck's most impressive works. For in
it, he solicits our sympathy for the weak and feeble-minded
while simultaneously showing how our world is a hard one;
how a simple pastoral vision of a farm with "a little house
an' a couple of acres" with "rabbits" is incongruous with the

facts of modern life. At the same time, through his presentation of the character of Slim, the jerkline skinner and
"prince of the ranch" who moves "with a majesty only
achieved by royalty and master craftsmen,"[11] Steinbeck asserts the inherent superiority of the simple human virtues to
the accumulation of financial wealth, of life-asserting to life-
denying.

Stylistically, Of Mice and Men is a masterpiece. It
shows Steinbeck as an original stylist, developing a medium
of expression uniquely his own. Indeed, the power of the
novelette derives from Steinbeck's ability to tell a story about
how the best laid schemes of mice and men "gang aft a'gley"
without explaining why. Originally, Steinbeck planned to call
his story "Something That Happened," and though he wisely
changed his mind, he tells his story of something that happened from a nonblaming point of view. Indeed, Steinbeck is
at his best as a writer of fiction when he writes from what
T. K. Whipple calls "the middle distance," in which he
places his characters "not too close nor too far away," so
that "we can see their performances with greatest clarity and
fullness."[12]

It is Steinbeck's ability to write in "the middle distance" which also accounts for the particular excellence of
the first of his political works, In Dubious Battle (1936),
which records a violent encounter involving strikers, Communist organizers, and land owners in a California fruit or-
chard. At the same time, Steinbeck's nonblaming point of
view makes In Dubious Battle a particularly brutal book, a
fact that Steinbeck acknowledged when he indicated in 1935
that it contained "no author's moral point of view." He said
that he had tried to write the novel "without looking through
the narrow glass of political and economic preconception" and
was not concerned with his protagonists as communists or
capitalists but rather as humans "subject to the weaknesses
of humans and to the greatnesses of humans."[13] Yet, despite Steinbeck's fears that In Dubious Battle would be attacked by both sides, it was a critical success and, as Peter
Lisca accurately notes, remains today as the best strike novel in our literature.[14]

It is true, of course, that In Dubious Battle marks a
kind of bottom in Steinbeck's political pessimism because,
while he shows that the kind of power which falls into the
hands of those who use raw violence is nihilistic and self-
defeating, he offers no alternative solutions which might

ameliorate the tragic predicament of a group of downtrodden
farm workers. As William Appleman Williams points out,
we were a traumatized society in the early 1930s, and in
In Dubious Battle Steinbeck encapsulates our passivity, our
inability to seek meaningful cures for our national depression. [15]

At the same time, by maintaining an objective stance
in which everything in the book is learned from the actions
and conversations of contrasting characters (Mac and Jim on
one side, Doc Burton on the other), within a strict enclosure
of the unity of time, Steinbeck presents a hard-headed analysis of two world-views, both of which are inadequate to deal
effectively with the explosive labor problems in California's
agricultural valleys. There are no heroes in In Dubious
Battle, though Steinbeck surely enlists our sympathy for the
poor and the dispossessed, and he identifies at least in part
with the scientist (Doc Burton) who translates many of Steinbeck's scientific principles of life (and particularly the organismal conception of W. E. Ritter which Steinbeck converted into what, in an as-yet unpublished essay, he called the
"Argument of Phalanx") into meaningful social and political
terms. At the same time, he shows how Burton (who is
patterned on Ed Ricketts) cannot work to alleviate the plight
of the pickers any more than the ruthless party organizers
can. Steinbeck's commitment is not to causes but to people,
and neither Mac and Jim nor Burton can work to achieve a
realistic solution to the strikers' dilemma.

Steinbeck's interest in California's agricultural problems led him to accept assignments to write an essay commissioned by Nation ("Dubious Battle in California," [1936])
and a series of articles for the San Francisco News ("The
Harvest Gypsies," [1936]). He and Carol purchased an old
house in Los Gatos, and in early 1937, after the success of
Of Mice and Men had enabled him to do some traveling, he
went to New York and then to England and Ireland. Upon his
return to the United States in August, he visited George
Kauffman's farm in Pennsylvania, where he finished work on
the stage version of Of Mice and Men which ran successfully
the following winter.

Not even waiting for production on Of Mice and Men
to begin, Steinbeck went to Detroit where he bought a car,
and then to Oklahoma where he joined a group of landless
tenant farmers on their trek to California. That trip was
the genesis of what would become his epic account of the

dispossessed and the disinherited, The Grapes of Wrath
(1939), which is without question Steinbeck's most ambitious
as well as his most successful novel. First, there was a
false start called L'Affaire Lettuceburg which Steinbeck
called "an experiment in trickery" and a "treacherous
book."[16] Then there was an offer from Life to do a story
about the migrants, which Steinbeck refused because he felt
he could not make money "on these people ... the suffering
is too great for me to cash in on it."[17] And there were the
days and weeks spent in Okie Hoovervilles, from the dust
fields of Oklahoma to the fertile California valleys, listening
to men talk and watching them work. There was the needed
help from people like Tom Collins of the Farm Security Administration, from Eric Thompson and George Hedley, and
most of all from Carol. And the result was the Pulitzer
prize-winning novel about the struggles of a band of dispossessed Oklahoma tenant farmers in which Steinbeck says just
about everything he knows and feels about man and the world
in which he lives. His study of the Joads' pilgrimage to California contains Steinbeck's belief in an ordered universe in
which all living things are inherently related, his reliance upon holistic and organismal thought as the best method of per-
ceiving this unity, and his Jeffersonian belief that land is the
greatest source of human freedom and enrichment.

Steinbeck's spokesman in the novel is the ex-preacher,
Jim Casy, a mystical philosopher-scientist who recognizes
that all that lives is holy, and through his disciple, Tom
Joad, employs the principles of his vision to alleviate the
plight of the disinherited. Casy comes to understand the nature of the group organism; he recognizes that the migrants
must regard themselves as a part of the whole; he replaces
superficial distinctions of good and bad, right and wrong with
a soundly-conceived gospel of direct social action. Through
Casy, Steinbeck assumes a believable theory of human society in which man is viewed not only in relation to the universe (as is the case in To a God Unknown) but also in relation to the human community. The migrants' needs give
birth to concepts and finally to action. They key into a moving, self-fulfilling social unit in which the break could never
come as long as fear could turn to wrath. Coming at the
end of a decade of despair and disillusionment, The Grapes
of Wrath is Steinbeck's clearest statement of faith in the enduring greatness of the human species; in man's ability to
suffer and die for a concept, for a belief. It contains his
ringing affirmation of man's ability to work, to create beyond
the single need. And it contains his intuitive recognition that

man, "unlike any other thing organic or inorganic in the universe, grows beyond his work, walks up the stairs of his concepts, emerges ahead of his accomplishments."[18]

IV

Within months of the publication of The Grapes of Wrath, Ed Ricketts' important ecological study of the marine invertebrates of the littoral of the central Pacific coast (Between Pacific Tides) was published by the Stanford University Press. Both men felt the need for some breathing space, and they agreed to work together on a small handbook about the marine life of San Francisco Bay. Ricketts planned the format and, with Steinbeck, made collecting trips to Tomales Bay and Moss Beach late in 1939 and early in 1940. Steinbeck wrote an as-yet unpublished preface which runs just less than 2,000 words and is valuable in that it shows that he, like Ricketts, viewed marine life ecologically. Indeed, Steinbeck noted in his preface that it is as pointless to study tidepool life by solitary investigations of individual organisms as it is to study family patterns in a large city simply by examining one family in that city.

Early in 1940, the San Francisco Bay project was abandoned in favor of a larger venture to the largely uncharted regions of the Gulf of California. Though Steinbeck was interested in the project, his primary reason for financing it was to enable Ricketts to continue his investigations of the Pacific littoral which he had begun so successfully in Between Pacific Tides. With the help of Webster Street, Steinbeck chartered Tony Berry's purse seiner, the "Western Flyer," and on March 11, 1940, Steinbeck, Ricketts and a crew of five (Carol Steinbeck made the entire trip, though she was never mentioned in the published account of the journey) sailed from Monterey harbor down the west coast of California and the Baja Peninsula to Cabo San Lucas, north to La Paz and Loreto, east to Guaymas, and then back to Monterey where they arrived six weeks later on April 20.

Soon after their return, Steinbeck began work on a narrative of the trip which he wrote from a journal kept by Ricketts. He took time off during the summer of 1940 to accompany documentarian Herbert Kline to Mexico in order to do a film study of rural health problems in that country. The result of that trip was The Forgotten Village, which Kline made into an award-winning film. Steinbeck was also preoccupied with his deteriorating marriage during 1940 and 1941, and this fact, combined with the difficulty Ricketts had in identifying all the specimens collected on the expedition, held off publication of Sea of Cortez: A Leisurely Journal of Travel and Research until December of 1941.

Sea of Cortez is among the most important if least understood works in Steinbeck's entire canon. The phyletic catalog, which makes up the bulk of the book, is a comprehensive ecological treatment of life in the faunal provinces of the Gulf of California. And the narrative is a true collaboration by two men who wished to "see everything our eyes would accommodate, to think what we could, and, out of our seeing and thinking, to build some kind of structure in modeled imitation of the observed reality."[19] The "structure" that Steinbeck and Ricketts build contains factual reports about the animals collected as well as philosophical reflections about "breaking through," the holistic structure of life, the organismal conception and "non-teleological thinking." It also contains highly serious (at times homiletic) statements about birth and death, history, navigation, and the virtues of the scientific method, sandwiched between less solemn commentaries about temperamental outboard motors, aphrodisiacs, and drinking. The "shape" of the book, as the authors remark about the trip itself, is "an integrated nucleus" from which "strings of thought stretched into every reachable reality."[20] And if Sea of Cortez is read in proper perspective (that is, with the recognition that Ricketts contributed much to the narrative section as well as to the phyletic catalog), those "strings of thought" can serve as a valuable index to the thematic design of much of Steinbeck's fiction. At the same time, it is also important as a biological record firmly anchored in scientific fact, "bright with sun and wet with sea water" and "the whole crusted over with exploring thought."[21]

Just days after Sea of Cortez was published, Pearl Harbor was attacked and Steinbeck quickly offered his writing talents to the State Department. In Sea of Cortez, he and Ricketts identified the coming war as a conflict "no one wants to fight, in which no one can see a gain...."[22] But the events at Pearl Harbor evidently convinced him that the role of the detached observer was no longer tenable.

Steinbeck's first contribution to the war effort was Bombs Away (1942) which is little more than propaganda for the Army Air Corps and which he wrote after visiting several training bases with photographer-flyer Jon Swope. Indeed,

even before the book was published, Steinbeck had some regrets about having written it. In 1943, he spent several
months in the European theatre as a roving correspondent for
the New York Herald Tribune and sent back dispatches which
were published at regular intervals and later collected and
published as Once There Was a War (1958). Most of Steinbeck's European reports (many of which stress human interest) were, by Steinbeck's own admission, "period pieces,"
"written in haste, and telephoned across the sea to appear
as immediacies." In 1958, Steinbeck reflected on these
pieces and identified the attitudes as "archaic," the impulses
"romantic," and "perhaps the whole body of work untrue and
warped and one-sided."[23]

Steinbeck did write two serious works which grew
from his war experiences. His story for Lifeboat, which
Alfred Hitchcock made into one of the more successful movies
of 1944 (thanks to fine performances by Tallulah Bankhead
and William Bendix), depicts a group of shipwrecked Americans (as well as the Captain of the German U-boat who sank
their ship) in a very small boat on a very big ocean and
shows how the free (if disorganized) Americans--mere flesh
and blood mortals--can resist the iron will of the Nazi mind.
In The Moon Is Down (1942), a highly controversial play-
novelette about the invasion of a small Scandinavian village
by a group of brutal, time-minded invaders, Steinbeck dramatized the conflict between free men and herd men, and gave
the ultimate advantage to the former. The book, and particularly Steinbeck's play (which opened in March, 1942), was
bitterly criticized, largely on the grounds that Steinbeck had
been soft on the Nazis. Nevertheless, it was translated into
many languages and was popular among resistance movements
throughout Europe. The king of Norway decorated Steinbeck
for it, and undoubtedly part of Steinbeck's enduring reputation in Scandinavia rests upon his celebration of the inherent
dignity as well as the resourcefulness of the townspeople in
The Moon Is Down.

V

Steinbeck's war experiences left him exhausted. He
had always loved to travel, and during the 1930s planned a
good many more trips than his finances permitted him to
take. Always, though, there were those long quiet periods
when there was time for reading, for long talks with Ricketts and other friends, for the kind of self-renewal a writer

must experience if he is to continue to be productive.   But
World War II changed all that.   First, he and Carol broke
up and Steinbeck married a singer named Gwen Conger in a
small ceremony in New Orleans.   Then, for two years,
Steinbeck was constantly on the move, at home only in a New
York apartment away from old friends, forced by personal
patriotism or by the urging of others into writing assignments
less attractive than he might have hoped.

Little wonder then that his first post-war book was,
at least on the surface, a nostalgic tribute to Monterey, to
Ed Ricketts (of whom he saw nothing during most of the war),
and to a group of simple indolent souls who, in a world
ruled by "tigers with ulcers, rutted by strictured bulls and
scavenged by blind jackals,"[24] still savor "the hot taste of
life."   Steinbeck wrote Cannery Row (1945) in a six-week
stretch early in 1944.   It is, as he suggests, "a mixed-up
book" with "a pretty general ribbing in it."[25]   And yet, beneath Steinbeck's casual tone and the book's ostensible good,
clean fun is the novelist's evaluation of man's unsuccessful
attempt to escape the reality of modern life.   There is no
doubt that Steinbeck enjoys the pleasurable world of Doc and
Mack and the boys, but his vision is not so naive that he is
blinded to its transiency.   When Malcolm Cowley suggested
that Cannery Row might be a "poisoned cream puff" thrown
at "respectable society," Steinbeck replied that if Cowley
would read it again, he would find how very poisoned the
cream puff really was.   And while Steinbeck's surface venom
is an indictment of what we call the "civilized world," his
underlying poison consists of his admission that while Doc is
the heroic scientist, and while Mack and the boys are "the
Virtues, the Graces and the Beauties," they live in a vacuum, in a fantasy-world beset on all sides by an ever-ex-
panding materialistic society which will eventually seal their
doom.

Even before Cannery Row was published, Steinbeck
was at work on a novelette to be called "The Pearl of La
Paz," which was based upon a legend he and Ricketts heard
during their trip to the Sea of Cortez, about a poor fisherman who found a great pearl which he thought would guarantee him wealth and happiness but which almost destroys him
before he wisely throws it back into the sea.   Steinbeck's
story first appeared in Woman's Home Companion as "The
Pearl of the World" in December of 1945.   It was finally
published in book form in 1947 as The Pearl, and it was
some years later that Steinbeck finally noted that it was
"gathering some friends."[26]

"I tried to write it as folklore," Steinbeck said of
The Pearl, "to give it that set-aside, raised-up feeling that
all folk stories have."[27]   And The Pearl differs from Cannery Row in that it is a simple, lyrical tale which Steinbeck
called "a black and white story like a parable."[28]   But because the parable is about the search for happiness and the
nature of man's need to choose between the benign natural
life and the frantic, self-centered modern world, Steinbeck's
central thematic concerns are the same in The Pearl as in
Cannery Row.   In essence, The Pearl contains Steinbeck's
definition of the modern dilemma: it is a parable of the
agony involved in man's recognition of the vanity of human
wishes.

This same theme pervades Steinbeck's next novel,
The Wayward Bus, which was not published until 1947 although Steinbeck had been thinking of it for some time. Like
The Pearl and Cannery Row, it is concerned with an exami-
nation of the assumptions which underlie post-war American
society, and it contains the novelist's belief that man be able
to overcome his pettiness and self-interest and act in behalf
of the human community.   Assuming as its epigraph a quota-
tion from Everyman, The Wayward Bus is a complex allegory of man's wayward journey through the modern world in
which a diverse group of men and women (thrown together
on an old bus bound from one California highway to another)
are forced by circumstances to re-examine themselves and
inspect the way in which they relate to one another.   Before
the end of their trouble-filled journey, they either destroy or
in some way redeem themselves, depending upon their willingness to alter and re-channel their thinking.

Though the early post-war years were busy and productive ones for Steinbeck the novelist, they were difficult
years for Steinbeck the man.   His marriage to Gwen Conger
deteriorated and finally broke up.   What complicated matters
more was that Steinbeck was deeply concerned over the future of his two sons, Tom and John IV.   Then, in May of
1948, Steinbeck's long-time friend and confidante, Ed Ricketts, was killed in a freakish car-train accident near his laboratory in Pacific Grove.   Steinbeck heard about the accident at his home in New York (after the war he and Gwen
settled permanently in a town house on the upper East Side
of the city) and was emotionally crushed.   He flew to California for the funeral and to clear up some of Ricketts' personal affairs, and friends of both men remember that he
acted as if the flesh had been torn from his body.   Initially,

Steinbeck found it difficult to adjust to the fact of his friend's
death, and back in New York, disbelief turned first to anger
and then to a deep sense of personal loss. Gradually, though,
as the impact of the immediate thing dulled, Steinbeck
claimed to be developing a new feeling of life again. He
wrote friends in late May of growing new tissue; of having a
new energy that would force him to work as he had not
worked in years. [29]

Actually, Steinbeck had done little writing since the
summer of 1946, when he completed work on The Wayward
Bus. There was a trip to Russia in 1947 with photographer
Robert Capa which resulted in their collaboration on A Russian Journal (1948), an interesting essay about Russian life
interspersed with some unusually fine photographs by Capa.
As might be expected, Steinbeck's text celebrates the Russian people, and particularly the simple farmers of Georgia
and the Ukraine, while denouncing the Russian bureaucracy
with its regimentation and its restraints on individual freedom. It was some time after Ricketts' death before Steinbeck really began new work. He did write a film script for
The Red Pony and started another for a story of the Mexican agrarian reformer, Emiliano Zapata, in whose life and
career he had long been interested. And he was doing background work on what he claimed would be his biggest novel,
to be called Salinas Valley.

But it was not until mid-1949 that Steinbeck really
began to feel that his life was turning around. And even
then, he admitted later, he often felt that "every life force
was shriveling. Work was non-existent.... The wounds
were gangrenous and mostly I didn't give a damn."[30] What
changed things was a remarkable woman named Elaine Scott
whom he met on Memorial Day in 1949 and whom he later
married. She filled the void, and Steinbeck went back to
work with a new enthusiasm.

First there was the completed script for his study of
Zapata which Elia Kazan made into one of the best films of
1952. Then there was the reissue of the narrative section
of Sea of Cortez, prefaced by a moving tribute to Ed Ricketts, a tribute which, though Steinbeck distorts some of the
facts about Ricketts' life, testifies to the strength of their
friendship and to the impact of Ricketts' ideas on Steinbeck's
fiction. There was a third experiment in the genre of the
play-novelette, a parable on the theme of sterility entitled
Burning Bright, which was produced by Rodgers and Ham-

merstein in October of 1950 and was a miserable failure.
And there was a great deal of work on "the big book," in
which Steinbeck planned to tell what he called "perhaps the
greatest story of all--the story of good and evil, of strength
and weakness, of love and hate, of beauty and ugliness."[31]

Renamed East of Eden in the summer of 1951, Steinbeck's "big book" was published in 1952. What began as the
novelist's "story of my country and the story of me"[32] had
been transformed into a sprawling study of the presence of
good and evil in the world (through a symbolic representa-
tion of the Cain-Abel story) and a decisive statement of
man's free will by which the individual can purposefully as-
sert his creative impulse. Steinbeck's authorial role as a
moralist in East of Eden, in which he makes right and wrong,
good and evil into moral absolutes, does constrict the range
of his vision. On the other hand, the novel as a whole
seems almost a paean to man and earth in which Steinbeck
once again asserts his belief in man's potential greatness despite his fallibility, so that "although East of Eden is not
Eden, it is not insuperably far away."[33]

During the composition of East of Eden, Steinbeck
wrote Pat Covici that he felt his duty as a writer was to
"lift up, to extend, to encourage. If the written word has
contributed anything at all to our developing species and our
half-developed culture," said Steinbeck, "it is this: Great
writing has been a staff to lean on, a mother to consult, a
wisdom to pick up stumbling folly, a strength in weakness
and a courage to support sick cowardice."[34] And in East of
Eden, as in virtually all of his novels, Steinbeck is a novelist of affirmation as he celebrates man's ability to master
his destiny as he is given "the glory of the choice" between
right and wrong, good and evil. To the end of his life,
Steinbeck refused "to view our times with professional despair"[35] or surrender to the popular disease of acute literary
pessimism. He asserted the greatness of man's moral will
which, he felt, would insure the slow, painful progress of
the species.

Steinbeck's career as a writer of fiction tailed off
markedly after East of Eden. Perhaps he meant seriously
his insistence in 1951 that there was nothing beyond East of
Eden since it contains "all in the world I know" and has in
it everything "of which I am capable--all styles, all techniques, all poetry--."[36] Rather, though, it seems that
Steinbeck wrote less in the 1950s because he did more. He

had become a New Yorker and had to satisfy his love of
things rural in Sag Harbor (a sort of "Cannery Row East")
where he and Elaine purchased a summer home. The Stein-
becks traveled widely in Europe and for a time even considered moving to London.

Out of those trips came such minor pieces as "How
to Fish in French," "Vegetable War" (a critique of the way
the English cook Brussels sprouts), and "Yank in Europe,"
a defense of the behavior of American travelers in Paris.
There was also a pleasant short story entitled "The Affair at
7 Rue de M---," which tells of his son John's escape from
a cancerous blob of bubble gum. Finally, there was a light-
hearted moral fable about French politics entitled The Short
Reign of Pippin IV (1957), which, as the dust jacket announces, tells "what happens to a retiring middle aged astronomer suddenly drafted to rule the unruly French...."
Finally, Steinbeck spent eleven months in England during
1959 researching Malory, and did some writing on the Arthurian legends which, unfortunately, has not been published.

Steinbeck's only full-length fictional work to be published after East of Eden in the 1950s and set in the United
States is Sweet Thursday (1954), which on the surface seems
a sentimental and sapless remake of Cannery Row. The fact
is, however, that Sweet Thursday (adapted by Rodgers and
Hammerstein into a play entitled Pipe Dream, which opened
a successful run in the fall of 1955) is among Steinbeck's
least understood novels. For though the setting and most of
the characters are similar to those in Cannery Row, the novel is less a look back at a lost past than it is a bittersweet
lament for the death of an era Steinbeck cherished. And in
his portrayal of Doc (who, like the Doc of Cannery Row, is
based upon Ed Ricketts) as a character more acted upon than
acting, and whose fate as the reluctant bridegroom of a reformed whore seems less tragic than pathetic, Steinbeck once
and for all is laying down the ghost of his closest friend.
Sweet Thursday ends with Doc's leaving Cannery Row, with
the Row itself limping into an uncertain future, and with
Steinbeck heading east toward New York and Paris where in
his remaining years he will write but two more novels and
two books of nonfiction, all of which are best described as
footnotes in terms of his career as a whole.

One of those novels is The Short Reign of Pippin IV
which Steinbeck himself admitted would probably have a very
limited audience. The other is The Winter of Our Discon-

tent (1960), an analytical and occasionally perceptive study of what Steinbeck saw as the moral vacuum in contemporary American society. The Winter of Our Discontent--with its references to Shakespeare's Richard III, the life of Ethan Allen (the Green Mountain patriot) and Eliot's The Waste Land --portrays man's fall from grace and the replacement of all meaningful codes of morality and human decency by a more lucrative fast-buck philosophy. It is, as Reloy Garcia notes, a record "of the country's malaise, of the country's unfulfilled dreams and unmet obligations, and of what happens to principles, to dreams, and to ideals in the care of moneylenders."[37]

Though The Winter of Our Discontent was Steinbeck's last work of fiction, the novelist remained active during the last eight years of his life. His long-time scientific interest, in hibernation since Ed Ricketts' death ended plans for a trip to explore the fauna of the Queen Charlotte Islands in northern British Columbia, was re-activated. He joined Willard Basom's Mohole project in 1962 and wrote an interesting and fact-filled account of the travels of "the elite and motley crew" of Cuss I for Life.[38] Elaine Steinbeck has noted that her husband wanted to go on a scientific expedition to the Great Barrier Reef, and in 1965 he considered accompanying Bascom on another scientific expedition to South Africa.[39]

When Lyndon B. Johnson committed American troops to aid South Vietnam, Steinbeck not only supported the move but also traveled to Vietnam as a correspondent for Newsday. He sent back occasional pieces about the American soldiers, which in tone and subject matter resembled his World War II dispatches for the New York Herald Tribune. But Vietnam was an unpopular war and Steinbeck incurred the wrath of his liberal admirers who concluded that he had abandoned his depression-style, radical militancy. By mid-1967 Steinbeck had changed his mind about the war and even told his agent, Elizabeth Otis, that the people running it didn't understand what they had undertaken, and so were leading the country into a quicksand.[40] Unfortunately, there are no published statements which record this shift in Steinbeck's thinking.

Steinbeck did write two works of nonfiction during the 1960s. The first is the very popular Travels with Charley in Search of America (1962), which is an account of Steinbeck's travels across the United States in a camper with his French Poodle, Charley. The other is America and Americans (1966), an extended essay about America interspersed with some unusually fine photographs by some of America's best photographers. Neither is an important work in comparison with Steinbeck's greatest fiction. Yet both contain memorable passages about Steinbeck's love of the country and its people, and about his faith in the ultimate progress of the human species. Steinbeck's optimism is occasionally betrayed by a feeling of bewilderment toward a world he no longer seems to understand fully. Indeed, Steinbeck looks at the world around him and attempts to make sense out of the nonsense he sees by predicting that good will ultimately come out of the present chaos. Still a man in search of the "happy valley," Steinbeck admits that the roads of the past have come to an end and that we have not yet discovered one to the future. But, he insists at the conclusion of America and Americans, we will find one, though "its direction may be unthinkable to us now."[41]

John Steinbeck died on December 20, 1968 in New York City, and his body was taken back to Salinas for burial in the Steinbeck family plot. Over the course of a long career as a master story teller who, better than any other novelist on record, portrayed life in California's rural valleys and along its central coast, Steinbeck gradually developed a coherent, meaningful view of man and the world in which he lives, a philosophical perspective that gives depth and breadth to his many memorable pictures of American life. He was a man in motion--complex and full of contradictions. But always he was his own man.

He wrote books not the way books are written, as he once remarked about The Grapes of Wrath, but about the way lives are lived. [42] And the subject of those books is the human condition. His message is that we must understand and help one another create the conditions appropriate for a meaningful life. In his own time and with his own voice, John Steinbeck shows man struggling--sometimes successfully, sometimes not--but always struggling to master his inner problems and outer conflicts and so attain a lasting paradise of the mind and heart.

NOTES

1. John Steinbeck, East of Eden (New York: Bantam Books, 1955), p. 1.

2. Frederick Manfred in conversation with Richard Astro, 10/13/73.

3. Steinbeck to Elizabeth Otis, 4/15/36 as quoted in Peter
    Lisca, The Wide World of John Steinbeck (New Bruns-
    wick, N.J.: Rutgers University Press, 1958), p. 26.

4. Lewis Gannett, "John Steinbeck's Way of Writing,"
    Steinbeck and His Critics, eds. E. W. Tedlock and
    C. V. Wicker (Albuquerque: University of New Mex-
    ico Press, 1957), p. 24.

5. Steinbeck to Elizabeth Otis, 2/?/33, as quoted in Gan-
    nett, p. 26.

6. Joseph Campbell in conversation with Richard Astro,
    4/2/71.

7. Steinbeck to Elizabeth Otis, 3/?/34, as quoted in Gan-
    nett, p. 27.

8. Gannett, p. 28.

9. Steinbeck and Edward F. Ricketts, The Log from the
    Sea of Cortez (New York: Viking Press, 1952), p.
    96.

10. Steinbeck, "Suggestion for an Interview with Joseph
    Henry Jackson," written during 1939 and published in
    The Viking Critical Edition, The Grapes of Wrath, ed.
    Peter Lisca (New York: Viking Press, 1972), p. 861.

11. Steinbeck, Of Mice and Men, Compass Books edition
    (New York: Viking Press, 1963), p. 37.

12. T. K. Whipple, "Steinbeck: Through a Glass Though
    Brightly," Study Out the Land (Berkeley: University
    of California Press, 1943), p. 106.

13. Peter Lisca, "John Steinbeck: A Literary Biography,"
    in Tedlock and Wicker, p. 10.

14. Ibid.

15. William Appleman Williams, "Steinbeck and the Spirit
    of the Thirties," a talk given at a conference on
    "Steinbeck and the Sea" at the Oregon State University
    Marine Science Center, Newport, Oregon, 5/4/74.

16. Gannett, p. 33.

17. Lisca, "John Steinbeck: A Literary Biography," p. 17.

18. Steinbeck, The Grapes of Wrath, Compass Books edition (New York: Viking Press, 1958), p. 204.

19. Steinbeck and Ricketts, The Log from the Sea of Cortez, p. 2.

20. Ibid., p. 270.

21. Ibid.

22. Ibid., p. 88.

23. Steinbeck, Once There Was a War (New York: Bantam, 1960), p. vi.

24. Steinbeck, Cannery Row (New York: Bantam, 1959), p. 9.

25. Gannett, p. 36.

26. Steinbeck, "My Short Novels," Wings, 26 (October, 1953), p. 8.

27. Lisca, "John Steinbeck: A Literary Biography," p. 17.

28. Gannett, p. 36.

29. Steinbeck to Ritch and Tal Lovejoy, 5/27/48.

30. Steinbeck, Journal of a Novel (New York: Viking Press, 1969), p. 95.

31. Ibid., p. 4.

32. Ibid., p. 3.

33. Ibid., p. 116.

34. Ibid., pp. 115-16.

35. Steinbeck, "Well, Max, Here's Why I'm a Columnist," Seattle Times Sunday Supplement, 12/5/65.

36. Steinbeck, Journal of a Novel, p. 8.

37. Reloy Garcia, "Steinbeck's The Winter of Our Discon-
     tent," A Study Guide to Steinbeck: A Handbook to
     His Major Works, ed. Tetsumaro Hayashi (Metuchen,
     N. J. : Scarecrow Press, 1974), p. 245.

38. Steinbeck, "High Drama of Bold Thrust through Ocean
     Floor," Life (April 14, 1961), pp. 110-18.

39. Elaine Steinbeck in conversation with Richard Astro,
     3/24/71.

40. Steinbeck to Elizabeth Otis, 8/31/67.

41. Steinbeck, America and Americans (New York: Viking
     Press, 1966), p. 142.

42. Steinbeck to Pascal Covici, 1/9/39 as quoted in the
     Viking Critical Edition, The Grapes of Wrath, p. 858.

DICTIONARY
OF
FICTIONAL CHARACTERS

ABBEVILLE, HORACE. A worried gentleman who had two
wives and six children, and who through the years
managed to build a grocery debt second to none in Monterey. In payment for his debt, Abbeville signs over
a building to Lee Chong which Lee eventually "rents"
to Mack and the boys (CR).

ABRA BACON See BACON, ABRA (EE)

ACADEMICIAN. Member of the planning committee for the
constitutional convention to draft the Code Pippin. His
name and wisdom are bywords in the world. He supports Jean Veauvache's argument for royal costumes at
the convention by pointing out that the greatest intellect
in the world would evoke giggles from a gathering of
the most serious kind by neglecting to button his fly
(SRP).

ACADEMICIAN POITIN See POITIN, ACADEMICIAN (SRP)

ADAM TRASK See TRASK, ADAM (EE)

ADAMS, JOE ("The White Quail"). Joe offers Harry Teller
an Irish Terrier pup which Harry wants to accept.
Harry becomes ashamed when the vision of a dog in
her garden makes Mary ill (LV).

AGGIE WAINWRIGHT See WAINWRIGHT, AGGIE (GW)

AGNES. One of the regular girls at the Bear Flag. She
seems to have the longest record of service among the
girls. She has an uncle in a mental institution. She
feels that Doc has changed for the worse since he returned from the war. When she appears it is usually
in the company of Mabel and Becky. She is probably
the "Alice" who receives the news of Doc's broken arm
while drinking orange juice with Mabel and Becky (ST).

AL. Cook at a lunch stand on Route 66. He is a composite
character typical of Joe or Carl or some other short-
order cook. He is moody, silent, rarely speaking,
never laughing. Though he is morose, he is compassionate and tells Mae to sell a needy migrant family a
15-cent loaf of bread for a dime (GW).

AL JOAD See JOAD, AL (GW)

ALBERT, ST. When the English dropped hundreds of tiny
    parachutes, each with dynamite and chocolate, one
    landed on the top of the head of the village statue of
    St. Albert, the Missionary (MID).

ALBERT JOHNSON See JOHNSON, ALBERT (IDB)

ALBERT RASMUSSEN See RASMUSSEN, ALBERT (TF)

ALBERTSON, JUDGE. Monterey judge who discharges the
    seer on the recommendation of the Safeway manager
    (ST).

ALEX HARTNELL See HARTNELL, ALEX (LV)

ALEXANDER MORDEN See MORDEN, ALEXANDER (MID)

ALF NICHELSON See NICHELSON, ALF (EE)

ALFIO MARULLO See MARULLO, ALFIO (WOD)

ALFRED. Watchman in the Bear Flag Restaurant. Alfred
    is a genial fellow who is well liked by everyone on the
    Row. He is particularly friendly with Mack and the
    boys and is often a guest at the Palace Flophouse (CR).

ALFRED ANDERSON See ANDERSON, ALFRED (IDB)

ALICE See AGNES (ST)

ALICE GARCIA See GARCIA, ALICE (TGU)

ALICE WICKS See WICKS, ALICE (PH)

ALICIA WHITESIDE See WHITESIDE, ALICIA (PH)

ALLA DAKIN See DAKIN, ALLA (IDB)

ALLEN, ELISA ("The Chrysanthemums"). A Salinas Valley
    farm wife whose sturdy flowers provide an insufficient
    substitute for unfilled emotional needs. Aggressively
    self-reliant, Elisa is betrayed when she lets down her
    guard. She represses her desire to counter male chau-
    vinism and weakly accepts her stereotyped role (LV).

ALLEN HAWLEY See HAWLEY, ALLEN (WOD)

ALLEN, HENRY ("The Chrysanthemums"). A Salinas Valley
    farmer who fails to understand his wife's need for in-
    tellectual companionship (LV).

ALLEN HUENEKER See HUENEKER, ALLEN (PH)

ALLEN, T. B. The storekeeper. He and Pat Humbert and
    John Whiteside find the Mustrovic house deserted. He
    is one of the town "regulars" (PH).

ALVAREZ, JOSE. One of the inhabitants of Our Lady. When
    the rain finally comes, he carries a deer's horns that
    he will wear in the ritual celebration of the event (TGU).

ALVAREZ, MISS ALMA. When day-and-night opposites come
    in contact, the likely result is not crisp intersection
    but an ambiguous zone charged with frictional incident.
    This phenomenon, agitated focus veiled from the strain-
    ing eye of an observer, fascinates Steinbeck. Thus in
    Tortilla Flat, at the start of Chapter V, he devotes a
    special paragraph to the twilight period when "all Mon-
    terey began to make gradual instinctive preparations
    against the night." The paragraph records Steinbeck's
    vain but commendable effort to freeze an on-going pro-
    cess, to compress the passage of time into a snapshot.
    Correspondingly, the image of "Little Miss Alma Al-
    varez, who was ninety years old," taking "her daily
    bouquet of pink geraniums to the Virgin on the outer
    wall of the church of San Carlos," captures the mo-
    ment when an individual life merges lyrically with the
    endless rounds of existence. The church is a meeting
    place where extreme old age can present fresh fragrance
    and color, and so the vignette supports the atmosphere
    of unity the whole paragraph projects (TF).

AMES, CATHY. She is also known as Catherine Amesbury
    and Kate. Cathy is born a psychic and moral monster,
    innately evil, without a conscience to make her aware
    of the fact. By contrast, she has an innocent face,
    golden hair, wide-set hazel eyes with drooping upper
    lids, a thin delicate nose, high cheekbones, and a
    small chin. Her small, rosebud mouth is set in a
    heart-shaped face, and she has tiny, lobeless ears.
    Her teeth are small, sharp, and vulpine. Cathy has
    a slender, boyish figure, thin ankles, and round and

stubby feet with fat insteps like hoofs. Her voice has a husky, soft sweetness but can rasp like a file when she is angry. She is a consummate liar and learns to use selfishness, lust, and fear to manipulate people. As a teenager, she drives her Latin teacher to suicide. When at sixteen she runs away from home, her father brings her back and whips her. In return, she locks her parents in the house and burns them to death. She then becomes the mistress of Mr. Edwards, the whore-master, but torments him so that he beats her nearly to death. He breaks her left arm and three ribs, cracks her skull and tears open her forehead, and knocks the teeth out of her left side. She bears a scar on her forehead for life, like the mark of Cain. When Charles and Adam Trask take her in and nurse her to recovery, she marries Adam and becomes the mother of his twin sons, after an unsuccessful attempt at abor-tion. Two weeks after their birth, she shoots Adam and leaves, to sign up as a girl in Faye's brothel in Salinas. After winning Faye's confidence and becoming a daughter to her, she poisons her and becomes the new madam. She now calls herself Kate. Kate rejects all affection and trusts and confides in no one. She pros-pers as a madam but begins to age prematurely. Her cheeks become chubby, her stomach and shoulders plump, and her legs and feet thick and bulging. Her hands become crippled with arthritis. Still in her thir-ties, she commits suicide after worrying that evidence may turn up to convict her of Faye's murder and after her son Aron meets her and turns away with revulsion (EE).

AMES, MRS. Cathy's mother. She has only one child and therefore believes that other parents have similar prob-lems with their children. Even when she discovers her ten-year-old daughter having sexual relations with two boys, she believes in her daughter's innocence. She never understands up to the moment when Cathy burns her to death (EE).

AMES, WILLIAM. He operates a small tannery in Massa-chusetts. Though he feels uneasy about his daughter, he keeps his suspicions to himself, even after James Grew tries to see him the night of his suicide. When Cathy runs away to Boston, he has her apprehended and whips her. In return, she locks her parents in the house and burns it to the ground (EE).

AMESBURY, CATHERINE See AMES, CATHY (EE)

AMY HAWKINS See HAWKINS, AMY (LV)

ANDERS, JACK. Jack Anders wrecks a car in an attempt
    to frustrate the invaders' attempts to mine the coal.
    As punishment Jack is shot and the soldiers are at-
    tempting to round up the rest of the family when Jack's
    brothers, Will and Tom, plan their escape (MID).

ANDERS, TOM. After their brother Jack is shot, Tom and
    his other brother, Will, escape from the village in
    Corell's boat with the help of Mayor Orden and Doctor
    Winter. Tom is surprised when the Mayor asks them
    to tell the English to send explosives so the villagers
    can fight the invaders (MID).

ANDERS, WILL. A fisherman who, with his brother Tom,
    plans to steal Corell's boat and escape the village.
    They hope to take Corell and drown him, but he is able
    to elude them after being severely injured (MID).

ANDERSON. Husband of Una Hamilton. We never learn his
    first name. He is "an intense dark man" obsessed
    with doing research on photography to invent color film.
    In the meantime, he and his wife live in poverty. He
    is embarrassed by the Hamilton family because of their
    warmth, humor, and imaginativeness. He has fear and
    contempt for intellectual speculation. When Una dies,
    her body worn out by hardship and poverty, the family
    thinks her death is caused by despair over her mar-
    riage (EE).

ANDERSON, ALFRED. A Party sympathizer who owns and
    operates Al's Lunch Wagon in Torgas. He helps per-
    suade his father to let the strikers camp on his land.
    Later Al is badly beaten, but he continues to support
    the strikers and asks for Party membership (IDB).

ANDERSON, MR. Anderson reluctantly allows the strikers
    to set up camp on his land and in exchange the strikers
    harvest his crop. His joy is short-lived because the
    vigilantes burn his barn, destroying his apples. He in-
    creasingly comes to resent the strikers (IDB).

ANDREWS, MABEL. Has a regular habit of reporting a
    burglar to Joe Blaikey, the town constable, who knows

whether it is a burglar, a rat in the dining room, or
just wishful thinking (ST).

ANDY.   A ten-year-old boy from Salinas who, while visiting
Monterey, saw the old Chinaman flap-flapping across
Cannery Row one evening and who teased him once in
a shrill falsetto: "Ching-Chong Chinaman...." A long,
vacant look from the old man terrifies Andy into a vision of desolate cold aloneness. Andy never teases
the old Chinaman again (CR).

ANGELICA.   Chapter XIII introduces the mother of Teresina
Cortez. At best a dubiously angelic "vieja," she seems
stupid, not stoic, as she provides for Teresina's an-
nually increasing brood. Like other old people in the
novel, especially old women, she is inured to hardship
and contributes to the backdrop of changeless, unreflec-
tive routine against which Danny and his crew play their
countless variations. Angelica has "nerves of steel"
and once each month piously confesses the "sins" she
has no spare time to commit. When crops fail, she
shifts allegiance from the Virgin to Santa Clara, then
returns to the Virgin following the "miracle" of the
(filched) manna. Skirting any trace of sentimentality,
the portrait consistently satirizes shallowness and su-
perstition (TF).

ANGELICA VASQUEZ   See   VASQUEZ, ANGELICA (TF)

ANGELO, FATHER.   Priest of Our Lady. Although he is a
stern priest of the church, he is a tender and humorous man. He is a tolerant opponent of the pagan rites
occasionally practiced by his people. He reacted an-
grily to the fiesta in the rain which celebrated the end
of the ten-year drought. He said the townspeople let
the devil into their souls. He comes to Joseph Wayne's
New Year's fiesta and brings the instruments of his religious service which includes a crucifix and a Mother
and Child which he had carved and painted himself. At
the fiesta, he warns Joseph Wayne against pagan rites,
but he admits that the old ways continue secretly in
a land newly converted to Christ. At Juanito's request
that Joseph visit the priest during the drought, Joseph
asks Father Angelo to pray for rain and the land.
Father Angelo tells him that the Church is concerned
with the soul and not the land, but after Joseph leaves,
he admires the priestly power of the man and prays

for the rain. When the rain comes, he does not inter-
fere with the wild celebration and retires to think of
Joseph Wayne's happiness now that the drought is ended
(TGU).

ANNIE. The Ordens' cook who characterizes the people of
the village in her fierce independence. She is able to
carry messages from the Mayor throughout the village,
thereby fanning the sparks of resistance (MID).

ANNIE LITTLEFIELD See LITTLEFIELD, ANNIE (GW)

ANTOINE (The Other Burgundian). A tall, one-armed pirate
and partner of Emil. (Long ago, Emil cut off Antoine's
arm after finding Antoine making love to his wife.) He
is a loyal member of Morgan's brotherhood. In the end
he is hanged along with Emil by Morgan (CG).

APOLONIA TOMAS See TOMAS, APOLONIA (P)

ARABELLA GROSS See GROSS, ARABELLA (TF)

ARON TRASK See TRASK, ARON (EE)

ARTHUR MORALES See MORALES, ARTHUR (TF)

ATHATOOLAGOOLOO. Headhunter in South America that
Fauna remembers from her missionary days. He was
a natural-born head-hustler who would push monkey
heads on his customers (ST).

B

BACON, ABRA. She first appears as a ten-year-old girl
wearing a blue-checked sunbonnet and a flowery dress.
Her father explains that she is named for a character
in a poem by Matthew Prior. She has dark hair, level
brows, a firm chin, and a wide mouth. Her eyes are
hazel, intelligent, and fearless. Abra is forthright and
honest in her emotions. She wants to be an adult and
even as a child simulates adult speech, attitudes, and
emotions. Aron immediately falls in love with her; and
while still in elementary school, they plan eventually to
marry. Abra grows into a beautiful girl with a calm,
warm face and a self-confident nature. As Aron first
decides to be a celibate priest and then goes away to
college, they move increasingly apart and she is drawn

more to his brother Cal. Her features have a "bold
muscular strength," and Lee feels strength, goodness
and warmth in her. He praises her for her loveliness,
courage, wisdom, and ability to know and accept things.
Her nature is a foil to that of Cathy (Kate), and her af-
firmative womanliness redeems Cal from the fate of
Cain (EE).

BACON, MR. Father of Abra. He is a county supervisor
given to pronouncing tiresome clichés about education as
the torch of learning. When Adam Trask loses his
money in an attempt to ship refrigerated lettuce, Bacon
turns against Aron and disapproves of his going with
Abra. He himself becomes psychosomatically ill with
fear after he embezzles from his company (EE).

BACON, MRS. Mother of Abra. When she first appears,
she is wearing the fanciest clothes Cal and Aron Trask
had ever seen--a black silk dress covered with black
lace. She disapproves of Abra's going with Aron Trask
and chases Cal Trask away from the house (EE).

BAKER, MR. As president of the First National Bank and
as the latest standard-bearer of an illustrious lineage,
Mr. Baker has assumed the stewardship of New Baytown's public probity and social manners. Behind the
scenes, he pulls the strings of the community's financial and political intrigues. The Baker history makes
a whiff of chicanery. The banker's father co-owned a
whaling ship, the Belle-Adair, with Ethan's grandfather.
When the vessel burned to the water line and the under-
writers made good on the insurance, old Cap'n Hawley
suspected arson and carried the grudge to his grave.
        During the span of the novel, Baker is initially
high-handed with Ethan and lodges a blistering accusation to ignite his fighting spirit: "Your blood has lost
its guts." After Mary inherits a modest legacy,
Baker's ultimatum to Ethan is a shocking caricature of
Christ's advice to his disciples: "lose it if you have
to but risk it." Elsewhere, Steinbeck's rhetoric buttresses this satirical inversion. Like Moloch in the
moralities, or a figure in Jonson's plays or Spenser's
poetry, Baker genuflects in the presence of the "Great
God Currency" before the shrine of his bank vault. On
a local scale, Baker is one of the "great artists of finance" that Ethan reluctantly admires. In secret, he
once made "a grammatically correct but obscure pass"

at Margie Young-Hunt.

A cagey speculator, Baker plans for an airport to service the population explosion he anticipates. He is thwarted in his scheme to bilk Danny Taylor and gain possession of the land where the Taylor family home burned to the ground years ago, but he successfully goads Ethan to usurp Marullo and ascend to the privileged station befitting a Hawley. When the time is ripe, on the eve of the critical Independence Day weekend, Baker springs his trap. Having engineered the ouster of his corrupt puppets from the municipal government, he nonchalantly departs for a holiday in Maine. On his return, he proposes that Ethan outflank "the egghead fringe" and cap his repaired fortunes by running for town manager. He is astonished and mortified when Ethan produces the grimy but perfectly legal deed to Danny's property and demands the lion's share in Baker's ventures. The old guard changes in dismay and relinquishes its grasp to a new generation of Machiavellian ruthlessness, personified by Ethan.

Baker's characterization suffers from the same thinness and polemical stridency that spoiled the late Twain. To be sure, Baker is a recognizable pharisee, snob, and hypocrite, but as a dramatic creation he is a sketchy patchwork of superstitions and eccentricities and lacks the incisive gestures and in-depth psychology of the true villain. Regrettably, the defects of the contemptible type Baker certainly represents proved contagious and occasioned false steps in Steinbeck's craftsmanship (WOD).

BANKS, MRS. Wife of Raymond Banks. She laughs a great deal and loves to work with her flowers (PH).

BANKS, RAYMOND. Owns the one most admired farm in the valley. He is a strong, forty-five-year-old man with thick short arms. He is always chosen to play Santa Claus at the school's Christmas party. He is also unusually attracted to the drama of the kill. The warden at San Quentin is an old friend and invites him to watch executions (PH).

BARTENDER. He serves whiskey to Juanito and Joseph Wayne. He tells them of the misfortune of his brother-in-law and how the people are leaving the town of Our Lady because of the drought. His business has deteriorated because his former customers take a bottle home and drink alone. If the rain comes, he will put a barrel of free whiskey out on the porch (TGU).

BARTENDER'S BROTHER-IN-LAW. He has lost every single
    head of cattle during the drought. The bartender
    passes this information on to Joseph Wayne and Juanito
    (TGU).

BARTOLOMEO PORTUGUES See PORTUGUES, BARTOLO-
    MEO (CG)

BATTLE, GEORGE. He came west in 1863 and settled on a
    farm in "The Pastures." He marries Myrtle Cannon,
    a thirty-five-year-old spinster with a small fortune.
    She bears him a son, John, before she is declared in-
    sane and institutionalized. George is old at fifty,
    pleasureless, and bent; but his farm remains beautiful
    (PH).

BATTLE, JOHN. Son of George and Myrtle. He leaves the
    farm to become a missionary; his father never misses
    him. When George dies, John comes home to claim
    the land. He inherits his mother's epilepsy and her
    mad knowledge of God. He lurks about the farm fight-
    ing devils. One evening he is bitten by a snake and
    dies (PH).

BATTLE, MYRTLE CAMERON. A thirty-five-year-old spin-
    ster with epilepsy whom George Battle marries. She
    bears him a son, John. After twice trying to burn the
    farmhouse, she is confined in a sanitarium where she
    spends the rest of her days crocheting a symbolic life
    of Christ (PH).

BEAR, JOHNNY ("Johnny Bear"). A half-wit, more beast
    than man, except for his uncanny ability to imitate any-
    one he hears speak. Johnny eavesdrops on Loma's citi-
    zens and then goes to the bar to act out the scene he
    has witnessed in the hope someone will buy him whiskey.
    It is all "fun and games" until Johnny brings conversa-
    tions of the town's respected aristocrats--the Hawkins'
    sisters. His revelation is, at least to Alex Hartnell,
    a threat to the very fabric of society in Loma (LV).

BECKY. One of the regular girls at the Bear Flag. She
    seems to have the sharpest tongue among the girls.
    She was badly bitten in the shoulder during a fight with
    a customer. Doc's treatment of the wound saved her

arm. She subscribes to "Pen Pals" and has a lively correspondence all over the world. When she appears, it is usually in the company of Agnes and Mabel (ST).

BENEDICT, FATHER ("Saint Katy the Virgin"). The Abbot of the monastery who desires pork and is distressed that Katy cannot be slaughtered because she is a Christian (LV).

BENTICK, CAPTAIN. A member of the invading army whose advance in rank had not kept pace with his years. He attempts to emulate the stereotype of the English gentleman; instead, he becomes one of the first casualties of the occupation. Attempting to intercede in behalf of Captain Loft, Bentick is killed by Alexander Morden (MID).

BERNICE PRITCHARD See PRITCHARD, BERNICE (WB)

BERT MUNROE See MUNROE, BERT (PH)

BERTHA RILEY See RILEY, BERTHA (IDB)

BIG BILL. A truck driver who stops at Al's lunchroom on Route 66, jokes with Mae, and tells of all the uprooted families going west. When Mae gives a migrant family nickel candy two for a penny, he tips her a dollar. He represents the generosity and cameraderie of the truck-driving fraternity (GW).

BIG JOE PORTAGEE See PORTAGEE, BIG JOE (TF).

BIG MIKE SHEANE ("The Raid"). Big Mike had told Root that although he couldn't think of anything to say at a meeting, once he stood up "... the words came out like water out of a hydrant" (LV).

BIGGERS, HUGH (?). "A spare man, a perpetually young man who had never been young, a smart dresser, hair gleaming thickly against his scalp, eyes merry and restless." Biggers is "a drummer" who represents the shadowy "B.B.D. and D." organization, evidently a wholesale concern that supplies merchandise to independent grocers. Broad hints are dropped that "B.B.D. and D." is a front for muscling gangsters. With some aid from Margie Young-Hunt and with the preliminary bait of a new wallet containing $20, Biggers approaches

Ethan on Good Friday and teases him with a dubious
proposition that amounts to a bribe: in return for an
under-the-counter commission, Ethan will secretly
transfer Marullo's business from a legitimate supplier
to B.B.D. and D.

At first, Ethan firmly rejects this flagrant appeal
to his awakening acquisitiveness. Later, he earns
Bigger's admiration by planting the (false) impression
that he has entered negotiations with B.B.D. and D.'s
competitors. This second confrontation prompts the
following curious exchange: (Biggers) "Jesus, I thought
I was conning a country boy"; (Ethan) "I will not sell
my master short." The two-edged quality of the language, the double entendres, Biblical and Faustian, that
Ethan, at least, must be supposed to recognize, suggest that Biggers is a pivotal character, a catalytic
tempter who feeds Ethan's own duplicity.

In an obvious sense, Biggers is a middle-man, a
seamy go-between. More subtly, Steinbeck fortifies
his descriptions of the entrepreneur with a remarkably
bi-polar vocabulary reminiscent of Orwell's "double-
think," a loaded diction that encodes and implements the
novel's persistent air of discord. Biggers' hands are
"immaculate," and he wears a "big cat's eye" in a
"gold" ring. Such language becomes conspicuously suspect in a novel where the prevailing motif is drab im-
purity, feline stealth, and universal counterfeit. To
Biggers, currency is "nice clean green cabbage," and
the coarse idiom demolishes any lingering hope that the
produce in Marullo's market is a symbol of a benign,
organic relationship between Ethan and his customers.
In the end, Ethan drives a hard bargain and accepts
Biggers' offer.

As a character, Biggers is ironically insignificant
and "little," but as a salient landmark in Ethan's parable and as a molecular model of the way Steinbeck's
style works hand-in-hand with his theme--the deplorable
secularization of human reverence--Biggers should not
be overlooked or underestimated. He reminds us that
for Steinbeck, a cardinal sign of a corrupt society is
language adrift from its natural moorings; and he offers
a convenient clue to the skill and merit of the novel's
technical machinery (WOD).

BILL WHITESIDE See WHITESIDE, BILL (PH)

BILLINGS, JOSH. A great humorist who, before he died,

once lived in Monterey. The city feels it must honor
Billings' memory. When a young boy is discovered
carrying Billings' liver to the waterfront to use as fish
bait, a town committee insists that the French doctor
who had embalmed Billings collect the writer's discarded parts (CR).

BILLY BUCK See BUCK, BILLY (LV)

BISHOP, THE. Supervisor of missionaries in South America during Fauna's tour of duty. He scolds her for
buying Athatoolagooloo's monkey heads (ST).

BLACK DEMON See DEMON, BLACK (LV).

BLACK HAT. A resident of the Weedpatch government camp.
He is a broad-shouldered man with a stringy neck and
bristled chin. He tells the Joads about prejudice in the
schools against "Okie" children and explains the way in
which farmers use surplus labor to lower wages. He
tells a story of how Appalachian mountain people stopped
vigilante violence against workers in the rubber companies of Akron, Ohio, by organizing 5,000 mountain
marksmen to have a Sunday turkey shoot (GW).

BLAIKEY, JOE. A good small town constable. He is well
liked and trusted by everybody. He knows more about
his town than anyone else and usually prevents most
crimes from ever happening. He knows everyone in
Monterey and can size up a stranger almost instantly.
When Suzy arrives in town, he advises her to stay off
the streets if she intends to hustle. When she leaves
the Bear Flag, he stakes her to twenty-five dollars until she establishes herself with a new job and a new
home (ST).

BLANKEN (Family). A clan of feuding, dispossessed emi-
grants from the Kentucky Appalachia, the Blanken family christened "Rebel Corners" when they located their
smithy on the spot and cast their fortunes with the Con-
federacy during the Civil War. Flushed with pride and
obstinate prejudices reminiscent of Faulkner's Yoknapa-
tawphans, the family profile presents an ironical image
of self-annihilating independence. In defeat, the Blank-
ens are reabsorbed into "blank" anonymity. The sur-
viving legend of their dynasty implicitly comments on
the current resident, rebel, and man of iron, Juan Chicoy (WB).

BLIND TOM See TOM, BLIND (LV)

BOLTER. During the pickers' strike, Mr. Bolter is chosen
     as the new president of the Torgas Valley Fruit Grow-
     ers' Association and tries to get the strikers to come
     back to work. Bolter offers the pickers twenty cents,
     but the strikers demand their raise. When he sees
     that the strikers will not accept his offer, he threatens
     to call in troops (IDB).

BORDONI. A Swiss immigrant who owned the Sanchez ranch
     of 900 acres between San Lucas and King City. He has
     squinting eyes and gets a little drunk every afternoon
     on red wine. Adam Trask buys his ranch (EE).

BOSS, THE. A little stocky man who walks with his thumbs
     stuck in his belt. He wears a soiled Stetson hat and
     boots with spurs to prove he is not a laborer. He
     warns George and Lennie not to make any trouble
     (OMM).

BOSTON, MILTON. When Van Brunt contemplated suicide,
     he purchased strychnine from this San Ysidro pharma-
     cist. Van Brunt and Boston are brothers in the "Blue
     Lodge," but the latter has attained a more exalted de-
     gree in the lodge hierarchy. The name Milton Boston,
     with its overtones of long-established, Eastern afflu-
     ence, may signify the poisonous atmosphere of middle-
     class snobbery and help account for Van Brunt's cor-
     rosively satirical social manner (WB).

BRAZILIANO, ROCHE. A Hollander with a chubby face who
     was driven from Brazil by the Portuguese. A kind and
     gentle man and a beloved captain, he is raised to fury
     by the sight of Spaniards. It is said that once he
     roasted Spanish prisoners on spits over a slow fire
     (CG).

BREED, MR. Practical-minded proprietor of Breed's Gen-
     eral Store and "unofficial custodian" of the bridge that
     obstructs passage of the bus to San Juan de la Cruz.
     Breed's name connotes universality and by inference en-
     hances biblical parallels to the flood and the mythic di-
     mensions of Chicoy's multifaceted trial (WB).

BREED, MRS. Insulated, conventional wife of Mr. Breed,
     the storekeeper. "Her legs swelled up in the after-

noon." A hapless "Oh, my God!" is her conditioned response to calamity (WB).

BREMAN, TOM. Takes Katherine and Alice Wicks to a
dance at the schoolhouse while "Shark" is away at his
aunt's funeral (PH).

BROTHER CLEMENT See CLEMENT, BROTHER (LV)

BROTHER COLIN See COLIN, BROTHER (LV)

BROTHER PAUL See PAUL, BROTHER (LV)

BRUNO, MRS. As soon as Jesus Maria Corcoran makes
common cause with Pilon and Pablo at the end of Chapter IV, he becomes "their feeder of lines, their opener
of uneasy situations." The metaphor of a "feeder" is
presently objectified when Pilon dispatches Jesus Maria
on a scavenger mission: "Maybe Mrs. Bruno, on the
wharf, will give you a fish." From the start, Pilon
casts the newcomer in a role of subordination and com-
pliance (TF).

BUCK, BILLY ("The Red Pony"). A hired hand on the Tiflin ranch, Billy is a natural man who is Jody's friend
and mentor. Unlike Jody's father, Billy can sense the
magnitude of Jody's joy or grief, and Billy invariably
makes the appropriate responses. Having failed to save
the life of the red pony in "The Gift," Billy successfully delivers the colt in "The Promise" at the expense of
the life of the mare. The contrast between Billy Buck
and Carl Tiflin pervades "The Red Pony" (LV).

BUCK, MULE-TAIL ("The Red Pony"). In "The Leader of
the People" Jody's grandfather recalls Billy Buck's father, old Mule-tail Buck, who packed mules. In "The
Promise" Billy had mentioned his father as a government packer (LV).

BUCKE, MISS. First grade teacher at Pacific Grove. She
creates a scandal when one of her students is discovered with his crayons wrapped in the dust cover of the
Kinsey report. She later confesses that her father
signed a petition in 1918 for the release of Eugene V.
Debs (ST).

BUD. Alice Chicoy's first lover, he shattered her fragile

illusions of romance. Alice's squalid seduction and
moral downfall, recollected during her drunken reverie,
were accomplished with the aid of a picnic in the country and the promise of apple pie. The wounded nos-
talgia prompted by this episode is a key to Alice's bitterness and self-pity (WB).

BUGLE, MILDRED.   Thirteen-year-old.   Head of her class
in Beginning Botany, Los Angeles High School. She
picked some interesting leaves in the Plaza in Los Angeles which turned out to be Cannabis Americana, the
marijuana that Joseph and Mary Rivas secretly grew
and sold (ST).

BULLET ROSENDALE   See   ROSENDALE, BULLET (TF)

BULLITT, JESSIE.   Chairperson of the Ladies' Committee of
Sanitary Unit Number Four at the Weedpatch government
camp. She is "a mammoth lady, big of hock and but-
tock, big of breast, muscled like a drayhorse, powerful and sure." She has a booming voice.   Kindly and
dignified, she explains the operation of the camp to Ma
Joad (GW).

BURKE.   A leader of the migrant strikers who supervises
the guards stationed around the camp.   He supports
Dakin and at one point accuses London of betraying the
strikers.   When he confronts London and accuses him
of selling out, London hits him so hard that he breaks
his jaw.   At Jim's motivation, London takes further
control and molds the individual strikers into one body
anxious to feed on blood (IDB).

BURTON, DOC.   Although not a Party member, Doc Burton
supervises the medical and health needs in the strikers'
camp.   Described as a young, golden-haired man with
delicate features, he acts the "devil's advocate" in discussions with Mac.   Doc's presentation of group man is
rooted in medical/biological vision, and in this respect
he is one of Steinbeck's early fictional characters modeled on Edward F. Ricketts.   Once Doc organizes the
camp and gets it operating, he simply disappears and
is assumed to be kidnapped or killed (IDB).

BURTON WAYNE   See   WAYNE, BURTON (TGU)

BUS DRIVER, THE.   Drives the sightseeing bus that passes

"The Pastures" at the end of the novel. He wonders
what life would be like on a farm in the valley (PH).

C

CACAHUETE RIVAS See RIVAS, CACAHUETE (ST)

CALEB TRASK See TRASK, CALEB (EE)

CAMILLE. A figure from Elizabeth's childhood. She was
a little girl with a skin as soft as camellias. Elizabeth thought Camille was the loveliest name in the world
and gave her dog the same name. The girl became
very angry (TGU).

CAMILLE OAKS See OAKS, CAMILLE (WB)

CAMP, GEORGE. Early in the novel, Joy attacks a policeman and is jailed for assault. Mac tells Dick to call
George Camp and have him pose as an attorney to get
Joy released as a drunk before he is booked and the
sanity board gets hold of him (IDB).

CANDY. An old crippled farm hand, referred to in the early
part of the narrative as "the old swamper." He cleans
up around the ranch. He has saved some money and
wants to be included in George and Lennie's plan to buy
a place of their own. His old dog is crippled and soon
will die. Carlson convinces him that the old dog
should be shot (OMM).

CAPORAL, SEÑOR. Chapter X is a self-contained sermon
that takes Jesus Maria's bedraggled humanitarianism as
its theme. The history of "Señor Caporal" and his ail-
ing infant, Manuel, furnishes the text with a suitable
exemplum. Having left Mexico in an unsuccessful effort to find work, the sixteen-year-old father and non-
commissioned officer is now stranded in Monterey. Im-
pulsively, Jesus Maria invites the youth to join Danny's
household. While the paisanos make inept attempts to
care for the baby, the Caporal tells his tale. A short
time ago, he married a beautiful and virtuous girl who
was dazzled by his military rank. Subsequently, his
commanding officer exercised a kind of droit de seigneur
and seduced the bride. The Caporal's protests were
met with threats on his life, and he was forced to flee.
Through the power of constantly drummed suggestion,

he hopes to raise his son to be a general.

The paisanos are profoundly moved by the story and are stunned when the baby suddenly dies. To comfort the Caporal, they vow vengeance on the dastardly commanding officer; but the good soldier is mystified by their assumption that his plans for his son outline a sophisticated scheme of retribution. On the contrary, "if that capitan, with the little epaulets and the little sash, could take my wife, imagine what a general with a big sash and gold sword could take!" After a prolonged silence, the paisanos "digested the principle." The Caporal leaves to rejoin the army, and the six friends declare themselves "proud to have known such a man."

The episode is clearly a key one, but it is subject to widely differing interpretations. On the one hand, the Caporal is manifestly the victim of dehumanizing social institutions; but on the other, the paisanos conditioned recourse to ritualized violence signals a fatal flaw in their own culture. Furthermore, Steinbeck complicates the picture with a clash of probably incompatible literary modes, harsh realism and mordant satire. The reader is baffled by a satirical thrust that slashes both ways and made uneasy by a clinical account that leaves his sympathies in the lurch when, without warning, it decomposes into poisonous ribaldry. In fact, readers' expectations about the proper course of conventions may be the target of this dark comedy. Perhaps Steinbeck is saying something about the fundamental instability of all artificial structures, social and literary. But one wonders if the risks he runs are worth the effort. In any event, Chapter X reaffirms the important lesson that, in Tortilla Flat, character and personality are decidedly subordinate to the ulterior demands of theme, atmosphere, technique, and arrangement (TF).

CAPTAIN. Owner of a parcel of land near the Carmel River where Mack and the boys set up a trap to catch frogs. Initially, the Captain, who is a dark, large man who patrols his property with a shotgun over his arm, insists that Mack and the boys leave his land. But when Mack cures the Captain's sick bird dog, the Captain and Mack's brigade become fast friends. Finally, the Captain helps Mack and the boys map strategy for their frog hunt (CR).

CAPTAIN BENTICK See BENTICK, CAPTAIN (MID)

CAP'N HAWLEY See HAWLEY, CAP'N (WOD)

CAPTAIN LOFT See LOFT, CAPTAIN (MID)

CAPTAIN SAWKINS See SAWKINS, CAPTAIN (CG)

CAPTAIN ZEIGLER See ZEIGLER, CAPTAIN (CG)

CAPTAINE PASMOUCHES See PASMOUCHES, CAPTAINE (SRP)

CARL, FAT ("Johnny Bear"). Owner and operator of the Buffalo Bar who sells only one brand of whiskey yet inevitably asks, "Well what's it going to be?" (LV).

CARL TIFLIN See TIFLIN, CARL (LV)

CARLSON. A powerful, big-stomached ranch hand. He encourages Slim to give one of his pups to Candy in an attempt to convince Candy to shoot his old, smelly dog. It is Carlson's Luger that George uses to kill Lennie at the end (OMM).

CARRIAGA, ALBERTO. Father of Johnny Carriaga. He receives sixty-two cents, the price of a gallon of wine, for the use of his first-born at the masquerade (ST).

CARRIAGA, JOHNNY. Selected to draw Doc's winning raffle ticket at the masquerade. He is dressed as Cupid for the occasion. Whitey No. 2 gives him lessons in the art of palming cards, but he drops the winning ticket before he has a chance to carry off the deception. After the raffle he joins in the spirit of the "tom-wallager" by firing his rubber-tipped arrows at random targets (ST).

CARRIAGA, MR. A Monterey citizen who discovers what turns out to be Josh Billings' liver in the possession of a young boy who intends to use it as fish bait (CR).

CARSON, "PIMPLES," "Ed," "KIT." Seventeen years old, a "particularly violent battleground of adolescence," Pimples Carson is less a handyman to Juan Chicoy than a protegé, almost a filial attendant. When the prospect of squiring Camille Oaks presents itself, Pimples decides to join the excursion to San Juan. For him, the adventure ends in mortifying defeat when a rehabilitated

Norma indignantly fends off his oafish advances.

Pimples' authentic knack with machinery, his idol-
ization of Chicoy, and his indomitable, pioneering energy all speak in favor of his emerging manhood. But he
is still the personification of callow youth, held in the
grip of maudlin sensibilities and violent, lustful impulses
that he cannot resist or comprehend. The mark of his
inexperience is a polarized consciousness that vacillates
between melodramatic self-condemnation and timid fantasies of sexual prowess. With others, he is alternately a vainglorious nuisance and a self-pitying, hyper-
sensitive romantic. Pimples' acute chagrin about his
ravaged appearance wins Chicoy's easy-going sympathy,
but such tactful encouragement merely leads the youth
into renewed excesses of arrogance and remorse.

Whether his dawning initiation will turn him in
the direction of his heroic ancestor, Kit Carson, and
of Chicoy, or will deflect him toward the spiritually
diminished, neon glitter of Hollywood, is a salient question that the novel dramatizes but does not answer.
Pimples entertains the ambition of becoming an electron-
ics expert. Perhaps he will ride this wave of the future, but just as likely he will founder in the trashy
chimeras that presently cluster around him (WB).

CASY, JIM. A former fundamentalist preacher who goes
with the Joads to California. He has "a long head,
bony, tight of skin, and set on a neck as stringy and
muscular as a celery stalk." His forehead is abnor-
mally high and pale, and his hard, beaked nose
stretches the skin tightly over his face. He has red
and raw lids stretched over heavy and protruding eye-
balls. His clean-shaven cheeks are brown and shiny,
and he has a full, sensual mouth. His stiff gray hair
looks as if he has combed it back with his fingers. He
wears overalls and a blue shirt, a denim coat, spotted
brown pork pie hat, and canvas sneakers. Casy used
to be a hell-fire revivalist but lost the call and decided that "There's just stuff people do." He is converted
from Protestant Christianity to a Transcendental belief
that all people are part of one soul, and he gives up
preaching about the hereafter in order to help people
who are hungry and oppressed in the present. In some
ways, he parallels Jesus Christ; he has the same initials, and he has had an analogous period of solitude in
the wilderness that converts him to a new gospel of
love. In California, he becomes a labor organizer try-

ing to help the farm workers strike for higher wages
and better working conditions. Like Jesus, he is killed
as a martyr, but Tom Joad is converted to his views
and becomes Casy's disciple, for the cause of the downtrodden migrants (GW).

CATHY AMES See AMES, CATHY (EE)

CHANGO See JOSEPH (TGU)

CHAPPELL, ED ("The Harness").   Peter Randall's only confidant after Emma's death, Ed was embarrassed to
learn of the San Francisco weeks.   Ed learned that for
Peter, Emma would always be alive (LV).

CHAPPELL, MRS. ("The Harness").   The closest neighbor
to the Randalls, Mrs. Chappell was with Emma at her
death.   She telephoned her husband and the doctor when
Peter became hysterical (LV).

CHARLES II.   King of England who pardons Morgan and appoints him Lieutenant-Governor of Jamaica (CG).

CHARLES MARTEL See MARTEL, CHARLES (SRP)

CHARLES TRASK See TRASK, CHARLES (EE)

CHARLIE GUZMAN See GUZMAN, CHARLIE (TF)

CHARLIE JOHNSON See JOHNSON, CHARLIE (WB)

CHARLIE MARSH See MARSH, CHARLIE (TF)

CHARLIE MEELER See MEELER, CHARLIE (TF)

CHICOY, ALICE.   Juan Chicoy's wife, Alice, is a disheveled,
profane woman furiously resisting her passage into middle age.   She oversees the lunch-room phase of the
Rebel Corners service station with the raucous efficiency of a mess-sergeant, but her inner existence is a
frequently losing struggle against hysteria.   Behind the
random flow of incident that the narrative surveys, Alice detects a malicious agency, a sinister opponent bent
on sabotaging her routine, throwing her mind into confusion, and jeopardizing her precarious relationship with
her husband.
      Provoked beyond endurance by the building pres-

sure of events, she opens the floodgates of her wrath
on the hapless Norma. When her passion has run its
course, Juan comforts his wife tenderly and she sinks
into wailing, tear-drenched slumber. After the travelers leave for San Juan, Alice shuts herself into the
lunch room and methodically drowns her sorrows in
strong drink. At first she reviews the love affairs that
have been the milestones of her life, but then she is
haunted by memories of her mother's agonizing paraly-
sis and death. She attempts to repair her battered appearance with cosmetics but is appalled by the frightful
results that her mirror reflects. Before lapsing into
boozy oblivion, Alice virtually demolishes the lunch
room in a futile attempt to swat an elusive house fly.

Alice's besetting weakness is that her personal relationships effectively blot out any more spacious frame
of reference: "Alice was not very aware of things or
people if they did not in some way either augment or
take away from her immediate life." She is the prison-
er of her own caprice and volatile impressions: "Alice
could only love, like, dislike, and hate." Her cruelly
jealous, abandoned devotion to Chicoy is transparently
understandable, but why this self-contained, splendidly
sensual man links his destiny to a nagging, irascible
frump is an enigma that Steinbeck wisely refrains from
clarifying. One can only hazard the guess that the Old
Adam in Chicoy, the resolute but far from saintly everyman, cleaves to some correspondingly elemental humanity in Alice (WB).

CHICOY, (Father). The fragmentary sketches of Juan Chicoy's Mexican father suggest a guileless, fatalistic
everyman, the soldier of fortune who sacrificed his life
to a cause whose name he neglected to learn. The legacy of his machismo is a principal component of Juan's
makeup (WB).

CHICOY, JUAN. Fifty years old, of Mexican-Irish descent,
Juan Chicoy operates a bus franchise on a secondary
road that links Rebel Corners and San Juan de la Cruz.
He rises early and repairs his disabled bus with the aid
of his assistant, Pimples Carson. Chicoy's wife, Alice,
is out of joint because she has had to improvise sleeping arrangements for the marooned passengers, and matters are further complicated by a torrential downpour
that threatens to destroy two bridges on the way to San
Juan. At mid-morning, the Greyhound from San Ysidro

arrives and deposits a lone traveler, Camille Oaks, and a load of pies destined for San Juan. With eight passengers, Chicoy leaves for Breed's general store, a way station situated at the Rebel Corners end of the first bridge. Alice remains at home and soothes her ruffled disposition by launching a monumental binge.

By the time they reach Breed's, the passengers have established a sense of communal rapport and mapped out the circuitry of their social arrangements. Diverted by the atmosphere of entertaining adventure, they drop their formal masks and unwrap the casual version of themselves they would normally suppress in unfamiliar surroundings. The bridge is unsafe, and Chicoy proposes two alternatives: return to Rebel Corners or face the unpredictable hazards of the "old road" to San Juan. When the travelers split into two factions, resolute and timid, devil-may-care and prudent, they become fully conscious of the temperamental alignments that have come into play and that Chicoy now knows he will have to navigate. The majority rules in favor of the old road.

Exasperated by his wife's trying behavior, fed up with the petty frictions now developing among his keyed-up convoy of strangers, Chicoy deliberately scuttles his bus many miles from Breed's. He sets off on foot, ostensibly to secure a relief party but actually with the intention of putting the present behind him and fleeing to Mexico.

Mildred Pritchard, a buxom college girl who has caught Chicoy's eye, follows him, finds him, and they make love. At one with himself again, philosophically resigned to accept whatever responsibilities may lie in his path, Juan returns to the bus. He patches up quarrels where he can, dresses wounds where he can do no more, and galvanizes frayed nerves by setting everybody to the work of extricating the bus. Liberated at last, the party completes its trek to San Juan.

Much like John Steinbeck, Juan Chicoy is a dialectical maverick, a jarring hybrid of the practical and the visionary. Poised at the summit of his maturity, seasoned but still vigorous, he scans the intuitively American metaphysic that he has forged from time and spirit. On the one hand, his idiom is Franklinesque, rooted in actuality. He is a "magnificent mechanic," immersed in the solvent details of human chemistry. On the other hand, he is speculative, Emersonian, eligible to ride the crest of Steinbeck's surging allusiveness.

The twentieth-century climate, according to Theodore Dreiser's tight-lipped forecast, would become a "trap of circumstance," a petrified forest of immobilized actors. To be sure, the pragmatic component of Chicoy's makeup returns him in the end to the landlocked compromise of Alice and axle grease. Steinbeck's denouement, if ambivalent, tenders unmistakenly pedestrian options. The potential Odysseus, the trailblazing pilot who rescues the probationaries among his clientele from the slough of despond and consigns the remnants to the damnation of Vanity Fair, remains, as he began, the maimed, veteran skipper of a brokendown hack.

But Steinbeck's far-ranging, many-faceted eloquence is more than an ironical rubric contrived to underscore the limitations of his battle-scarred protagonist. The initials of Juan Chicoy's name convey a trace of authentic if adumbrated charisma, and the name of his destination animates a tantalizing promise that Chicoy may yet celebrate an epiphany and enter the mystique of his glorious namesake, Saint John of the Cross.

At a critical moment in the novel, Chicoy concludes his musing soliloquy: "I will take off my old life like a suit of underwear." Steinbeck's metaphor runs grave risks of exposure to the same contaminating grimness that renders many of his characters little more then celluloid filmstrips. The book that ventured to flay Hollywood became a moderately successful movie, after all; The Wayward Bus became a promotional vehicle for Marilyn Monroe. Perhaps Chicoy is foolhardy, skin-deep at best, and perhaps Steinbeck was merely being opportunistic, meretricious, when he pitted "the great power of Jesus" against the "Sweetheart" confections of modern life.

But for many readers Chicoy will continue to personify Steinbeck's uncompromising, at times gallant fusion of normally scattered currents that cascade through the national consciousness. Mechanical and creative, prosaic and lyrical, profane and sacred: such an inventory, sweeping up the author, the book, and the dominating character, converges in the single channel of a true native vernacular (WB).

CHICOY (Mother). Juan Chicoy's Irish mother had wholly adopted the ways of her husband's Mexican heritage. She "had made the Virgin of Guadalupe her own personal goddess" and was thus the source of Juan's lingering attachment to that symbol of spiritual omniscience. By default, the meagerness of her characterization emphasizes Chicoy's Promethean isolation (WB).

CHILDERIC DE SAÔNE See SAÔNE, CHILDERIC DE (SRP)

CHIN KEE See KEE, CHIN (TF)

CHINAMAN. An unnamed old man who wears a flat straw hat, blue jeans, and heavy shoes and who every morning in the dawn and every evening in the dusk crawls out from the piles where he lives and flap-flaps across Cannery Row. A mysterious figure, some people thought he was God, very old people thought he was Death. And children thought he was a funny old Chinaman (CR).

CHITLING, WILLIE. A movie producer and customer of Charles Martel's art gallery and antique store. He builds the entire bar in his ranch house in Palm Springs with the furniture, paneling, and thirteenth-century altar from the chapel of the Chateau Vieilleculotte (SRP).

CHONG, LEE. Owner of the grocery store on Cannery Row. Lee is a round-faced, courteous man who speaks a stately English without using the letter R. An unwittingly shrewd businessman, Lee has accounts from nearly everyone on the Row. Lee's grocery is not a model of neatness, but it is a miracle of supply. Within its walls, there is virtually everything a man might want and need to live and be happy. Lee also owns the old Abbeville building which he "rents" to Mack and the boys and which they convert into the Palace Flophouse. In Steinbeck's symbolic delineation of life on the Row, Lee is described as "more than a Chinese grocer.... Perhaps he is evil balanced and held suspended by good-- an Asiatic planet held to its orbit by the pull of Lao Tse and held away from Lao Tse by the centrifugality of abacus and cash register..." (CR).

CHONG, LEE. Former owner of the grocery store (see CR). One day he sold out and bought a schooner. He wanted to go trading in the South Seas and fulfill his dreams of palms and Polynesians. He loaded the entire stock of his store aboard his dream ship and set sail into the sunset. Mack blames the movies for his actions. He never missed a movie (ST).

CHRISTINE.   Christine is the cook in the household next door
     to the Ordens' and, although she is a better cook than
     Annie, she is as angry about the occupation as any vil-
     lager (MID).

CLARK DEWITT   See   DEWITT, CLARK (LV)

CLEMENT, BROTHER ("Saint Katy the Virgin").   A monk
     who fell in a pond and drowned when he would not drop
     the sack of salt he was carrying.   The monk's dilemma
     caused Roark, Katy's original owner, to laugh until he
     had to go to bed (LV).

CLERK AT THE COMPANY STORE ON THE HOOPER
     RANCH.   He is a tiny man with a blue-white bald head
     and large, brown eyebrows.   His long, thin nose is
     "curved like a bird's beak," and his nostrils are
     "blocked with light brown hair."   He wears a blue shirt
     and black sateen sleeve protectors.   When he explains
     the company store's exorbitant prices and poor quality
     to Ma Joad, he laughs and giggles until Ma asks him
     why he makes fun of his own people.   Ma shames him
     into sympathy, and he violates orders to give her a
     dime's credit (GW).

CLOTILDE HERISTAL   See   HERISTAL, CLOTILDE (SRP)

CLOUGH, MAYOR.   At the opening of the novel, Danny is
     freshly mustered out of the army.   After a gloriously
     destructive celebration, he spends a predictable stint in
     the Monterey jail.   He amuses himself by "playing a
     satiric game.   He caught a bedbug, squashed it against
     the wall, drew a circle around it with a pencil and
     named it 'Mayor Clough.' "   The jailor "was scandal-
     ized; but he made no complaint because Danny had not
     included either the justice of the peace who had sen-
     tenced him or any of the police force.   He had a vast
     respect for the law."
          The Mayor's Anglo surname underscores the rela-
     tive powerlessness of the paisano enclave, but the more
     important features of Steinbeck's language are his ref-
     erence to satire and his satirical irreverence "for the
     law."   For example, satire can become a literary law
     unto itself that limits the freedom of the writer, just
     as the written statutes of Anglo law impinge on the elas-
     tic social ties of paisano culture.   Moreover, the impli-
     cation is that the powers of orthodoxy will indulge the

ironical perception of a downtrodden minority only so long as they refrain from hitting their intended mark. That is, the American majority prefers to shunt criticism aside, disguise it, pull its fangs.

Steinbeck's overt references to satire are as tendentious as they are infrequent. At the very least, they indicate that he respects the need for form but chafes under the restrictions that form imposes. On a rhetorical level, the argument is between the imperatives of systematic communication and the romantic impulse toward self-expression. On a political level, the argument is between the legitimate claims of law and order and the private dictates of conscience that lead to civil disobedience (TF).

COEUR DE GRIS. A young Frenchman under Morgan's command and the only member of his company whom Morgan does not regard with contempt. An expert swordsman who rejected the pirate cutlass in favor of the long thin blade. Coeur de Gris answered orders with a smile that indicated respect. He becomes Morgan's only friend until, in an irrational moment, Morgan kills him (CG).

COLIN, BROTHER ("Saint Katy the Virgin"). A monk collecting tithes with Brother Paul. When Roark gives Katy to the monks, Brother Colin visualizes the sausage he will get as a reward. Katy attacks Brother Colin, biting off a piece of the calf of his leg (LV).

COLONEL LANSER See LANSER, COLONEL (MID)

COMTE DE JOUR See JOUR, COMTE DE (SRP)

COMTE DE PARIS See PARIS, COMTE DE (SRP)

COMTE DE TERREFRANQUE See TERREFRANQUE, COMTE DE (SRP)

CONCIERGE, THE. A brooding provincial who refuses to believe in Paris even after living there for years. He admits Pippin Héristal into his old house at Number One Avenue de Marigny after his disposal as King of France. When he asks Pippin how the political situation is going in the country Pippin quickly excuses himself (SRP).

CONNIE RIVERS See RIVERS, CONNIE (GW)

CONTRACTOR, THE. He tries to recruit workers from the
    Hooverville camp near Bakersfield in which the Joads
    spend their first night in California. He wears khaki
    trousers, a flannel shirt, a flat-brimmed Stetson hat,
    and carries a sheaf of papers in his shirt pocket. He
    arrives at the camp in a new Chevrolet coupe, accom-
    panied by a deputy sheriff. When Floyd asks him to
    show his license and give the men a contract, the con-
    tractor has the deputy try to arrest Floyd as an al-
    leged car thief (GW).

CORCORAN, JESUS MARIA. As his amiable blurry name
    suggests, Jesus Maria is not calculated to impart sharp
    focus to the narrative. On the contrary, he is the es-
    sence of mellow harmony, always compassionate, al-
    ways helping to blend Steinbeck's fictive ingredients.
    He enters the mainstream of events in Chapters IV, V,
    and VI, and his genial presence at once settles the nov-
    el in its suitable course. Jesus Maria will subdue the
    sometimes too rapid pace of things and leaven sluggish
    passages. With minimal fuss, he will animate a buffer
    zone between Pilon and Danny, between misaligned cor-
    ridors of logical sequence and the heedless trajectory
    of "an artist who consumes himself to become divine."
    "Jesus Maria," the book never tires of saying, "was a
    humanitarian, and kindness was always in him."
        When Pilon and Pablo stumble on Jesus Maria in
    Chapter IV, he is satiated with love and wine. Gener-
    ous to a fault, he surrenders the rest of his wine and
    cheerfully accepts the proposal to sub-let the house that
    Pilon has rented from Danny and earlier sub-let to Pi-
    lon. Rather than resist the inevitable, Jesus Maria
    bends to a "philanthropic cause" and permits himself to
    be relieved of two of the three dollars that were to pur-
    chase a brassiere for Arabella Gross. He takes his
    leave to renew his courtship of Arabella but returns
    shortly in a terrible state. Truculent soldiers have
    routed the tryst, and Jesus Maria, the man to whom
    things happen, has beaten a bloody retreat: "Pablo and
    Pilon rushed to him. 'Our friend! He is hurt. He has
    fallen from a cliff. He has been run over by a train!'
    There was not the slightest tone of satire, but Jesus
    Maria knew it for the most deadly kind of satire." In
    light of Jesus Maria's solicitude for Arabella's bosom
    and the abundance of his own milk of human kindness,
    his retort, "Both thy mothers were udderless cows,"
    is peculiarly fitting.

Part of the "satire" is that the "cliff" reference
is already preparing for the end of the novel, but
Steinbeck's technique is no more impatient than Jesus
Maria's as he tells of his misadventure: "The story
was gradually taking shape.   Pilon liked it this way.
It ruined a story to have it all come out quickly.   The
good story lay in half-told things which must be filled
in out of the hearer's own experience."

Jesus Maria is the very soul of the picaresque,
of the suffering but resilient Candide who sets the craft
in motion but then abides the directions of others or
drifts whither the wind blows.   After the rented house
burns and all move in with Danny, it is Jesus Maria
who "in a frenzy of gratefulness, made a rash promise" and pledged the friends' allegiance to Danny:
"Never shall our friend go hungry."   His burst of poetic inspiration enfranchises the company with a moral
consciousness.   Henceforth, Jesus Maria will nourish
the narrative--provide for the Caporal's baby or for
Teresina's clamoring multitude--but claim no reward
except the pleasure of his own benevolence.   He is the
midwife of incident and the maternal nurse of episode,
truly an "opener of uneasy situations" and a "feeder of
lines."   His is the accent of the full term, forestalling
premature conflict, that Steinbeck must have attended
during the novel's period of gestation (TF).

CORELL, GEORGE.   The "popular storekeeper" whose arrangements made it possible for the invader to take
over the town with very little bloodshed.   Corell wanted
to be given authority in the occupation of the town;
once his perfidy became known, he became persona non
grata and several attempts on his life were made (MID).

CORNELIA RUIZ   See RUIZ, CORNELIA (TF)

CORPORAL, THE.   A Spaniard who stops in 1776 to wonder
at the beauty of a long valley floored with green pas-
turage.   He names the valley "the green pastures of
Heaven."   He leaves and never returns.   Twenty families within one hundred years will have settled in the
valley (PH).

CORPORAL KEMP   See KEMP, CORPORAL (EE)

CORTEZ, MR. ALFRED.   When Teresina was sixteen, "Mr.
Alfred Cortez married her and gave her his name and

the two foundations of her family Alfredo and Ernie.
Mr. Cortez gave her that name gladly. He was only
using it temporarily anyway. His name, before he came
to Monterey and after he left, was Guggliemo. He
went away after Ernie was born. Perhaps he foresaw
that being married to Teresina was not going to be a
quiet life."
      Mr. Alfred's appearance in the novel is as brief
as his appearance in Teresina's life but similarly fruit-
ful in light of the significant episode he engenders.
Perhaps his pioneering spirit takes a backward glance
at the famous Spanish adventurer, Cortez. As with
Teresina, Steinbeck seems to admire a life force that
peoples the earth without standing on ceremony, but the
latent note of condescension towards paternal irrespon-
sibility may well disturb thoughtful readers. From
what perspective does Steinbeck propose to overlook
Cortez' behavior? (TF).

CORTEZ, TERESINA (MRS. ALFRED). "Her body was one
of those perfect retorts for the distillation of children."
Teresina is the earthy, serenely unwed mother of nine
(going on ten) offspring who astonish local school officials by thriving on a diet that consists solely of beans
and tortillas. Until now, the family has gathered its
sustenance from obliging farmers as casually as Teresina has repeated her remarkable feats of maternity,
but disaster strikes when the bean crop is rained out.
Right on cue, Jesus Maria enlists the aid of Danny's
liegemen. After the false start of providing indigest-
ible delicacies, the paisanos pilfer 400 lbs. of beans
and save the day. Pregnant as usual, Teresina "won-
dered idly which one of Danny's friends was responsible."
      The account is rendered in a tone of wry imparti-
ality. Teresina's uninhibited fertility scarcely complements Steinbeck's own self-conscious, disciplined literary production, but he is too good-humored not to tip
his hat in the direction of a fabulously self-vindicating,
lilies-of-the-field abundance. The tale, a kind of Chau-
cerian märchen in miniature, immediately follows the
climactic episode in Chapter XII of the Pirate's offering
to St. Francis and serves as comic relief and coda for
the paisanos' crowning act of generosity (TF).

COYOTITO. Infant son of Kino and Juana who is stung by a
scorpion in the beginning of the story. His mother
sucks the poison from the bite. The town doctor re-

fuses to see him because his father has no money. He
is shot to death at the end of the story (<u>P</u>).

CRISTY, MAYOR. Mayor of Pacific Grove. He leaves town
after being discovered as he fled with an overcoat and
a blonde from a hotel fire in King City (<u>ST</u>).

CROOKS. The black stable boy with a crooked back. He is
proud and aloof; he keeps his distance from most white
people and expects them to reciprocate in kind. He
sleeps in the harness room and spends a great deal of
time reading. The ranch hands will not let him play
cards with them because he is black (<u>OMM</u>).

CURLEY. The Boss's son. He is a thin young man with a
brown face, brown eyes, and tightly curled hair. Like
the Boss, he wears high-heeled boots. He loves to pick
fights and develops an instant dislike for Lennie because
of his massive size. He wears a glove full of vaseline
on his left hand. It is intended to keep his hand soft
for his wife. Lennie crushes his hand after Curley
picks a fight with him. Lennie accidentally kills Curley's wife (<u>OMM</u>).

CURLEY'S WIFE. A flirt who likes to give men "the eye."
She is heavily made up, with full rouged lips and taunt-
ing eyes. Lennie is attracted to her because she is
soft like a rabbit. In his attempt to pet her hair, he
panics and accidentally breaks her neck (OMM).

CYRUS TRASK <u>See</u> TRASK, CYRUS (<u>EE</u>)

D

DAFYDD. A bent, feeble man who visits the Morgan home
in Wales and tells young Henry about his many years as
a pirate in the Indies. Dafydd is old and tired. He is
gray-white and toughened like a dry hide. Still, it is
his wild tales about life in the Indies that help Henry
reach his decision to leave home (<u>CG</u>).

DAKIN. The leader of a group of migrant workers who is
elected the first general leader of the strike. Dakin so
identifies with his new truck that when it is destroyed
he loses his mind and is jailed (<u>IDB</u>).

DAKIN, ALLA. Like her husband, Mrs. Dakin is a strong

and proud woman. She shares everything with her husband and is disappointed when she is not included in
the strikers' planning sessions (IDB).

DAN. An old migrant who lives in his past and derides the
attempts to organize the workers. He uses the "group
man" concept to describe his belief in what he thinks
will eventually occur to the workers. Dan breaks a
hip because of a weak ladder and becomes a cause
célèbre among the workers (IDB).

DANE, SERGEANT AXEL. San Jose recruiting officer. He
has been made unfit for war by two hitches in the
peacetime army. Dane signs up Aron Trask, falsify-
ing his age as 18 (EE).

DANNY. "This is the story of Danny and of Danny's friends
and of Danny's house." At the start of the preface, the
narrator takes occasion to announce three primary ingredients: a protagonist, a texture, and an architec-
tural structure. Each corresponds roughly to one of
the three principal sections of the novel. The opening
section, through Chapter VI, dwells on the material
premises that stake out the book's foundations. Danny
returns from the wars, aged about 30, to discover he
has inherited two houses. This real property poses a
twofold threat: it will excite the envy of his former
friends, and it will hem in his activities. A partial
solution is to rent one of the houses to Pilon and, casually, to Pablo and Jesus Maria. But the burden of
ownership continues to press. Danny feels compelled
to court the relatively affluent Mrs. Morales in order
to accelerate the treadmill of his success. He is much
relieved when his three tenants burn down their rented
residence and join him in the remaining house. In
Chapter VI, Jesus Maria arrives on the scene to complete the nucleus of Danny's following. At the end of
the Chapter, Jesus Maria articulates the embryonic ambience of the group: " 'Never shall our friends go
hungry,' " and clinches the basic design of ensuing
events.
        The center of the narrative, Chapters VII through
XIV, is an orderly series of mock-heroic episodes that
gradually shift in tone from comic to tragic as their
cumulative impact begins to make itself felt. The Pirate and Big Joe Portagee finish the circle of Danny's
roundtable. Each character in turn sponsors a tale

that adds to the growing cycles of narrative. Danny's is the story of temporary apostacy. Still uncomfortable in the role of leader, he deserts his companions and romances Sweets Ramirez. But the friends rescue him from this web of seduction, and Danny resumes his rather passive supervision of affairs. Throughout the section, it is Danny's first-lieutenant, Pilon, who lays out plans of attack and executes tactical stratagems.

The final section, Chapters XV through XVII, belongs to Danny. Pride of ownership has long since lost whatever allure it might have possessed, and the consummation of the Pirate's dream for Saint Francis has exhausted fraternal staying power. Danny runs amuck, like the Berserkers of old, desperately seeking a supreme moment of self-realization. At a loss for a cure, the paisanos arrange a splendid celebration. The idea is to rekindle the quenched flame of brotherhood and welcome Danny back to the fold. Danny rises to epic heights of drinking, wenching, and fighting. Then, transported, he stalks off to face the Opponent: " 'I will go out to The One who can fight. I will find The Enemy who is worthy of Danny!' " Moments later, he falls to his death. Tattered and demoralized, the paisanos lurk around the fringes of Danny's funeral. But Danny has already passed into legend, and the former friends sink into oblivion, an aimless, lonely crowd: "no two walked together."

Steinbeck insisted that Arthurian legend is the key to Tortilla Flat, but critics disagree whether the apparatus of literary parallel promotes a sympathetic glorification of the paisanos or a patronizing, satirical gesture of dismissal. The prevailing view is that Steinbeck refuses to be pinned down. He rummages through fictive formats, the emerging realism of the opening, the collectivism of the middle section, the apocalyptic narcissim of the denouement, with an irritable nervousness that rivals Danny's own. Finally, the reader, too, is infected with indecision. Is Tortilla Flat an example of sentimental realism, a book that reduces the distance between art and life, or is it within the genre of stylish artifice, a self-conscious satire that deploys the resources of art to snipe at the folly of a special culture?

Perhaps the answer is that Danny, for all his local paisano color, epitomizes a dilemma that is intrinsically American and that hinges on the different meanings of competition and economy. For a time, Danny springs loose from the commercial ethic of Torrelli.

He renounces the ambition to bury all contenders, get
the better of his opponent, crow in triumph. For a
while, too, he embraces the scheme of compact, cooperation within a chivalrous structure. In the mid-
section of the novel, adversaries become indispensable
foils who collaborate with the principals and, however
reluctantly, assist their efforts. The texture becomes
a warm, artistic medium, a superstructure that supports imaginative performances. But at the end, Danny
retreats within himself. He is isolated, introverted,
as he launches an inner-directed drive to perfect some
self-ordained ideal. He becomes the pioneer in uncharted space.

However phrased, in social terms, political, or
literary, the struggle is between the classical, formal
component of life and the romantic aspiration for un-
fettered liberty. Pilon represents mentality, conformity, convention, and proves bankrupt. His perceptions
of law and order briefly identify apathy and inertness
as the constant factor in his conservative equation, but
there is a procedure of response, a dynamic symbiosis,
that eventually forces Danny's radicalism. The intui-
tion of Tortilla Flat is that the constitutional compro-
mises of any social covenant aim at rational freedom
but ultimately encourage the creative energies of the
liberated individual, unconscious, primarily irrational
vibrations that demolish themselves and the surroundings that give them life in spectacular exhibitions of
self-assertion. When the critical mass becomes too
congested, it detonates a shattering holocaust of pyro-
technic display. And the story must end.

Three eminent American critics, Cleanth Brooks,
R. W. B. Lewis, and Robert Penn Warren, use their
anthology of American literature to contend that Arthurian legend informs our thinking from William Bradford
to William Faulkner: "Faulkner describes ... a community dedicated to the great virtues of courage and
humility and pride and the rest, but one which likewise
went down and disappeared before the encroachment of
men impatient with these virtues and bent on 'the en-
riching of themselves.' And behind both Bradford and
Faulkner, and other narratives like theirs, one makes
out the ancient legend of the Round Table at Camelot--
of the rise, triumphs, troubles, and dissolution of that
model community." If the American experiment is destined to recurrent cycles of visionary Camelot, of utopia

doomed to violent destruction for whatever reason, failure of good will, the pressure of narrow materialism,
the precarious instability of the trial itself, then Steinbeck has tapped the nerve center of a nation in Tortilla
Flat. His sympathy and his satire are the opposite
sides of a single coinage and currency (TF).

DANNY (His Grandfather). Danny's Grandfather "was an important man who owned two small houses in Tortilla
Flat and was respected for his wealth." When Danny
returned from the Army, he learned that "the viejo ...
had died, leaving Danny the two small houses on Tortilla Flat." In a formal as well as a material sense,
this property is the donné of the novel. The Grandfather's apparent generosity in fact lurks in ambush like
the ghost of an incubus and becomes a chilling obstacle
to Danny's spiritual welfare. Danny "had bitter memories of the viejo," perhaps because the old man had
the malignant instincts of a dragon safeguarding a treasure horde. The Grandfather's shadowy influence is a
curse from the past that diminishes Danny's life even
as it enriches the texture of Steinbeck's narrative (TF).

DANNY TAYLOR See TAYLOR, DANNY (WOD)

DEAL, WILLIAM. A villager who escaped to England one
night (MID).

DEBORAH, GREAT-AUNT. Ethan's great-aunt Deborah combined the intellectual gusto and vigorous curiosity of his
father's family with the bedrock Calvinism of his mother's flinty ancestors. Perhaps this fusion accounts for
Steinbeck's declining to specify whether she was a Hawley, but in fact Deborah salutes us from the universe
of myth as much as she hails from a world of flesh and
blood detail: "She was named for Deborah the Judge of
Israel." Ethan appeals to her as the steadfast advocate
of moral choice and the unflinching touchstone of conscience: "If she wanted immortality, she had it in my
brain"; but her paramount role is to trace the dynamics
of the puritan plain style and strenuous doctrine of cove-
nants.
        One vector of Deborah's dialectical thrust aims at
Ethan's tentative conviction that "the laws of thinking
are the laws of things." Words are the raw material
of thought, and Deborah "cared deeply about words and
she hated their misuse as she would hate the clumsy

handling of any fine thing." She was thus an empiri-
cist and technician, "a precise machine with words,"
who rebuked slovenly departures from unvarnished truth.
For her, sin was synonymous with disobedience to the
immutable laws of verbal systems, and ignorance was
no excuse. More than once, Ethan's darker side teems
with images of firearms. Consequently, his comment
that "Aunt Deborah was a great wing shot on a covey
of lies" is especially significant of the editorial pressure she exerts on the grammar of his spirit.

But Deborah was no plodding literalist. Her mind
set the stage for an energetic Hawthornian equilibrium.
The eagle-eyed alertness to surface mixed in comple-
ment with the detection of motive and the surgical prob-
ing of psychological roots. Her gaunt, chiseled consciousness serves as a clearing-house for Steinbeck's
freight of allusions; and her peculiar strength is to
practice what she preaches. Familiar with the secrets
of symbolism, she is herself the living symbol of a
past continuous with the present. To her, Ethan's talisman "means what you want it to mean": if words have
fixed values, they also gain the magical versatility of
runic totems when subjected to the prismatic diffrac-
tions of individual experience.

Deborah's distinctive mode is to express herself,
Christ-like, in clever parables or to send Ethan bur-
rowing among etymologies. She is stern, ascetic, and
witty. There is a haunting link between her and Margie
Young-Hunt: both are kin to a "pythoness." Indeed,
Ethan cannot elude the implications of Deborah's quot-
ing the Old English poet Caedmon's translation of Genesis, "Me beswac fah wyrm thurh faegir word" ("The
evil serpent enticed me with fair words"), any more
than he can cease being disturbed by her cryptic cita-
tion of King Alfred's translation of Boethius, "Seo leo
gif heo blades onbirigth abit aerest hire ladteow" ("The
lioness, if she taste blood, will tear her keeper first").

Ethan's vision of his mentor becomes blurry when
he swerves from the straight and narrow trajectory of
her dogma, but a whispered debate with her memory is
never entirely silenced. His own abortive criminality
testifies to her wisdom. To every plot hatched by the
sons of Cain, there corresponds an apocalyptic narrative designed by an eternal architect.

The passages about Deborah carry Steinbeck's in-
quiry into regions of elemental relationships between
the voice of a speaker and the inner ear of an audience;

between the normative, stable meaning of a word and
its metamorphosis within a transmuting imagination;
and between archetypal fables and their local adapta-
tions as the stories of particular men and women. Deborah "read the Scripture to me like a daily newspaper
and I suppose that's the way she thought of it, as something going on happening eternally but always exciting
and new." In her capacity as Ethan's guide to such
mysteries of language as the marriage of tenor and vehicle in metaphor, Deborah has much to teach us. As
a primer on Steinbeck's art, she suggests that his allusiveness in The Winter of Our Discontent is anything
but merely decorative and that the novel valiantly
strives, almost as a valedictory effort, to incorporate
the critical assumptions that are the foundation of his
fiction (WOD).

DEEMS, MR. A philanthropist who gives the elderly citizens
of Pacific Grove two rogue courts. When the gift creates havoc in the town, he hires a bulldozer to bury the
courts. The townspeople run him out of town and every
July 30 they burn him in effigy (ST).

DE LA NARIZ, JOSE. At the start of Chapter X, Jose de la
Nariz is cited as an example of Jesus Maria's established role as Good Samaritan: "He it was who carried
Jose de la Nariz four miles when Jose's leg was brok-
en." Jesus Maria's quixotic impulses often cause much
inconvenience (TF).

DEMON, BLACK ("The Red Pony"). In "The Promise" Jody
dreams that Nellie's colt becomes a magnificent animal
that he calls Black Demon, but he more often dreams
of the horse simply as "Demon" (LV).

DEPUTY, THE. A deputy sheriff who accompanies the contractor trying to recruit workers from the Hooverville
camp near Bakersfield. When Floyd asks for a con-
tract, the deputy tries to arrest him on a trumped-up
charge. He threatens to have vigilantes break up the
camp. When he tries to take Floyd, the latter strikes
him and Tom Joad trips him. Firing from the ground,
the deputy shoots the knuckles off the hand of a migrant
woman. Casy then kicks him in the neck and knocks
him unconscious. The contractor calls the deputy Joe,
but the police call him Mike. Casy is arrested for
hitting him (GW).

DEPUTY SHERIFF, THE.   Forces "Shark" Wicks to put
    down the gun with which he plans to kill Jimmie Mun-
    roe (PH).

DESSIE HAMILTON   See   HAMILTON, DESSIE (EE)

DEUXCLOCHES, M.   Leader of the Communist bloc although
    he holds the humble position of Cultural Custodian.   At
    a group caucus during the conference of parties to se-
    lect a new French Government, he argues that it would
    be to the Communists' advantage if the French monarchy
    were restored because it would hasten a revolution. His
    statement is roundly accepted as policy by the mem-
    bers.   After Pippin IV is crowned, he outlines in a
    secret meeting a series of political traps which would
    bring disaster to the king (SRP).

DEWITT, CLARK ("The Harness").   Clark DeWitt and Peter
    Randall were the two most highly respected Monterey
    County farmers.   DeWitt indicated that Randall's plant-
    ing sweet peas showed his mental instability (LV).

DICK ("The Raid").   An older, experienced socialist labor
    organizer who counsels Root about a raider: "... it
    isn't you he's busting. He's taking a crack at the Prin-
    ciple" (LV).

DICK HALSING   See   HALSING, DICK (IDB)

DOC.   Owner and operator of the Western Biological Labora-
    tory, Doc is the center of life on Cannery Row.   He is
    small, wears a beard, and his face is half Christ and
    half satyr.   Not only is he a competent marine biologist,
    he is the fountain of science and art and philosophy on
    the Row.   Though he has a complicated personality, his
    mind has no horizon and his sympathies have no warp.
    Everyone who knows Doc feels indebted to him and wants
    to do something for him.   Consequently, Doc is the re-
    cipient of a party thrown by the Row's denizens which
    takes place in Doc's laboratory and is the novel's high
    point.   The book ends with Doc reflecting on the events
    of the party, knowing that he has savored the hot taste
    of life.   The character of Doc is based on Edward F.
    Ricketts, the marine biologist who was Steinbeck's
    closest friend for more than two decades (CR).

DOC.   A benign and pleasant man who is the most beloved

and most preyed-upon citizen of Cannery Row. He has
an IQ of one hundred and eighty-two and a master's and
a Ph.D. from the University of Chicago. Before the
war he was at ease with the world. He liked his work
collecting and preserving various marine animals and
selling them to colleges and museums and he enjoyed
his life observing and participating in a world full of
excitement and interesting people (See Cannery Row).
He was drafted and during the war served as a tech
sergeant in a V.D. section. When he returns to Western Biological Laboratories, he discovers that old
Jingleballicks has failed to keep up the place and it is
now in ruins. He restores the place to its old form,
but he discovers from Mack that Cannery Row has
changed and that he, too, feels a new sense of restlessness and depression. He is haunted by three voices of
intellect, feeling, and instinct, but it is the voice which
comes from his marrow that tells him that he is a
lonely man. Everybody in Cannery Row thinks that he
needs a woman, but Doc turns to the study of emotions
in octopi and puts his soul into researching a paper on
"Symptoms of Some Cephalods Approximating Apoplexy."
The flame of science burns in him for a time, but his
bottom voice mourns his loneliness. He meets a seer
who tells him that there are things that a man cannot
do without love, and his friends begin a plot to find him
a good woman.

He becomes interested in Suzy, the only completely honest human he has ever met, but her honesty creates hostility between them. But Mack hints that Suzy
likes him, and Fauna arranges a dinner for them at
Sonny Boy's. During the date, he confesses to Suzy
that he is lonely. Old Jingleballicks unexpectedly arrives to disrupt Doc's world for a time, but at the
masquerade he embarrassingly accepts Suzy as his girl
only to be rejected by her. He is shocked and hurt by
her actions, but eventually realizes that his failure is
his own fault. He learns from her that she needs a
man who will totally need her and that she feels she
would only spoil Doc's private life. He is sick with his
loss because he now feels that he cannot be whole without her. His dilemma is solved by Hazel who sneaks
into Western Biological while Doc is sleeping and breaks
his right arm with an indoor-ball bat. Suzy comes to
him and agrees to drive him to La Jolla for the spring
tides so that he can find more octopi. He now has the
girl he needs to be emotionally whole, and Old Jingle-

ballicks has set up a foundation for him at Cal Tech so
that he may also pursue his intellectual needs. Mack
and the boys complete his joy by presenting him with
the gift purchased from the raffle money. It turns out
to be a telescope rather than a microscope, but Doc
with choked voice admits that it does not matter whether
you look down or up--so long as you look (ST).

DOC BURTON See BURTON, DOC (IDB)

DOC WILKINS See WILKINS, DOC (ST)

DOCTOR, THE. A wealthy physician known for his prejudice, cruelty, avarice and sins, who refuses to treat
Coyotito's scorpion bite until Kino finds the pearl and
can guarantee payment (P).

DR. EDWARDS See EDWARDS, DR. (EE)

DR. H. C. MURPHY See MURPHY, Dr. H. C. (EE)

DOCTOR HOLMES See HOLMES, DOCTOR (LV)

DR. HORACE DORMODY See DORMODY, DR. HORACE
(ST)

DR. HORACE LIEBHOLTZ See LIEBHOLTZ, DR. HORACE
(WB)

DR. MARN See MARN, DR. (LV)

DR. PHILLIPS See PHILLIPS, DR. (LV)

DR. PHILLIPS See PHILLIPS, DR. (PH)

DR. TILSON See TILSON, DR. (EE)

DR. WICK See WICK, DR. (ST)

DOCTOR WINTER See WINTER, DOCTOR (MID)

DOCTOR'S SERVANT, THE. Opens the gate for Kino when
he comes to see the doctor (P).

DOGGEL, WALTER. With William Deal, he escaped to England in a boat (MID).

DOLORES ENGRACIA ("SWEETS") RAMIREZ See RAMI-
REZ, DOLORES ENGRACIA ("SWEETS") (TF).

DON GUIERMO See GUIERMO, DON (CG)

DON JUAN PEREZ DE GUZMAN See GUZMAN, DON JUAN
PEREZ DE (CG)

DON PEDRO See PEDRO, DON (CG)

DORA FLOOD See FLOOD, DORA (CR) (ST)

DORA WILLIAMS See WILLIAMS, DORA (TF)

DORMODY, DR. HORACE. Examines Doc after he returns
to Cannery Row, but discovers no secret infection
which might be causing his restlessness and sense of
failure. He also treats Doc for a broken arm caused
by a blow from a club. On the second Sweet Thursday
he whistles over an appendectomy and tells a political
joke to the anesthetist (ST).

DOUBLEBOTTOM, ELSIE. A whore at the Bear Flag who,
during a busy season on the Row, makes a novena and
is suddenly useless in her profession (CR).

DOUBLETREE MUTT See MUTT, DOUBLETREE (LV)

DOUXPIED, M. Secretary of the French Communist party.
A titular leader of the party since M. Deuxcloches holds
the actual leadership. At a group caucus during the
conference of parties to select a new French government
he warmly clasps the hand of M. Deuxcloches as a symbolic gesture of agreement after being assured the
French party would privately but not officially advocate
the return of the monarchy (SRP).

DUC DES TROISFRONTS See TROISFRONTS, DUC DES
(SRP)

DUCHESSE DES TROISFRONTS See TROISFRONTS, DUCH-
ESSE DES (SRP)

DUENNA. An old woman who tends La Santa Roja (CG).

E

EASTER ("The Red Pony"). Carl Tiflin says Easter, his
thirty-year-old horse, is too old to live and should be
shot. When Carl also rejects Gitano, the old man
takes Easter and goes into the Great Mountains (LV).

EATON, WILLIE. Chairman of the entertainment committee
at Weedpatch government camp. His eyes are gray and
sunburned from the Texas panhandle. He is a stringy
man with long, loose arms and legs, "a long fragile
jaw, and dust-colored hair." Willie prevents the infiltrators from starting a riot at the Saturday night dance
(GW).

ED. Deputized to patrol the road by the strikers' camp, Ed
is told to cover Mac and Jim with his rifle. Knowing
they are to be shot, Jim trips the deputy guarding him
and the two escape (IDB).

ED CHAPPELL See CHAPPELL, ED (LV)

ED, FRIEND See FRIEND ED (BB)

EDDIE. One of Mack's group of vagabonds who occasionally
fills in as bartender at La Ida. While working, Eddie
keeps a large jug under the bar with a funnel in its
mouth. Anything left in any glass Eddie pours into the
funnel, so that on most nights he takes back to the
Palace Flophouse a mixture of rye, beer, bourbon,
scotch, wine, rum and gin, spiced with a little angus-
tura. Obviously, Eddie is a much-admired member of
Mack's group (CR).

EDDIE. One of the inhabitants of the Palace Flophouse.
During the war he stayed on as bartender at the Cafe
La Ida where out of sentiment he emptied the winning
jug into a series of little kegs which he buried (see
Cannery Row). He wishes that Doc owned the Palace
Flophouse and unwittingly inspires Mack's plan to save
their home from the greed of Joseph and Mary. He is
the one who is sent to tell Suzy about Doc's broken
arm. His main function in the group is to provide a
jug for the meetings. He tends to say little during
Mack's strategy sessions (ST).

EDGAR. Youthful clerk at the San Ysidro Greyhound termi-

nal. A cog in the apparatus of mechanized transporta-
tion and delivery, he tips his hand when he apprentices
himself to an irreparably flawed model, Louie the bus-
driver and would-be pacesetter. By emulating Louie's
unlikely fashion of growing one fingernail to grotesque
length, Edgar participates in a recurrent motif of the
novel, a nervous tick about fingers and, inferentially,
about the entire body and its natural functions. Because it sponsors vicarious images of sexual competition and conquest, Edgar's relationship to Louie ap-
proximates Pimples' relationship to Chicoy. But Edgar
is no more than a contemptible facsimile of Pimples, a
mere parody or understudy (WB).

EDWARD MANSVELDT See MANSVELDT, EDWARD (CG)

EDWARD WICKS See WICKS, EDWARD (PH)

EDWARDS, DR. A physician who tends Adam Trask after
     his stroke (EE).

EDWARDS, MR. Manager of a circuit route of prostitutes.
     With his wife and two children, he lives in affluence in
     a good Boston neighborhood. In his late forties, he is
     large, powerful, slightly fat but in good condition.
     When Cathy Ames, calling herself Amesbury, applies
     for a job with him, he violates his own rule of never
     mixing his professional life with his private pleasures
     and falls in love with her. Though "as coldblooded a
     whoremaster as ever lived," he keeps her in luxury.
     She in turn makes him miserable with her restlessness
     and dissatisfaction, and taunts and maneuvers to steal
     from him. When he makes her drunk, she reveals her
     true nature, mocks him, and cuts his cheek with the
     broken edge of a champagne glass. In turn, he takes
     her into the country and beats her nearly to death. Af-
     terwards he returns to his wife and dies at the age of
     67 from strangling on a chicken bone (EE).

EDWARDS, MRS. Wife of Mr. Edwards, the whoremaster.
     She believes that her husband is an importer. To her,
     Mr. Edwards is coldly thoughtful, neither warm nor cru-
     el; and she is content with life, devoting herself to her
     sons, to housekeeping, and to the church (EE).

ELEGANT, JOE. Cook for the Bear Flag and budding novel-
     ist. Since his services are never required late at night,

he retires early and rises at four. This gives him
three or four hours to write his novel, The Pi Root of
Oedipus. His book is a composite of dark moods, pale
odors, decaying dreams, and guilt-ridden characters fit
for mental wards. He dresses Hazel in a hideously
grotesque version of Prince Charming for the masquerade. His revenge on mankind is blunted, however, by
the guests who refuse to laugh at Hazel and by the cold-
ness he receives when he returns from the safety of his
hiding place (ST).

ELISA ALLEN See ALLEN, ELISA (LV)

ELIZABETH. A pretty young girl in Wales for whom Henry
    longed. Her womanly character frightens and embar-
    rasses Henry. When he tries to visit her on his last
    night home and sees through her window the outline of
    her figure through her dress and the fine curve of her
    legs and swell of her hips, a wild shame fills him and
    he runs away into the night (CG).

ELIZABETH McGREGGOR See McGREGGOR, ELIZABETH
    (TGU)

ELIZABETH MORGAN See MORGAN, ELIZABETH (CG)

ELIZABETH WAYNE See WAYNE, ELIZABETH (TGU)

ELLA. Waitress-manager of the Golden Poppy. She works
    around the clock and cannot remember a time when her
    feet and back did not ache and she did not feel tired.
    After Suzy is hired as a waitress, she undergoes a re-
    markable change. She surrenders to her fatigue and
    eventually rediscovers an interest in her own well-being
    (ST).

ELLA SUMMER See SUMMER, ELLA (GW)

ELLIOTT PRITCHARD See PRITCHARD, ELLIOTT (WB)

ELSIE DOUBLEBOTTOM See DOUBLEBOTTOM, ELSIE
    (CR)

EMALIN HAWKINS See HAWKINS, EMALIN (LV)

EMIL (The Burgundian). A fat little pirate (partner of An-
    toine) with a very red face, who is nervous and excit-

able.   Before he joined Morgan's army, Emil was married to a lovely woman in Burgundy whose sexual indis-
cretions forced Emil to murder two of her lovers and
cut off the arm of a third.   Emil is hanged by Morgan
after Morgan becomes Lieutenant-Governor of Jamaica
(CG).

EMILIO MURIETTA See MURIETTA, EMILIO (TF)

EMILIO TORRES See TORRES, EMILIO (LV)

EMMA RANDALL See RANDALL, EMMA (LV)

ERNEST HORTON See HORTON, ERNEST (WB)

ERNST STEINBECK See STEINBECK, ERNST (EE)

ETHAN ALLEN HAWLEY See HAWLEY, ETHAN ALLEN
   (WOD)

ETHEL.   A former prostitute in Kate's brothel.   After some
   years away, she returns to blackmail Kate with details
   of Faye's murder.   Ethel is lazy and sloppy but goodhearted.   Never very pretty nor very bright, she has
   become fat and heavy, with poverty-stricken clothing.
   When she infected a customer with venereal disease, he
   hurt her nose and knocked out four teeth.   Ethel sees
   Kate bury the eye-dropper and smashed medicine bottles
   that contained the poison Kate used to kill Faye.   She
   digs up the broken glass and saves it for evidence.
   When Ethel tries to blackmail Kate into giving her $100
   a month, Kate has her framed for stealing the money,
   and the judge runs her over the county line.   Ethel is
   drowned at Santa Cruz, but Joe conceals this fact from
   Kate and harasses her with hints that Ethel is still
   around threatening to get revenge by revealing the facts
   of the murder.   This fear is one of the factors behind
   Kate's suicide (EE).

EUSKADI, JULIUS.   A farmer of Basque extraction who ac-
   companies Horace Quinn to examine the shooting of
   Adam Trask.   Julius has a knack for investigation and
   for weighing evidence, and Horace deputizes him.   When
   Quinn goes to Salinas to see the sheriff, he leaves
   Julius in charge at the Trask ranch (EE).

EVA.   One of the prostitutes at Kate's brothel.   She is a

drug addict, with a soft voice and a sharp face that reminds Adam Trask of a predatory animal. When Adam
first goes to Kate's place, Eva is the girl who greets
him (EE).

EVA FLANEGAN See FLANEGAN, EVA (CR)

EVELYN, JOHN. British diarist and confidant of King
    Charles the Second who is present when Morgan appears
    before the King. Evelyn realizes that Morgan is a fool-
    ish man whose folly and whose distorted vision were the
    source of his greatness (CG).

EXPRESSMAN, THE. Delivers to the Palace Flophouse a
    large crate which contains the instrument Mack and the
    boys have purchased for Doc's study of the octopi (ST).

EZRA HUSTON See HUSTON, EZRA (GW)

                              F

FAFNIR, BERTHA. Third grader remembered by Hazel.
    She used to draw pictures of turkeys on the blackboard
    during the Thanksgiving season (ST).

FAT CARL See CARL, FAT (LV)

FAT MAN. A filling station attendant in Oklahoma. He has
    red arms and face, wears brown corduroys, suspenders
    and polo shirt, and has a silver cardboard sun helmet.
    He complains of beggars and is dumbfounded by all the
    poor families moving west, who want to barter goods
    for gasoline. He repeatedly says he doesn't know what
    the country is coming to (GW).

FATHER BENEDICT See BENEDICT, FATHER (LV)

FATHER HAWLEY See HAWLEY, FATHER (WOD)

FATHER MURPHY See MURPHY, FATHER (ST)

FATHER MURPHY See MURPHY, FATHER (TF)

FATHER RAMON See RAMON, FATHER (TF)

FAUNA (FLORA) FLOOD See FLOOD, FAUNA (FLORA)
    (ST)

FAYE. Madam of the third whorehouse in Salinas. She is
"the motherly type, big-breasted, big-hipped, and
warm." Her house specializes in genteel sex, reassur-
ing wayward husbands and adolescent initiates in a soft
and casual way. Faye herself is "a nice woman, not
very bright, highly moral, and easily shocked." She
becomes a stable citizen of Salinas and contributes
heavily to the local charities. Taking advantage of
Faye's gullibility and good nature, Kate works her way
into the madam's affections and becomes her adopted
daughter. When Faye wills all her money to Kate, the
latter poisons her. Years later, fear that evidence of
the murder will be revealed is a leading factor in
Kate's suicide (EE).

FENCHEL, MR. A tailor in Salinas. He is short, round,
and has a thick German accent. When World War I
breaks out, he is the victim of anti-German hysteria.
The Home Guard rejects him, and a mob of vigilantes
tears down his white picket fence and burns the front
out of his house (EE).

FLANEGAN, EVA. A whore in the Bear Flag who, during
a particularly busy season on the Row, takes a vacation to St. Louis and so leaves Dora shorthanded (CR).

FLOOD, DORA. A very large woman with flaming orange
hair who is the madam of the Bear Flag Restaurant
where people have actually tried to purchase sandwiches.
Dora has been a girl and madam for fifty years, and
through her special gift of honesty, tact, charity and a
certain realism, she has become respected by the
learned and the intelligent and the kind of Monterey.
Dora leads a ticklish life, for, because she operates
against the law, she must be more law-abiding than
most people. Moreover, she must be especially phil-
anthropic, since everyone solicits money from her.
She is a good woman, kind to her girls. And she is a
bright woman, who understands Doc's complicated needs
(CR).

FLOOD, DORA. Former owner of the Bear Flag (see Cannery Row). She died in her sleep. Her girls were so
broken-hearted that they put on a lady-drunk which
lasted three days (ST).

FLOOD, FAUNA (FLORA). Former silent partner of the

Bear Flag. She took over the place when her sister
Dora Flood died in her sleep (See Cannery Row). She
gave the Bear Flag its name by insisting that if you
were hustling a state, you should do honor to it. She
reads horoscopes and continues, after hours at least,
to transform the Bear Flag into a kind of finishing
school for her girls. At her former business, a Mid-
night Mission, a bum told her, "Flora, you seem more
a fauna-type to me." She was Fauna forever afterward. She is an astute judge of character. She hires
Suzy but knows she is not a born hustler. When Joseph
and Mary Rivers warn her against Suzy, she points out,
with the aid of a parable about her missionary days in
South America, that people need to be a patsy now and
then. Her horoscope readings lead Hazel to believe he
will be a nine-toed President of the United States.
They also generate a romance between Doc and Suzy.
She is a benevolent and public-spirited woman who
takes pride in the ladies from the Bear Flag who marry
well, and she sets about trapping Doc for Suzy. She
gets Doc to take Suzy out to dinner on Sweet Thursday,
and arranges all the details. She gives Mack the idea
of a masquerade for the raffle and, after suggesting
the theme of Snow White and the Seven Dwarfs, decides
to dress as a witch-like fairy godmother and present
Suzy as a kind of bridal Snow White for Doc. Her plan
fails miserably, but later she gives Hazel the beginning
of an idea when she tells him that Doc and Suzy should
go to La Jolla together. After Hazel acts to bring off
the trip by breaking Doc's right arm, she relieves
Hazel of any further thinking by telling him that her
horoscope was wrong. She also points out that Hazel
has ten toes (ST).

FLOSSE, M. Right Centrist and a member of the committee
    that carries word to Pippin Arnulf Héristal of his elec-
    tion by proclamation as King of France. He emotional-
    ly tells Pippin that a king is needed to restore continu-
    ity to the French government (SRP).

FLOWER, JAMES. A planter in Barbados who buys Henry
    Morgan as an indentured servant. He is a soft man
    and not a very bright one. His whole life had been a
    search for ideas--any ideas--and he hadn't found any.
    He has a large library and reads a great deal, but his
    learning was pointless because it formed no design of
    the whole. "His mind," notes Steinbeck, "was a sad

mass of unrelated facts and theories." He indulges young Henry, and unwittingly permits him to use his period of indenture to plan for a life as a buccaneer (CG).

FLOYD KNOWLES See KNOWLES, FLOYD (GW)

FRANCISCO, SUSIE. On occasion, Pilon varies his role as resident metaphysician by offering moonlight services as a necromancer. He "had a big round sugar cookie in a bag, that Susie Francisco, who works in a bakery, had given him in return for a formula for getting the love of Charlie Guzman." Susie's ultimately successful intrigue for Charlie is a trifling, comic affair in the novel, but it is nevertheless a mark of Steinbeck's tightly knit technique. When he first visits the Pirate, Pilon brings a candle to shed light on the Pirate's secret treasure. Presently, the Pirate explains that his horde will purchase a sacred candle to honor Saint Francis. Furthermore, Pilon relies on Susie's sugar cookie to lure the Pirate away from his chaste mission. The apparent link between Susie's seduction of Charlie and Pilon's rapacious plans for the innocent Pirate indicates that Steinbeck's choice for Susie's last name is anything but haphazard (TF).

FRANKIE. A young boy, mentally handicapped, who forms a strong attachment to Doc. He has large eyes and dark wiry hair. Alone and unwanted, Frankie has no place to go. He cannot attend school and his parents (or parent) refuse to pay for his upkeep in an institution. Consequently, he spends his days at Doc's laboratory and sleeps in an old excelsior crate. In an act of love, Frankie breaks into a jewelry store and steals a large black onyx clock which he wants to give to Doc. He is apprehended and committed to a mental institution (CR).

FRANKLIN GOMEZ See GOMEZ, FRANKLIN (PH)

FRIEND ED. Joe Saul's close friend and confidant. He is a clown, a farmer, and a sailor. He is a reflective man, taller and heavier than Joe Saul and slower in speech. He attempts to make Saul understand why Mordeen has committed adultery with Victor. He attacks Saul's inflated ego and his inability to receive, and he eventually convinces Saul that he should accept "The Child." Shortly before the book ends, Friend Ed tells Joe Saul he has

his "sailing orders," so that Saul must make his commitment to Mordeen and to her child without him. Before he goes, however, he pushes the threatening Victor overboard (BB).

FROST, RICHARD. A high-strung, if brilliant, young man
who is deeply troubled when he cannot understand how
a flagpole sitter at a local department store eliminates.
When he finds that the sitter keeps a can up with him,
he is content (CR).

G

GABILAN ("The Red Pony"). Jody calls his red pony Gabilan, a name derived from the jolly Gabilan Mountains
to the east of the Tiflin ranch (LV).

GALVEZ. In Chapter III, Galvez' "bad bulldog" forbears at-
tacking the "wistful and shining" version of Pilon but
presently regrets the oversight when Pilon reverts to
his customary "cunning mixture of good and evil." At
the end of the novel, Galvez himself personifies self-
righteous respectability when he buys elegant finery for
Danny's funeral and parades past the unkempt, humili-
ated survivors of Danny's household. The bit performances of Galvez and his bulldog function as a burlesque
but not insignificant moral chorus. In Tortilla Flat,
Steinbeck does not specify moral norms that in turn generate action. Rather, readers must infer normative values from a dialectical play of character and incident.
The reading activity is inductive and strenuously experi-
ential, not a passive response to authorial dictate. Even
Galvez' bulldog is faced with dainty problems of moral
perception. Correspondingly, the reader must decide
whether to love Galvez' cur is to love Galvez, or whether Galvez' ostentation is the antithesis of the bulldog's
scrupulous discriminations. In addition, the reader
must fashion a response to an author who addresses
matters of high principle at the level of beast fable and
low comedy (TF).

GARCIA, ALICE. Wife of Juanito. She is courted and won
by Juanito in the traditional Spanish manner. She is seduced by Benjamin Wayne, who is killed by Juanito during the act. She mourns the loss of her husband who
has fled after killing Benjy because she is carrying a
child at the time. Elizabeth brings her to Joseph

Wayne's house and puts her to work in the kitchen.
She becomes happier and shares in the general activity
of the ranch with the children. She returns to her
home to bear her baby and brings her son back to the
Wayne ranch. She eventually goes back to Nuestra
Señora to wait for the return of her husband. After
serving a dinner of the famous beans that Elizabeth
loved so well to Juanito and Joseph Wayne, she asks
Joseph to bless her child whom she has named in honor
of him (TGU).

GARCIA, JESUS. Father of Alice Garcia. His family can
prove at least one true Spanish ancestor. He listens
with a mixture of admiration and skepticism to Juanito's
mild boasts and formal words, and with a comely re-
luctance accepts Juanito as son-in-law. He claims to
have seen a fiery goat crossing the Carmel Valley one
night at dusk. When Juanito returns to his wife after
a period of self-exile, Jesus Garcia and his wife tactfully go visiting in San Luis Obispo. He loves his
grandson and calls him Chango (TGU).

GARCIA, MRS. Mother of Alice Garcia. She too listens
with a mixture of admiration and skepticism to Juanito's
mild boasts, and, as decorum suggests, she and her
daughter retire so that Juanito may speak formal words
to her husband. When Juanito returns to his wife after
a period of self-exile, Mrs. Garcia and her husband
tactfully go visiting in San Luis Obispo (TGU).

GARDENER, THE. A gardener at Versailles. He orders
Pippin IV to remove himself from the royal garden.
He does not recognize the king and assumes he is a
tourist (SRP).

GARRIGAS, MR. Salesman and regular customer at the
Golden Poppy. Suzy remembers his name and that he
likes cream of celery soup (ST).

GASTON, MRS. Has a kidney stone removed which is as big
as a hand and shaped like a dog's head, a beagle (ST).

GAY. One of the most interesting members of Mack's group
of vagabonds. Gay is an inspired mechanic who is one
of those few men who can look, listen, tap and make a
broken machine work. In flight from a domineering
wife, Gay spends a good deal of his time in jail for

beating her in self-defense. Actually, Gay enjoys his
stints in the new Salinas jail where there are radios,
good bunks and a nice sheriff (CR).

GAY. A former resident at the Palace Flophouse (see Cannery Row). He was killed by a piece of anti-aircraft
fallback in London. His wife remarried on his Army
insurance, but the boys keep his bed as it were as a
little shrine. He is remembered from time to time
when the boys think about the old days (ST).

GELTHAM, MR. Mentioned as having an affair with the
school teacher. Joe Blaikey, the town constable, knows
that he is sleeping with her and how often. Also mentioned as a customer at the Golden Poppy (ST).

GELTHAM, MRS. Mentioned as a woman who gives big
parties. Joe Blaikey, the town constable, knows why
she gives a party and who is likely to be there (ST).

GENDARME, THE FIRST. On duty at Versailles. He asks
Pippin IV to remove himself from a place in the shade
on a great stairway. He does not recognize the king
and tells him that the visiting hours are from two to
five (SRP).

GENDARME, THE SECOND. He intercepts Pippin Héristal
as he returns home after the Paris rioting. He examines Pippin's card of identity and remembers him as a
resident of Number One Avenue de Marigny rather than
as the disposed King of France (SRP).

GENERAL VICTOR GONZEL See GONZEL, GENERAL VIC-
TOR (SRP)

GEORGE. A vigilante who kills Casy. He is a short heavy
man who smashes Casy's head with a pick handle.
Tom Joad seizes the club and kills George with it (GW).

GEORGE. A Black menial at the San Ysidro Greyhound ter-
minal. On the bus he is cleaning, George finds a wallet containing $100. His scheme is to pocket the money
undetected and have himself a spree, but "a punk kid"
thwarts him, and afterward Louie even cheats him out
of his reward money. With George, Steinbeck dramatizes a stark vignette of racial and economic exploitation doing its grim work (WB).

GEORGE ("The Murder"). A neighbor of Jim Moore, George
reports the discovery of the slaughter of one of Jim's
cattle. The incident causes Jim to cancel his Saturday
trip to Monterey and leads to his discovery of Jelka's
infidelity (LV).

GEORGE BATTLE See BATTLE, GEORGE (PH)

GEORGE CAMP See CAMP, GEORGE (IDB)

GEORGE CORELL See CORELL, GEORGE (MID)

GEORGE HAMILTON See HAMILTON, GEORGE (EE)

GEORGE MILTON See MILTON, GEORGE (OMM)

GEORGE MORGAN See MORGAN, GEORGE (PH)

GEORGES DE MARINE See MARINE, GEORGES DE (SRP)

GIRL ON THE BUS. Mack's companion aboard an eastward-
bound bus which he takes because his Geiger counter
starts buzzing at the Monterey bus station. He travels
to Salina, Kansas with the girl until he discovers that
he has been following the radium of her watch (ST).

GIRL WITH NO NAME. Young lady companion with Doc on
his first trip to La Jolla. She grows disgruntled when
Doc shows more interest in the baby octopi he has
found than her. She is given no name because she never returns to Western Biological Laboratories (ST).

GITANO ("The Red Pony"). An old paisano who arrived at
the Tiflin ranch stating, "I am Gitano, and I have come
back." Having been born on that land, he had returned
to die. Carl sends him away; and taking an old horse
that is also used up, Gitano goes into the Great Mountains to await the end (LV).

GOGI. A high-wire man. Very handsome, but nervous, former lover of the Duchess of P_____ (SRP).

GOMEZ, FRANKLIN. Rancher who pulls his whiskers a
good deal. He takes in the baby, Tularecito, found by
his ranch hand, Pancho. Although he raises the boy, he
never claims to be able to understand him (PH).

GOMEZ, MANUEL. One of the inhabitants of Our Lady.
When the rain finally comes, he carries a wet coyote
pelt that he will wear in the ritual celebration of the
event (TGU).

GONZEL, GENERAL VICTOR. World's authority on the proper use of the muzzle-loading pistol. Because of the increased interest in the aristocratic arts and graces
caused by the return of the French monarchy, he gives
daily instructions in the use of the pistol to half a hundred budding courtiers (SRP).

GRACIE MONTEZ See MONTEZ, GRACIE (TF)

GRAMPA JOAD See JOAD, GRAMPA (WILLIAM JAMES
JOAD) (GW)

GRANMA JOAD See JOAD, GRANMA (GW)

GRAVES, MISS. Fourth grade teacher who sings the lead in
the butterfly pageant in Pacific Grove. She sees her
first leprechaun on Sweet Thursday. She loses her
voice two days before the arrival of the butterflies, but
regains it on another Sweet Thursday in the spring (ST).

GRAVES, MULEY. A neighbor of the Joads, who has been
evicted from his farm. He is a short, lean man with
quick jerky movements. His face is smooth and un-
wrinkled, but his little eyes and small, tight mouth are
scowling and petulant. He wears worn blue jeans, a
ragged black suit coat, and a stained black hat with a
torn and flopping band. Muley is the first farmer Tom
Joad meets after leaving prison, and Muley explains to
him the circumstances under which his family and neigh-
bors have lost their land and are planning to migrate to
California. He informs Tom that he can find his family at Uncle John's place. Muley refuses to leave his
own land; his family heritage and roots are there, and
he insists that "Places where folks live is them folks."
Muley is embittered at the bankers and officials who
have "chopped folks in two for their margin a'profit."
The Joads invite Muley to go with them to California,
but he insists on staying behind, alone, even though
Noah predicts that he will die out in the field (GW).

GREAT-AUNT DEBORAH See DEBORAH, GREAT-AUNT
(WOD)

GREW, JAMES. Latin teacher at Cathy Ames's high school. He is "a pale intense young man" who becomes a teacher after failing in divinity school. In some unspecified way, Cathy has a relationship with him that makes him briefly ecstatic but quickly reduces him to feverish dejection. When Mr. Ames refuses to talk to him in the middle of a desperate night, he blows his head off before the altar in the church. He is Cathy's first victim (EE).

GRIPPO. The pirate captain of the Ganymede. Grippo is a weak captain who is afraid of his own shadow. Back in port after an expedition on which he took no prize, he sells his captaincy to Henry (CG).

GROSS, ARABELLA. In Chapter IV, Arabella Gross in the passing object of Jesus Maria's fancy, and for the remainder of the novel she is the intermittent topic of daydream and dalliance. Along with Sweets Ramirez and Cornelia Ruiz, Arabella is a member of a loose sisterhood of eligible younger women who casually bestow sexual favors on Danny and his followers. It is unclear whether the women are pitiable victims or predatory opportunists. The exotic allure of the name Arabella does not rule out gross violence when four soldiers, Arabella's latest suitors, administer a savage beating: "Arabella Gross helped too. She hit me on the head with a rock," Jesus Maria laments. Such sirens are clearly dangerous, but often the perilous vortex of courtly romance proves weaker than the chivalrous code that unites Danny's group in a cameraderie exclusively masculine. When Jesus Maria discloses his intention to buy a $3 brassiere for Arabella, Pilon and Pablo garnish $2 so that Danny can give candy to Mrs. Morales. Eventually, the money goes for wine, the brassiere goes into safe-keeping, and the four inseparables go on a bachelor carouse. Danny's rented house and his courteous attentions to Mrs. Morales have just been reduced to ashes on the same eventful evening, but Danny's sudden escape from the twin burdens of property and sex brings immense relief, not even feigned anger. The episode is a gathering point for the motifs of violence and sexual exploitation, and the Arthurian apparatus of the narrative seldom becomes more explicit (TF).

GROSS, MR. Regular customer at the Golden Poppy. Suzy becomes so distraught when she hears of Doc's broken

right arm that she forgets who Mr. Gross is. She
calls him "you" and sickens him by serving his eggs
straight up (ST).

GUARD ON THE FLATCAR. Mack wins a few dollars from
him on his return to Monterey after his Geiger counter
adventure. Mack uses the money to get the Palace
Flophouse ready for the return of his friends from the
war (ST).

GUGGLIELMO See CORTEZ, MR. ALFRED (TF)

GUIERRMO, DON. A citizen of Panama who fears Morgan's
invasion and tells tales of Morgan's power of evil (CG).

GUITTIEREZ, MRS. Mrs. Guittierez, who "cut little chiles
into her enchilada sauce," is a minor detail, a piquant
tidbit of local color, in the panoramic montage of Monterey at twilight that Steinbeck memorably depicts in
Chapter V (TF).

GUS. The driver of a large Mack dump-truck that pulls up
to the migrant camp toward the end of the novel.
Standing in the back of the truck with a submachine-
gun, the sheriff tells London that he will give the workers until daylight to get out of the county (IDB).

GUSTAVE HARMONIE See HARMONIE, GUSTAVE (SRP)

GUTIERREZ, MRS. One of the inhabitants of Our Lady. She
gives Joseph and Elizabeth Wayne a chicken as a wedding gift. When the rain finally comes, she carries a
moth-eaten bear skin that she will wear in the ritual
celebration of the event (TGU).

GUZMAN, CHARLIE. "Charlie was a Postal Telegraph mes-
senger and rode a motorcycle" and was the prey of
Susie Francisco's spider and fly campaign of seduction.
Charlie gets Susie's message only with the assistance
of Pilon's love potion. ("I guess it must have been the
poison oak in it that made Charlie Guzman sick.") It
is characteristic of Steinbeck's minor figures that they
etch an indelible impression, however fleeting their appearance on stage. With precision and dispatch, Steinbeck lampoons an Anglo society in which men flee to
machines to sublimate sex and in which the robust flow
of communication is stopped up by superfluous titles (TF).

GUZMAN, DON JUAN PEREZ DE. Governor of Panama
whose life was devoted entirely to being a complete
gentleman. He was a good soldier, if a poor military
campaigner. He dressed well, was proud and condescending. He had the richest blood and the fullest ware-
houses in the entire city. He is no match for Henry
Morgan who easily conquers the city (CG).

GWENLIANA MORGAN See MORGAN, GWENLIANA (CG)

H

H. W. JOHNSON See JOHNSON, H. W. (SRP)

HAL MAHLER See MAHLER, HAL (EE)

HALSING, DICK. A Party member, described by Mac as a
bedroom radical. He uses his charm on those who
sympathize with the labor movement to get the necessary food and supplies to support the striking laborers
(IDB).

HAMILTON, DESSIE. The third daughter of Samuel and Liza
Hamilton. Dessie is full of fun and laughter, and everyone loves her. She and her brother Tom are particularly close. She wears a gold pince-nez that falls off
the bridge of her nose when she bursts into laughter.
Dessie runs a dressmaking shop in Salinas, which is
immensely popular because of her relaxed and infectious
good humor. When she falls in love (no one knows with
whom), the affair becomes hopeless and drains the joy
and laughter out of her. When her business falls off,
she sells it and joins Tom at the ranch. For a while,
they regain their gaiety, but it does not last. Dessie
suffers from increasingly agonizing abdominal pains,
perhaps from appendicitis, perhaps from cancer. After
a severe bout, Tom doses her with salts; the treatment
brings on her death, and Tom, in guilt and remorse,
commits suicide (EE).

HAMILTON, GEORGE. The oldest son of Samuel and Liza
Hamilton. He is a tall and handsome boy with a courtly
bearing. George is neat in appearance and sinless in
conduct. He prospers in the insurance business but
learns in his middle-age that he has pernicious anemia
(EE).

HAMILTON, JOSEPH. The fourth and youngest son of Samuel and Liza Hamilton. The baby of the family, he
acts helpless to protect himself from work. He is a
mooning boy, given to lazy daydreams and to writing
verse. Spoiled and coddled, he gets what he wants
with a minimum of effort. He is inept at farming, so
the family sends him East to college. Upon graduation,
he becomes very successful in advertising (EE).

HAMILTON, LIZA. Grandmother of John Steinbeck, wife of
Samuel Hamilton, and mother of the Hamilton family in
Salinas Valley. She comes from Ireland with her husband but has a different nature. Where he is expan-
sive and inventive, she is Puritanical and constrained.
She believes that idleness, card playing, fun and laughter are sinful. A good cook and an immaculate housekeeper, she does not like work for its own sake but
does it as a duty. She has no sense of humor and
thinks that life is not to be enjoyed but to be endured
with uncomplaining fortitude. Her head is small and
round, and she wears her hair pulled back tight and
knotted in a bun. Liza reads only the Bible, which she
accepts without question. There is "a nail-hard
strength in her, a lack of any compromise, a rightness
in the face of all opposing wrongness" that makes her
universally respected but held in awe rather than
warmth. A militant teetotaler, she considers any consumption of alcohol to be a crime until in her seventies,
when the doctor prescribes port wine for medicine.
Thereafter, she consumes over a quart a day, is never
completely sober, and becomes much more relaxed
(EE).

HAMILTON, LIZZIE. Second daughter of Samuel and Liza
Hamilton. No one knows much about Lizzie, who seems
ashamed of her family, marries young, moves away,
and reappears only at funerals. Unlike the rest of the
family, she has "a capacity for hatred and bitterness"
that causes her to disown her son when he marries a
woman she disapproves of (EE).

HAMILTON, MOLLIE. Fifth daughter of Samuel and Liza
Hamilton. The most beautiful of the girls, she has
blond hair and violet eyes. As a small child, she has
a speech impediment. Her brother Tom sees that it
is caused by a membrane under her tongue and cuts it
with a pocketknife. When Mollie grows up, she marries

and lives in an apartment in San Francisco with a white bearskin rug, and smokes gold-tipped cigarettes (EE).

HAMILTON, OLIVE. Fourth daughter of Samuel and Liza Hamilton, and mother of John Steinbeck. She has a firm chin, button nose, and fine eyes. At the age of 18, she becomes a school teacher at Peach Tree, where she teaches first grade reading and eighth grade algebra. She also writes social notes for the Salinas Journal and runs the social life of the area. After marrying Ernst Steinbeck, she moves to Paso Robles, King City, and finally to Salinas. She is intuitive rather than rational. Though she belongs to the Episcopal Church, she believes in a mixture of Irish fairies and the Old Testament Jehovah. She has an abhorrence of debt. During World War I, she sells more Liberty bonds than anyone in the area and is rewarded with a flight in an army open-cockpit biplane. She is the mother of three daughters and one son, the author (EE).

HAMILTON, SAMUEL. Grandfather of John Steinbeck and father of the Hamilton family in the Salinas Valley. He emigrated from northern Ireland, where he was the son of small farmers. Despite his Irish upbringing, he does not have a brogue but speaks with a singing lilt. He has a rich, deep voice and a patriarchal beard that eventually turns white. His cheeks are pink from sunburn and his hands blackened from the forge. His blue eyes remain youthful looking and become surrounded by wrinkles from laughter. Samuel loves books and is artistic by nature but tries to make a living by ranching on waterless land on the barren hills above the Salinas River. Clever with the hands, he is a jack of all trades--blacksmith, carpenter, wood and metal worker, and a perpetual inventor whose models are stolen by manufacturers and whose profits are taken by the patent attorney. Unable to support his family by ranching, he hires out to do jobs--digging wells, threshing, repairing tools--for other farmers, many of whom never pay him, so that his family lives in marginal poverty. But everyone says he is "a comical genius." He serves as doctor for his family, delivers all his own children, and delivers the twins for Adam and Kathy Trask. He and Lee find a philosophical affinity, and he acts as a sort of mentor for Adam Trask, forcing him from the lethargic despair after Kathy's departure, persuading him to name the twins, and provid-

ing philosophical and psychological guidance. When he
dies, he is greatly mourned, and over 200 people attend his funeral (EE).

HAMILTON, TOM. The third son of Samuel and Liza Ham-
    ilton. Tom has extravagant joys and suffering and re-
    sponds to books and to the world around him with in-
    tense enthusiasm. A manic depressive, he has "a de-
    spairing quality of gaiety" and "a dour and brooding
    ghost." He is dark-faced, with swarthy red skin and
    dark red hair, beard, and flowering moustache, and
    startling blue eyes. He has powerful arms and shoul-
    ders and slim hips. Tom is a mixture of savagery
    and gentleness, fierceness and shyness. He has a
    strong sexual drive that makes him feel unworthy of
    marriage; instead he remains celibate between uncon-
    trollable orgies of sensuality. Though possessing phys-
    ical and mental skills, Tom lacks all competitiveness.
    When the other Hamilton children leave, he stays alone
    on the ranch, writing poetry secretly, sinking deeper
    into books, and becoming increasingly brooding. After
    her unhappy love affair, Dessie joins him on the Ham-
    ilton ranch. When she has severe abdominal pains,
    Tom doses her with salts and unwittingly brings about
    her death. Unable to endure his sense of sin, Tom
    commits suicide (EE).

HAMILTON, UNA. Oldest daughter of Samuel and Liza Ham-
    ilton. "A thoughtful, studious, dark girl," she is Sam-
    uel's favorite. She has little humor and marries a
    poverty-stricken photographer named Anderson who
    fears and scorns the Hamiltons because of their imagi-
    nativeness. Una goes to live with him near the Oregon
    border. There she dies young, worn out from hard-
    ship and poverty, possibly a suicide. Her death turns
    her father into an old man (EE).

HAMILTON, WILL. The second son of Samuel and Liza Ham-
    ilton. Will is dumpy and stolid, with much energy but
    little imagination. Reacting against his father's indi-
    vidualism, Will becomes a conservative and a conform-
    ist in society and politics. He considers ideas revolu-
    tionary and dislikes them accordingly. But he has a
    great knack for making money. Beginning with small
    business activities, he gets a one-third interest in a
    chain of stores and becomes the sole dealer for Ford
    automobiles in the southern half of the valley. He

loves the competitiveness of business and cannot understand the impracticality of other members of his family.
Will sells a car to Adam Trask and goes into partner-
ship with Cal Trask to help him make money contract-
ing the cultivation of beans (EE).

HARMONIE, GUSTAVE. Member of the French Communist
party. At a group caucus during the conference of
parties to select a new French government, he resolves
a seating dispute between M. Deuxcloches and M. Douxpied by declaring that the Communist party is the Communist party, but France is France (SRP).

HARRIET WAYNE See WAYNE, HARRIET

HARRY E. TELLER See TELLER, HARRY E. (LV)

HARRY NILSON See NILSON, HARRY (IDB)

HARTNELL, ALEX ("Johnny Bear"). A farmer in Loma,
California, and a friend of the narrator. Alex attacks
Johnny to protect the reputation of Amy Hawkins (LV).

HASCHI, WALTER. A Japanese amateur astronomer living
in California. The co-discoverer with Pippin Héristal
of the Elysée Comet. He is a regular correspondent
with Pippin. They compare photographs and techniques
(SRP).

HAWKINS, AMY ("Johnny Bear"). Pregnant, apparently by
one of her Chinese laborers, and despondent, Amy
hanged herself. Johnny Bear's relating various conversations he overheard at the Hawkins' house destroyed
the symbol which for years had sustained the town (LV).

HAWKINS, EMALIN ("Johnny Bear"). The older of the aristocratic maiden sisters of Loma, California. The
Hawkins women are symbols for the town. "They're
what we tell our kids when we want to--well, to describe good people." Johnny Bear overheard Emalin
and Dr. Holmes discussing Amy's suicide attempt (LV).

HAWLEY, ALLEN. Ethan's fourteen-year-old son reduces
the Hawley family disgrace to its lowest common denom-
inator. He plagiarizes his entry in the "National I Love
America" essay contest and lays the blame at every
door but his own when the sponsors expose his wrong-

doing. His actions and his attitude caricature the Hawley ancestors, marauding buccaneers who hungered for
loot behind a cover of patriotism. Unlike his sister,
Allen is out of touch with the past. He retains none of
the robust virtue of his namesake, Ethan Allen, and
his nation's literary heritage is little more than a junk-
yard vacated to plunder. His motto, "everybody does
it," with its endemic corollary that the only sin is in
getting caught, strikes the keynote of a generation of
bankrupt perceptions and institutionalized vandalism.

On the threshold of adolescence, Allen is already
the full-fledged wheeler-dealer and accomplished chame-
lon of self-justification. Perhaps he is an especially
unsightly version of the natural man, the pre-lapsarian
ignoramus, or perhaps he is the end-product of dashed
hopes, the enervated spawn of a worn-out liberalism.
Either as atavistic numb-skull or as cankered scion,
he mumbles a squalid language that has bartered away
its majesty and fallen from grace. Ethan stigmatizes
"my august and illiterate son" in words that make a
mockery of the elegant Shakespearian tropes adorning
the novel's title: "Now is the winter of our discontent/
Made glorious summer by this sun of York." In contrast to Richard III's menacing impostures, Allen's vice
is that he proved a "lousy" ventriloquist. He is slav-
ishly addicted to the pre-fabricated verbal and musical
monotonies foisted on contemporary youth culture.

Steinbeck's portrayal is disappointingly evasive.
It would be nonsense to hold Allen entirely responsible
for his own defects, and yet the distinction between
Steinbeck's authorial overtones of disapproval and Ethan's carping jibes at his son's expense is equivocal at
best. Allen is the victim of mass techniques of commercial propaganda, not-so-hidden persuaders insidious-
ly programed to overwhelm the nuclear family unit and
stunt the growth of self-supporting, inner-directed morality. Ethan is the negligent accomplice of circumstance and never faces the fact that he has betrayed his
son. Allen has internalized no durable code of conduct
primarily because his father has dodged the obligation
to offer one. Indignantly, Ethan mouths the platitudes
of a work ethic discredited by his own labor in Marullo's vineyards, a struggle that has been more a soothing alternative to hard choice than an aggressive asser-
tion of time-tested value.

On a solitary occasion, Ethan shows some sympathy for Allen: "He appeared what he had become--sul-

len, conceited, resentful, remote and secret in the
pain and perplexity of his pubescence, a dreadful, har-
rowing time when he must bite everyone near, even
himself, like a dog in a trap." But elsewhere he shows
no quarter and flails away with impunity, as though
Steinbeck, determined to advance nature over nurture,
were content to minimize one of Ethan's most glaring
shortcomings. Usually, the novel is explicit to a fault
when declaring its moral preferences. Steinbeck merely
augments the error if he makes a single exception and
asks his readers to parse Ethan's failure with Allen.
The internal conventions the narrative establishes re-
quire that Steinbeck spell out the reciprocation between
father and son: in warped fashion, the child shows himself father of the man when Ethan begins to ape the
rank behavior he has permitted to flourish in Allen.

Viewed from one nagging perspective, Allen personifies the writer as confidence man, as purveyor of
shoddy illusion contrived for debased ends. Steinbeck
may have been too close to his material when he drafted
his blueprint of Allen Hawley. He had been concerned
about the profile of his readership throughout his career, and writing as he was at the close of a decade
not noted for its moral uplift, he may have harbored
cynical doubts about his own efforts when he arranged
for Allen to seize on the "gimmick" of "audience interest." The revised edition of Holden Caulfield, de-
bunked and discredited, gives vent to Steinbeck's smold-
ering outrage only at the sacrifice of plausibility and
fair play (WOD).

HAWLEY, CAP'N. Cap'n Hawley was the elder statesman,
the venerable and sagacious Nestor, of Ethan's boyhood. Ethan's recollections of his grandfather summon
up the picture of "a fierce old man with a white whisker
fringe" whose whaling days had long since ended but who
stubbornly kept alive the traditions of a bygone era.
Drawing on his encyclopedic memory, he drilled Ethan
in the catechism of nautical lore and lay the foundation
of his masculine sense of duty. In keeping with the
iron law of his calling, the veteran mariner never forgave Baker's father for setting fire to their ship, the
Belle-Adair; but he was not vindictive and refused to
visit the sin of the father on the head of the son. Baker
recalls "a truculent man, some thought a quarrelsome
man"; but a more balanced portrait reveals a heroic,
larger-than-life figure who mastered the challenges of

everyday existence and preached the gospel of stout
self-reliance.

The Cap'n survives in Ethan's mind not just as a
quaint image but as the voice of certain authority: "He
didn't argue--never did. Just said I must, and so I
did." When this inner lode-star of his moral compass
begins to fade, Ethan has learned to mistrust his personal bearings: "I do know that when I am not friends
with myself old Cap'n doesn't come clear. That's a
kind of test of my personal relations with myself." As
a man, the Cap'n is the succinct spokesman for a fin-
ite fund of practical experience more than the eloquent
lyricist of the sea's fathomless mystique. As a character, he acquires dramatic stature through a steady
accumulation of concrete detail and is seldom the
mouthpiece for windy pontifications. Rhetoric is the
special province of the 19th century authors he recom-
mended when Ethan was a boy and who remain stored
--and memorable--in the attic of the Hawley manse.
Like the strong-ribbed ships he once commanded, the
Cap'n navigates the real world of human commerce
(WOD).

HAWLEY, ELLEN See HAWLEY (MARY) ELLEN (WOD)

HAWLEY, ETHAN ALLEN. In The Winter of Our Discon-
    tent, Steinbeck's fiction addresses the theme, "the state
    of the union, dead," during the restless period, Easter
    through July 4th, 1960. It is the time when thoughtful
    Americans are first beginning to make out the distinc-
    tive profile of the post-World War II era. From Stein-
    beck's seasoned vantage point, the Eisenhower years of
    the 1950s project a scene of unrelieved mediocrity,
    Cold War psychology, McCarthyism, and corruption.
    The providential splendor of a nation's birthright lies
    parched and wasted; estranged and dispossessed, an en-
    tire people squanders its energies on petty affairs; the
    sustaining metaphors of a once-proud patriotism have
    turned poisonous at their source. Steinbeck himself
    seems alienated within a hostile warp of time and des-
    perately determined, by dint of sheer effort, to estab-
    lish the imprint of his familiar literary perceptions on
    utterly uncongenial material.

        Placed against this troubled backdrop, the princi-
    pal actor is Ethan Hawley, Harvard graduate, combat
    veteran, exemplary family man and stymied disciple of
    the New England Way. Ethan's grocery business failed

shortly after the War, and he now operates the store
for its new owner, Alfio Marullo, a financially astute
immigrant from Italy. At Easter time, multiple tempt-
ations descend on Ethan like a storm of body blows.
Baker, president of the local bank and master of cere-
monies for the New Baytown gentry, chides Ethan to
invest the money his wife Mary's brother has left her
and rehabilitate the Hawley family fortunes. Mary and
the Hawley children, Ellen and Allen, chafe under the
presumed disgrace of Ethan's menial position and modest salary. For reasons that remain obscure, Margie
Young-Hunt, a divorcee of easy virtue, tells Ethan's
fortune and predicts sudden affluence. A man named
Biggers, representing underworld interests, proposes
a kick-back arrangement that will line Ethan's pockets.
Then Ethan's bank-teller pal, Joey Murphy, sketches
to Ethan his plan for a fool-proof bank robbery and
presently casts doubt on the legality of Marullo's citi-
zenship. Finally, Ethan learns that the family property
of Danny Taylor, his one-time bosom companion and
now the town derelict, will hold trump value for the
man who controls it when plans for a new airport ma-
terialize.

April proves the cruelest month, indeed. Ethan
celebrates his Epiphany, not with an apocalyptic regen-
eration or even a Faustian bargain with evil, but with
a tedious skein of improbable impulses and wretched
rationalizations that eventually compromise the under-
pinnings of the novel itself. By July 4th, Ethan has
cynically conspired with events to insure that Margie's
prophecy will be self-fulfilling. He gives Danny
$1,000, knowing that Danny will deed him the Taylor
property and then drink himself to death. Anonymously,
he notifies the authorities about Marullo. Meanwhile,
he advances Joey's bank robbery from fancied caper to
hard contingency.

All this comes to a head on July 4th weekend.
Danny destroys himself on cue, and Ethan, armed with
the Taylor deed, checkmates Baker and assumes a commanding posture in town affairs. At the eleventh hour,
Ethan aborts the bank break-in, only to learn that Marullo has retreated to Italy and left him the store.

The only weak link is Ethan himself, who can no
longer withstand his own moral collapse. He has clung
to the philosophy that he can regulate the cancer growing within him, that "the main thing was to know the
limited objective for what it was, and, once it was

achieved, to stop the process in its tracks." He has
soothed himself with the bromide that, with assassins,
"maybe the first time is always hard." But with his
own soul in ruins and the son he has neglected exposed
as a cheat, he flees to his "Place," a seaside cave,
and contemplates death by drowning. The image of Ellen, who promises to perpetuate the values of the past,
brings a temporary stay of execution, but the chances
for Ethan's spiritual salvation appear damaged beyond
repair.

Ethan's double consciousness charts the novel's
ruling dynamic: "I had the advantage of two worlds,
the layered firmament of dream and the temporal fix-
tures of the mind awake." A subjective, interior world
pits its visions of Promethean free will against the in-
tractable realities of predetermined fact and sequence.
The dramatic itinerary of The Winter of Our Discontent
is an on-going debate, a schedule of interfaces where
Ethan's psychic ballet collides with the inherited labels
of everyday life. But the centrifugal force of his latter-
day angst is puny; his mental gymnastics lack sufficient
leverage to forge a durable reconciliation between
massed, contending forces. Ethan is fond of "taking
stock," but his deliberations shirk the consequences of
good and evil and settle for the bland impotence of situ-
ational ethics: "Point of reference, that's it. If the
laws of thinking are the laws of things, then morals are
relative too, and manner and sin."

In The Winter of Our Discontent, the past assumes
the three-dimensional presence of a dramatic character.
Ethan's past, Steinbeck's past, the literary past, even
echoes of the novel's own past performance, all impinge
on the present moment. Ethan combines the gothic intu-
itions of Hawthorne with the satirical accents of Twain
("I never saw a boy accept greatness with more grace,")
and even triggers Margie's parting shot at Hemingway
("I think bullfights are for men who aren't very brave
and wish they were.") The Bible, Shakespeare, T. S.
Eliot, a gallery of unimpeachable guardians are inter-
cepted in their efforts to counsel a diminished everyman
at a moment of supreme trial that subsides into the flac-
cid aftermath of a non-event.

But it is the present moment itself that swallows
up the reader's interest. In 1961, Steinbeck entertained
a dialogue with himself, soliloquized a last will and testament from the nucleus of certainty that this protagonist had deserted. He articulated the rhythms of escala-

tion: "such a process may become a thing in itself, a
person almost, having its own ends and means and quite
independent of its creator." He anatomized the religion
of style: "it is not what you do, but how you do it and
what you call it." He flayed the invertebrate euphem-
isms of a bankrupt pragmatism: "no crime is committed unless a criminal is caught."

Steinbeck already knew what the 1970s learned to
their dismay, that the raucous materialism of contemporary life would sooner mimic the catchy assurances of
a computerized idiom than ponder the restraints of a
more classical phraseology. The upstart from California had every reason to suspect Madison Avenue and
its phalanx of Joey Murphy temporizers: "I think he was
a fairly well-educated man, but only because of his
process, his technique of thinking. His erudition hid in
a demiworld dialect, a language of the bright, hard,
brassy illiterate."

Almost invariably, the novel bogs down in Ethan's
attenuated folly, but Steinbeck himself may well have
weathered a treacherous ordeal and salvaged wisdom
from an artistic shipwreck. Ethan's cult of personality
excuses the decay of critical faculties as a victimless
crime. "The structure of my change," he says, "was
feeling," as he melts into a policy of disabling flux.
Steinbeck, however, to the end "more interested in what
is than in why it is," knew better than Ethan that "to
be alive at all is to have scars" and that betrayal is
far worse than failure. Ethan's experience "nudged and
jostled me in a direction contrary to my normal one";
but there is no "new Steinbeck" who "goes along with
the nation," only a nation that shrinks from his difficult
path (WOD).

HAWLEY, FATHER. In Ethan's words, his father "was a
kind of high amateur ancestor man and I've always noticed that ancestor people usually lack the qualities of
the ones they celebrate. My father was a gentle, well-
informed, ill-advised, sometimes brilliant fool. Single-
handed he lost the land, money, prestige, and future;
in fact he lost nearly everything Allens and Hawleys had
accumulated over several hundred years, lost everything but the names--which was all my father was interested in anyway." The passage is notable for the Faulk-
nerian cadences it invokes to introduce an oddly indis-
tinct bit-player who sounds as much like a Compson as
a Hawley. In contrast to the tough-minded Cap'n Haw-

ley, Ethan's father was a self-defeating egoist and romantic dilettante.

Mr. Hawley's impracticality is summed up by the
way he dug his own financial grave: "He put money in
munitions that were already obsolete. Then when the
contracts were canceled, he lost." It is painfully appropriate that his ruin stemmed from a gullible faith in
faulty armament and a textbook exhibition of compound
mistiming. A prominent duality the novel examines is
the contrast between permanence and change, between
an incorruptible, legendary sense of time and an opposite sense of time as hectic, immediately pressing,
ever-accelerating. The opening of the book enacts the
timeless drama of the Passion; the conclusion thrusts
us into the impetuous tempo of American life on the
nation's birthday, 1960. Steinbeck aligns his characters
along an axis that links the two extremes of surrender
to the past and heedless immersion in the present moment. Mr. Hawley ranges far in the direction of quixotic devotion to the past. Ethan, with the aid of a
hand-me-down timepiece that must have been utterly
worthless to his father, counts the seconds separating
him from his plunge into the promiscuous rush of
events. In both instances, Steinbeck insists that character, not chance, is the ultimate arbiter of destiny
(WOD).

HAWLEY, MARY. Mary Hawley's Irish-Protestant upbringing is a shorthand literary recipe for "lace curtain"
conventionality, but the ethnic stereotype barely screens
from view the chauvinistic prescription for feminine behavior that Ethan smugly consults as an index to every
phase of his wife's existence. At the end of the novel,
Margie Young-Hunt protests, "Mary? You don't even
know her." Not at all the defenseless pet that chirps
from the gilded cage of Ethan's carefully groomed image, Mary is, in Margie's words, "like a gull that uses
the wind to stay aloft and never beats a wing." The re-
cast formula establishes that Ethan, not Mary and not
Steinbeck, has generated the mists that obscure the novel's principal emblem of serenity, stability, and resourcefulness.

There is little reason to believe that the substance
of Ethan's critique, as opposed to the tone of the infer-
ences he draws, is inaccurate. Mary is unsophisticated
and parochial, contentedly middle-class. She lacks
Ethan's gift of imaginative speech and restless explora-

tion of psychological labyrinths. She is systematically
passive and determined to leave puzzling worldly matters in his hands, such as the prudent investment of the
money her brother left her. She is suspicious of sudden change, sublimely patient with the long-term rhythms
of fortune, and incurably optimistic. From what we can
gather, she is a complaisant spouse, a competent mother, an ideal if unspectacular housewife.

Notwithstanding these unassumingly pliant features,
Mary possesses a streak of hardiness that Ethan does
his best to nullify, usually by slighting her strengths.
With nervous, jaunty irony he patronizes her own sunny
disposition: "My Mary is no mocker and contempt is
not her tool." On the rare occasions when her understandable irritation with his endless "wallowing" in self-
pity break through the surface, he dismisses her plea
as the shrill note of yearning for status and affluence.
He perversely identifies her intuitive grasp of reality
with a failure of analytical cognition: "Mary doesn't use
her mind for organized thought and maybe this makes
her more receptive of impressions." But he turns a
deaf ear when she tries to unscramble his mad flights
of fancy: "I never know what you're thinking"; "You always mix me up"; "I'm not going to let you hide in your
words."

Ethan exploits Mary as a wellspring of figurative
expressions that finally separate him from the truth of
her nature, even though it is he who sententiously observes that "three things will never be believed--the
true, the probable, and the logical." "You hardly ever
use my name," she says in objection to his inexhaustible fund of diminutives and endearments. Ethan, rather
than Steinbeck, terms her Easter bouquet "the yearly
vernal offering to Eostre," as though the novelist, bow-
ing to the common-sense conservatism of Mary herself,
knew when to restrain his penchant for allegorizing. In
short, Mary Hawley is not simplistic but uncomplicated,
and her level-headed, prosaic consciousness offers a
calm alternative to her husband's season of Byronic
tempest (WOD).

HAWLEY, (MARY) ELLEN. Ethan's thirteen-year-old daughter Ellen is nonchalantly seductive during the day and
guardian of the family talisman, "a kind of mound of
translucent stone," by night. In ironic reversal of
Ethan's betrayal of Marullo, Ellen informs on Allen's
plagiarism to preserve the beleaguered Hawley honor.

At the close of the novel, Ellen secretly slips the talisman into Ethan's pocket. The act presently revives his
will to live by restoring his faith that the "light" of his
ancestors has a new owner and will not be extinguished.

Steinbeck's naturalistic depiction of the Oedipal
magnetism between father and daughter may try readers'
patience and commit violations of literary good taste.
Ellen's precocious erotic intuitions--"The blond hairs
on her arm shone like gold dust under the lamp"--sug-
gest a nymphet edition of Daisy Buchanan. Her infan-
tile witchery links her with Margie Young-Hunt, and her
somnambulistic ramblings evoke Gothic visions of Lady
Macbeth. Ethan's comment that, after fondling the talisman, Ellen "did not walk like a child but like a ful-
filled woman" may similarly overburden an essentially
frail vessel.

But the portrait, if occasionally saccharine, is often invigorating. Long after Ellen's sleep-walking
scene, Ethan recalls his Army friend Charley Edwards,
who used to review cherished memories "as though he
picked precious things one by one from a cabinet,
looked at each, felt it, kissed it, and put it back." Ellen's sympathetic bond with the talisman radiates a wave
of imagery that functions as a stylistic deterrent to the
disruptive forces at loose in the novel (WOD).

HAZEL. One of Mack's group of vagabonds. Hazel is a
young man of great strength but limited intelligence.
"Casting about in Hazel's mind," Steinbeck notes, "was
like wandering alone in a deserted museum." A product
of reform schools as well as grammar schools, Hazel
is as innocent of reform-school viciousness as he is of
fourth-grade mathematics. Hazel seems interested in
many things and is always asking questions. Really,
though, he is only interested in hearing the flow of conversation. Above all, Hazel is loyal. He helps Doc
collect marine specimens and is very good at it as soon
as he understands what Doc wants (CR).

HAZEL. One of the inhabitants of the Palace Flophouse. He
gave the Palace Flophouse its name (see Cannery Row).
During the war he was in the Army long enough to qual-
ify for the G.I. Bill. By making a check mark on an
application, he unknowingly enrolled for training in astro-
physics at the University of California. It took the university authorities three months to discover their mistake. A slow, simple-minded man, he is unaffected by

his years in grade school and reform school; however,
he suffers under a great burden because Fauna Flood
has discovered that his horoscope indicates that he will
become a nine-toed President of the United States. He
loves Doc, and with a heroic effort comes to the conclusion that since Mack knows Doc is in trouble, Mack
must either help Doc or be murdered. He inspires
Mack and the boys to help Doc. He elects to be Prince
Charming at the masquerade and unwittingly becomes
the victim of Joe Elegant who dresses him in a hideously grotesque costume. The guests, however, refuse
to laugh at him, and he interprets their silence as
awed approval. He has been slowly growing aware of
the world because of the terrible responsibility of becoming President, and when Mack and the boys refuse
to help Doc because of the masquerade's failure, he decides to act by himself. For the first time in his life
he listens to the answers people give to his questions
and forms the idea of getting Suzy to go with Doc to
La Jolla. The seer tells him that a friend should do
anything to help him even if it causes pain or death.
Hazel's moment of glory comes when he acts to save
Doc by creeping into the Biological Laboratory at night
where he breaks Doc's right arm with an indoor-ball
bat. The effort leads to a trip for Suzy and Doc; and
Hazel, who is exhausted by his mental effort, is relieved of his future burden by Fauna Flood who tells
him a fly speck caused her to make a mistake. She
proves her mistake by showing him that he miscounted
his toes, which now add up to ten (ST).

HAZEL JOHNSON See JOHNSON, HAZEL (SRP)

HEINE. Lieutenant Tonder gave Molly a poem which he
claimed to have written. When Molly questioned him,
he admitted that Heine had written it. The poem is
"Mit deinen blauen Augen," and it expresses Tonder's
fascination for Molly (MID).

HELEN. One of the regular girls at the Bear Flag. She
does sixty days for a lady fight that is discussed with
admiration in Cannery Row (ST).

HELEN VAN DEVENTER See VAN DEVENTER, HELEN
(PH)

HENRI. A French painter who is not French and whose name

is not really Henri. Steeped in stories of Paris' Left
Bank, Henri believes that he once lived there, though
he has never even seen Paris. As an artist, Henri
throws himself into artistic movements with such feroc-
ity that it is impossible to tell what kind of painter he
is. Henri is also a boat builder who "sculptures" boats
on land rather than build them for water. He lives on
one and brings women to share his quarters with him.
Over a period of time, two wives and a number of semi-
permanent liaisons break up because Henri refuses to
install a landsman's toilet on his shore-bound boat (CR).

HENRI THE PAINTER. Former resident of Cannery Row
(see Cannery Row). Mack and the boys played a trick
on him which led to his departure. They glued barna-
cles and seaweed to the bottom of Henri's boat. He
built the boat on land because he was afraid of the
ocean. After the practical joke, Henri sold the boat
and left town because he believed that the boat was going to sea while he was asleep (ST).

HENRY ALLEN See ALLEN, HENRY (LV)

HENRY MORGAN See MORGAN, HENRY (CG)

HERISTAL, CLOTILDE. Daughter of Pippin and Marie Héristal. She is twenty years old and described as intense,
violent, and overweight. She wrote the best selling
novel Adieu Ma Vie at the age of fifteen. She became
a Communist at the age of sixteen and a half. Before
she was twenty she also passed through a religious
phase and a brief film career in Rome where she acted
in three versions of War and Peace and two versions of
Quo Vadis. Her elevation as Princess Royale saves her
from her unsuccessful film career. She falls madly in
love with Tod Johnson, the son of America's Egg King
and regresses into a form of adolescence in her relationship with him. When Pippin IV is deposed, she
leaves France with Tod to begin a new film career in
Hollywood under his loving supervision (SRP).

HERISTAL, MARIE. Wife of Pippin Héristal. She is described as buxom and pleasant. Her main duty is to
keep a good, economical house for her husband and her
daughter Clotilde. She admires her husband and has a
good friendship with him that is not found in marriages
of passion. She grows unhappy with her life at Ver-

sailles as Queen of France because of the extravagance
of running the royal household. Her escape valve from
royal dust and royal freeloaders comes in her conversations with her old friend and schoolmate Suzanne Lescault, now Sister Hyacinthe, who becomes companion
to the queen. She is unmoved, however, by the idea
of being married to the King of France. She disappears during the turmoil after her husband is deposed,
but when Pippin returns to his old home at Number One,
Avenue de Marigny, he discovers that Madame has already returned to begin her housework (SRP).

HERISTAL, PIPPIN ARNULF. An amateur astronomer of
noble family who reluctantly becomes King of France.
He is fifty-four, lean, handsome, and healthy. He is
described as a gentle, inquisitive man. He lives in a
small house in Avenue de Marigny with his wife Marie
and his grown daughter Clotilde. His income derives
from vineyards that produce an excellent white wine.
He has a scholarly interest in progressive jazz and had
once shaken hands with Louis Armstrong. His life is
frugal and orderly except for the occasional extravagance of an instrument of astronomy. In 1951, he was
given credit with Walter Haschi for discovering a comet
designated the Elysée Comet. Even though he is not
political, he is forced into national prominence when
the political parties of France turn to his ancient and
noble family for their next head of state. Their desire
to return to a monarchy leads directly to the blood line
of Charlemagne and Pippin, the direct descendant from
the legitimate branch. He is elected, by acclamation,
King of France with the name Pippin IV. Pippin reluctantly becomes King of France. He becomes frustrated and unhappy and searches for ways to either as-
sert himself as king or escape entirely from his responsibilities.

He discovers that without the trappings of office,
he may be unrecognized by people. Dressed in his disguise, which is himself, he rides a motor scooter about
the country. On one such excursion, he meets an old
man who rescues statues that vandals push into a moat.
He learns from the old man that no man can stand being extinct. At the opening of the convention to deliberate the Code Pippin, he delivers a speech which asserts the need for reform in taxes, prices, housing,
public health insurance, and governmental organization.
The speech causes the expected governmental crisis

which leads to the overthrow of the monarchy. Pippin
quietly and unnoticeably returns to Number One, Avenue
de Marigny (SRP).

HILDA VAN DEVENTER See VAN DEVENTER, HILDA (PH)

HITZLER. On a trip through Cannery Row he reported to
    Doc that he saw Old Jingleballicks on a lawn in Berke-
    ley, on his knees, pulling a worm out of the ground
    with his teeth (ST).

HOGAN, RUPERT. At twilight, Rupert Hogan, "the seller of
    spirits, added water to his gin and put it away to be
    served after midnight." The glancing sketch of Hogan
    introduces the note of commercial deception to the Mon-
    terey pastoral that sets the stage for Chapter V. In
    contrast to the full-bodied, three-dimensional Torrelli,
    Hogan has a Northern name and projects a thin, adul-
    terated image. The paisanos prefer the wine of the
    warm South to the hard transparency of gin, and after
    midnight their own volatile spirits express no thirst for
    store-bought, Anglo-animation (TF).

HOLMAN, RABBIT. A farmer from San Ardo who is at
    Adam Trask's helping to fix up the old house when the
    twins are born. Years later, in Salinas for his semi-
    annual drunk, he meets Cal Trask and takes him for
    the first time to Kate's brothel (EE).

HOLMES, DOCTOR ("Johnny Bear"). The doctor in Loma,
    California, who realized that Amy Hawkins had attempted
    suicide. He also revealed that Amy was pregnant (LV).

HONEYMOONING COUPLE, THE. Passengers on the sight-
    seeing bus that passes "The Pastures" in the last chap-
    ter of the book. They would like to live in the valley
    but realize how impossible that would be (PH).

HORACE QUINN See QUINN, HORACE (EE)

HORTON, ERNEST. One of the travelers who spends the
    night at Rebel Corners, Horton is a drummer for a trick
    company, a wise fool who provides the moral index
    Steinbeck uses to gauge the mettle of the other principles.
    As his name and his dilemma in the novel suggest, Er-
    nest Horton is a man divided against himself, a man at
    the crossroads. On the one hand, he is the pitchman

for sensational novelty, a peddler in human frailty. He
sells a phony sock that feigns a hideously crushed foot,
and he plans to market a similarly ersatz set of ac-
couterments that will turn a business suit into a tuxedo.
Thus he converts the psychic maiming and cruel self-
delusions of others into cynical commercial fraud. His
chumminess with Mr. Pritchard and his smutty sex
jokes imply a degenerate entrepreneur, perched on the
dungheap of post-war hucksterism.

But he is genuinely "earnest," too, as the nostalgic disciple of his father's obsolete creed, "honesty
and thrift." He is conspicuously kind to Norma, de-
clines the invitation to play the traveling salesman of
stock comedy, chivalrously protects the girl from Alice's
wrath. Throughout, he is the uncomplaining optimist,
respectable in his shabbiness, tolerant of the failings he
understands so well.

The key to Horton is that he is a veteran, the
casualty of a between-eras-war that continues to rage
within him. The young man on the make, who seeks
"new wrinkles" and admires a "real hustler," is desperately "nervous," on the thin edge of self-control:
"he protected himself from insult with studied techniques." Pritchard's unflattering references to footloose
veterans evoke Horton's "slightly crooked smile." The
real insult, however, is self-inflicted--Horton's compromise with contemporary decadence. But his recourse
to the human values of the past goes a long way to redeem him. At the novel's close, he and Camille Oaks
have declared a separate peace, a turn of events that
Steinbeck does not evidently disapprove (WB).

HUBERT VAN DEVENTER See VAN DEVENTER, HUBERT
(PH)

HUENEKER, ALLEN. The ugliest, shyest man in the valley.
He walks like an ape. He rides a short way with Maria
Lopez. Shortly after, Maria's "restaurant" is closed
(PH).

HUGH BIGGERS See BIGGERS, HUGH (?) (WOD)

HUGHIE. A member of Mack's group of vagabonds. Hughie
does not work except to collect frogs and cats for Doc
(CR).

HUGO MACHADO See   MACHADO, HUGO (TF)

HUMBERT, PAT. Notices that the old Battle farm, now
owned by the Mustrovics, is deserted. At sixteen, the
work of the entire Humbert farm fell to him. His parents hated him for being young. His heart is broken
when Mae Munroe marries Bill Whiteside (PH).

HUNT, MARGIE YOUNG See YOUNG-HUNT, MARGIE
(WOD)

HUNTER. Mr. Hunter owns a big white house in Torgas.
When the vigilantes burn Anderson's barn, Sam slips into town and sets fire to Hunter's home. Jim Nolan
criticizes Mac for having encouraged Sam because it indicated that Mac had allowed himself to become personally involved (IDB).

HUNTER, MAJOR. An engineer and an arithmetician who is
second in command in the invading army. Major Hunter
spends most of his time at his drafting board and seems
only vaguely aware of the war. Major Hunter is responsible for the operation of the coal mine, but he
cannot replace the tracks as fast as the villagers destroy them (MID).

HUSTON, EZRA. Chairman of the Central Committee at
Weedpatch government camp. He has steel-colored eyes
"like little blades" and is "a tall spare man, wind-
blackened." He oversees the plan to prevent a riot at
the Saturday night dance that would let deputies come in
and close the camp (GW).

HYACINTHE, SISTER See LESCAULT, SUZANNE (SRP)

I

IDA, WIDE. Proprietor of Cafe La Ida. Described at various times as huge and mountainous, she is capable of
throwing a drunk out of her establishment without his
body touching the sidewalk. She is one of the conspira-
tors who try to rid Doc of his restlessness and melancholy. She attends the meetings called by Mack and also attends the masquerade where she wrestles on the
floor with Whitey No. 2. She fails in her own attempt
to get Doc to talk about his troubles (ST).

IGNACIA, TIA. In Chapter XI, Big Joe Portagee visits Tia
Ignacia, a lady "about forty-five, a widow of long stand-

ing and some success." Throughout the evening, the amorous widow plies Big Joe with generous libations of wine and domestic amenities, but unfortunately "Big Joe simply could not be warm and comfortable without going to sleep." At last, Tia Ignacia's Indian blood boils and she attacks the stuporous clown with a stick of firewood. Despite a torrential downpour, she pursues Big Joe into the middle of the muddy lane that passes her front door. Suddenly aroused, the Portagee possesses the lady amidst the highway filth, much to the astonishment of Jake Lake, who is doing his appointed rounds on his motorcycle. Steinbeck's tone is urbane and condescending, but the narrator's comic mask cannot disguise the incident's raw brutality. The suspicion that Steinbeck fully recognizes the unregenerate ugliness of Big Joe's conduct is confirmed in the next chapter, when the one lost soul among Danny's crew steals from the Pirate's untouchable treasure horde (TF).

IVY WILSON See WILSON, IVY (GW)

J

JACK. One of the sheriff's deputies patrolling the road at the strikers' camp. When Mac and Jim go out to talk to the deputies, the leader instructs Jack to get behind them with his gun (IDB).

JACK ANDERS See ANDERS, JACK (MID)

JACK, MISS ("The Harness"). A nurse who was called after Emma because unconsciously she said she couldn't handle Peter alone (LV).

JACKSON. A lean, bony Kansan at the Weedpatch government camp. The infiltrators who try to make trouble at the Saturday night dance claim that he invited them (GW).

JAKE LAKE See LAKE, JAKE (TF)

JAKE PEDRONI See PEDRONI, JAKE (IDB)

JAKOB STUTZ See STUTZ, JAKOB (PH)

JAMES CREW See CREW, JAMES (EE)

JAMES FLOWER See FLOWER, JAMES (CG)

JELKA SEPIC See SEPIC, JELKA (LV)

JENNEY RAMSEY See WAYNE, JENNIE (TGU)

JENNIE WAYNE See WAYNE, JENNIE (TGU)

JEREMY. A sad dark boy from Unit Two at the Weedpatch
     government camp. He helps prevent the riot planned
     by the Associated Farmers (GW).

JERRY. One of the migrant workers who supports the pick-
     ers' strike. Jerry affirms that failure of the apple
     pickers in striking will result in lower wages in the
     cotton fields later in the year (IDB).

JESS TAYLOR See TAYLOR, JESS (LV)

JESSIE BULLITT See BULLITT, JESSIE (GW)

JESUS GARCIA See GARCIA, JESUS (TGU)

JESUS MARIA CORCORAN See CORCORAN, JESUS MARIA
     (TF)

JIM CASY See CASY, JIM (GW)

JIM MOORE See MOORE, JIM (LV)

JIM NOLAN See NOLAN, JIM (IDB)

JIM RAWLEY See RAWLEY, JIM (GW)

JIMMIE MORGAN See MORGAN, JIMMIE (PH)

JINGLEBALLICKS, OLD. He is so rich that he does not
     know he is rich at all. He is a scientist of sorts, but
     his major contributions are the funds and grants he has
     given to foundations and universities. His eccentricity
     is that he gives millions away, yet insists upon spong-
     ing on a friend. Doc placed him in charge of Western
     Biological Laboratories during the war, but he returned
     to find the place deserted and in ruins. Old Jinglebal-
     licks arrives out of nowhere to freeload on Doc for as
     long as he can get away with it. He confesses that his
     miserly actions are part of the American state of mind

caused by the tax laws which permit him to give money
to an organization, but not to an individual. He believes that Doc's problem is a lack of fulfillment. He
attends the masquerade as a red dwarf; however, the
next day as a part of the general woe caused by the
party, he is ordered out by Doc and told never to return. He leaves the laboratory, but later arranges a
foundation for Doc at Cal Tech (ST).

JOAD, AL. The third son and Tom's younger brother. He
is sixteen years old, a smart aleck making out with
girls at every opportunity. Al is crazy about girls and
automobile engines. He walks with a swaying strut like
a randy rooster, wears a Stetson hat at a rakish angle,
and swaggers around in stiffjeans with the bottoms
turned up to show his boots. Despite his immaturity,
Al is an expert at automotive mechanics and repairs.
He is responsible for the maintenance and operating
condition of the family's old Hudson Super-Six truck. Al
repeatedly insists that he would like to leave the family
and get himself a job as a garage mechanic, but Tom
persuades him to stay and help. Al's adolescent thought-
lessness is a contrast to Tom's hard-learned maturity.
At the end, Al plans to marry Aggie Wainwright and get
a job in a garage (GW).

JOAD, GRAMPA (WILLIAM JAMES JOAD). He is "a lean,
ragged, quick old man" whose right leg comes out of
joint. His face is lean and excitable, "with little bright
eyes as evil as a frantic child's eyes." In tempera-
ment, he is "cantankerous, complaining, mischievous,
laughing." In his senility, Grampa is vicious, cruel,
impatient, lecherous, and gluttonous. He and Granma
constantly fight in a fond fashion. Grampa tells dirty
stories, leaves his fly unbuttoned, and is a hell-raiser.
When it is time to depart for California, Grampa refuses to go, insisting on staying in his own country.
Tom has to get him drunk on soothing syrup to get him
away. Just beyond Bethany, Oklahoma, Grampa has a
stroke and dies in the tent of Ivy and Sairy Wilson.
The family buries him themselves (GW).

JOAD, GRANMA. She is as mean as her husband and matches
his lechery with "a shrill ferocious religiosity." Her
conversation consists largely of "Hallelujahs" and "A-
mens." She wears a shapeless Mother Hubbard gown.
She never recovers from Grampa's death, has halluci-

nations during the trip west, and dies between Needles,
California and the inspection station at Daggett.   To
keep the family from being stopped there, Ma Joad
tells the inspectors that the old woman is very sick and
has to be rushed to a doctor.   She then sits up with
the dead body during the drive across the Mojave.
Granma is buried at Bakersfield.   The deaths of Granma and Grampa show the destruction of lives and the
break-up of families uprooted from their tenant farms
in the Dust Bowl (GW).

JOAD, MA.   The mother of Noah, young Tom, Rose of
Sharon, Al, Ruthie, and Winfield.   Her name is never
given; everyone, including her husband, calls her Ma.
She is "heavy, but not fat; thick with child-bearing and
work."   She customarily wears an ankle-length Mother
Hubbard with washed-out flowers on a gray background.
Ma has thin, steel-gray hair gathered in a knot.   Her
arms are strong and freckled.   She has hazel eyes and
a strong, kindly face.   Ma is the spiritual center of
the family, and she represents the qualities of patience,
endurance, understanding, and dignity of the migrant
families as a whole.   Ma symbolizes the best qualities
of the working people--their strength, compassion, common sense, and toughness.   As she tells Tom, "we're
the people that live ... we're the people--we go on."
When Pa agrees to let the family split up, Ma revolts,
threatens to hit him with a jack handle, and takes control as the new leader.   When Pa asks whether they
can all get to California, Ma answers, "It ain't kin we?
It's will we? ... as far as 'will,' why we'll do what we
will."   She refuses to be discouraged by obstacles (GW).

JOAD, NOAH.   The oldest child of Ma and Pa Joad.   He
gives the impression of being misshapen, though no part
of him is so.   Though he is not stupid, he seems not
to care about anything.   Pa blames himself for Noah's
strangeness, because he delivered the baby without forceps and twisted and warped the infant's head and body,
which the midwife later molded back into shape.   Noah
is tall and slow-moving.   He speaks seldom and very
slowly and has a strange, calm, wondering look on his
face.   He has never been angry or upset.   He has no
sexual urges and is listless towards life in general.
When the family arrives at Needles, Noah says he cannot leave the Colorado River.   He insists on staying
with the water and says he will go down river and live
off fish (GW).

JOAD, PA (TOM JOAD, SR. or OLD TOM JOAD). The titular head of the Joad family; father of young Tom, Noah,
Al, Rose of Sharon, Ruthie and Winfield. He has a
grizzled face with a pepper and salt stubble beard, a
forward thrusting chin, brown eyes with wrinkles at the
corners, and thin red lips. His forearm muscles are
bulging and powerful, his stomach and hips are lean,
and his legs are short, heavy, and strong. He wears
cracked and swollen shoes and well-worn work clothes.
Pa has been the leader and support of the family; but
once they leave Oklahoma, he ceases to play a domi-
nant role. Young Tom and Ma increasingly make the
major decisions; and when Pa proposes that the family
split up when the Wilsons' car breaks down, Ma refuses, has a showdown with him, and takes control. Pa
can still work hard, as he does during the final flood,
but something is broken in him when he loses his farm
(GW).

JOAD, RUTHIE. Youngest daughter of Ma and Pa Joad. She
is twelve years old and associates mainly with her
younger brother Winfield. Though she is entering pu-
berty, she is still an ignorant, excitable, and grimy
child who seems too immature for her years. At the
boxcar camp, she fights with some other girls and then
tells them that her brother Tom has just killed a man
and is in hiding. Her indiscretion precipitates Tom's
final departure in the book (GW).

JOAD, TOM. The second oldest Joad son and the male protagonist of the novel. He is about 30 years old, with
dark brown eyes, high and wide cheek bones, and a
long upper lip closed over protruding teeth. He has
spent four years in McAlester penitentiary for killing a
man in self-defense in a fight. As the novel opens, he
is returning home to his family, not knowing that they
have been evicted and are about to migrate to California. Tom goes west with them and becomes increasingly involved in opposing social and economic injustice.
Though he has violated parole in leaving Oklahoma, he
finds it difficult to remain quiet and inactive, and repeatedly speaks out in protest against corrupt or inhumane treatment. When a vigilante kills Jim Casy, Tom
in turn kills the murderer and thus becomes a marked
man. At the end, he is converted from thinking mainly of himself one day at a time, to Casy's belief in
group concern and action and in planning for the future.

Outlawed, Tom finally leaves the family to follow Casy's footsteps in helping migrant farm workers to organize and strike for decent wages and working conditions (GW).

JOAD, UNCLE. Pa Joad's brother. He is 50 years old, a lonely widower. His thin, strong body is tense, and his eyes are haunted and restless. Usually, he eats little, drinks nothing, and is celibate; but when his appetites build up to the breaking point, he indulges wildly in gluttony, drunkenness, and lechery, after which he feels guilty and repentant. He gives anonymous gifts and does anonymous work to make amends. His extreme self-denial and sensuality are part of the repressed life of Protestant fundamentalism and are a contrast to the common sense of Ma Joad and to Casy's new gospel of love and forgiveness (GW).

JOAD, WINFIELD. The youngest child of Ma and Pa Joad. He is ten years old, "kid-wild and calfish." He is usually grim and "a trifle of a snot-nose." At the Hooper Ranch, he is put to work in the fields, where he eats too many peaches and gets the "skitters." Winfield is something of a tattle-tale and reflects the naive, self-centered child's point of view (GW).

JODY TIFLIN See TIFLIN, JODY (LV)

JOE. One of the migrant workers "jungled up" by the river in Torgas. Speaking to Mac and Jim, Joe explains London's reaction when he learned the wages in the valley had been lowered (IDB).

JOE. Helen Van Deventer's Filipino houseboy (PH).

JOE ADAMS See ADAMS, JOE (LV)

JOE ELEGANT See ELEGANT, JOE (ST)

JOE SAUL See SAUL, JOE (BB)

JOE VALERY See VALERY, JOE (EE)

JOEY AND WILLARD. Two little boys on Cannery Row who one day peer into the window of Doc's laboratory and discuss Doc's collection of bottled babies (CR).

JOHN BATTLE See BATTLE, JOHN (PH)

JOHN EVELYN See EVELYN, JOHN (CG)

JOHN STEINBECK See STEINBECK, JOHN (EE)

JOHN WAYNE I   See WAYNE, JOHN I (TGU)

JOHN WAYNE II See WAYNE, JOHN II (TGU)

JOHN WHITESIDE See WHITESIDE, JOHN (PH)

JOHNNY BEAR See BEAR, JOHNNY (LV)

JOHNNY POM-POM See POM-POM, JOHNNY (TF)

JOHNSON, ALBERT. When Joy is killed by the vigilante's
    bullet, he is placed in Albert Johnson's truck. The
    migrant worker's truck becomes a hearse in the public
    funeral the strikers stage (IDB).

JOHNSON, CHARLIE. Mr. Pritchard's roommate in college
    and still his closest, perhaps his only real pal. "A
    natural comic," Charlie is much given to adolescent
    horseplay and practical joking. He enjoys a place of
    special esteem in the Pritchard family mythology, but
    his portrait conveys residual impressions of arrested
    development, hollowness, and failure of human engage-
    ment. Charlie is a kind of cheerleader for the sterile
    games the Pritchards substitute for life (WB).

JOHNSON, H. W. Tod Johnson's father. Known as the Egg
    King because he amassed his vast fortune in the chicken
    business. He is a self-made man who rose from pov-
    erty during the Depression to the head of a vast organi-
    zation. He becomes interested in the French monarchy
    and eventually develops what his son calls "duke fever,"
    the desire to purchase an aristocratic title (SRP).

JOHNSON, HAZEL. Daughter of the H. W. Johnsons. A
    beautiful girl who was crowned Egg Queen at the Peta-
    luma Poultry Pageant on three separate occasions.
    She is one of the chief stockholders in her father's vast
    chicken industry (SRP).

JOHNSON, MRS. H. W. Tod Johnson's mother. One of
    chief stockholders in her husband's vast chicken indus-
    try and part of his plan to create a dynasty in the
    American pattern (SRP).

JOHNSON, TOD. Wealthy boyfriend of Clotilde Héristal.
    He is the image of the ideal American young man--tall,
    good looking, well mannered, and soft spoken. He is
    the son of H. W. Johnson, the Egg King, of Petaluma,
    California. He attends four major American universi-
    ties including Harvard and Yale; after a brief period in
    New York to study the arts, he travels to France as
    part of a grand tour to acquire culture. He meets
    Clotilde at Les Ambassadeurs, and after a carefully
    nurtured friendship he announces his love for her by
    calling her a real dish. His interest in the French
    monarchy leads to a warm friendship with Pippin IV.
    He and the king discuss the business potential in the
    monarchy and drink themselves into happy oblivion. Af-
    ter the fall of the monarchy, he tells Pippin IV that he
    will return to America with Clotilde. He promises to
    take care of her--as much as anyone can take care of
    anyone (SRP).

JONES. A member of Mack's group of idle men. Along
    with Hughie, Jones sometimes collects cats and frogs
    for Doc (CR).

JONES. The Cockney, dwarf-like pirate who helps Morgan
    conquer Panama, but who is shot by Morgan when he is
    caught concealing spoils (CG).

JOSE. One of the ranch workers mentioned by name. He
    and Manuel are to dig a grave for Elizabeth Wayne
    (TGU).

JOSE DE LA NARIZ See DE LA NARIZ, JOSE (TF)

JOSEPH. The mayor's servingman, who is described as
    having a life "so complicated that only a profound man
    would know him to be simple." Joseph is totally com-
    mitted to Mayor Orden and to the routine and order of
    the household (MID).

JOSEPH. Son of Alice and Juanito. He is born at Nuestra
    Señora and brought back to the Wayne ranch. He is
    named after Joseph Wayne, but his grandfather calls
    him Chango. At Alice's request, Joseph Wayne blesses
    the small child by kissing his forehead and wishing that
    he grow big and strong (TGU).

JOSEPH HAMILTON See HAMILTON, JOSEPH (EE)

JOSEPH PATRICK ("JOEY") MORPHY See MORPHY,
    JOSEPH PATRICK ("JOEY") (WOD)

JOSEPH RIVAS See RIVAS, JOSEPH (ST)

JOSEPH WAYNE See WAYNE, JOSEPH (TGU)

JOUR, COMTE DE. Bonapartist and participant in the
    closed meeting of Royalist parties. He strongly objects
    to the proposal of another Bourbon king and heatedly
    asks if the sacred blood of Napoleon has run out (SRP).

JOY. A veteran of labor conflicts who had been beaten so
    many times that Mac called him "slug-nutty." When
    the owners bring in scabs to break the strike, Joy is
    among them and is the first to respond when the strik-
    ers urge the scabs to join the strike. Joy is immedi-
    ately gunned down, and Mac uses his body and his fu-
    neral to unify the strikers (IDB).

JUAN, OLD. An old Mexican whom Joseph Wayne meets af-
    ter he records his homestead. He sees Joseph's new
    outfit and asks if there is a fiesta someplace. He is
    told that after Joseph builds his house he will make a
    fiesta. He appears again some years later as a ped-
    dler and asks Joseph Wayne if he made a fiesta. He
    inspires the New Year's fiesta and spreads the word
    among the people of the coming event. He builds the
    altar for Father Angelo and directs much of the prepa-
    ration for the fiesta. Joseph Wayne starts the fiesta by
    performing a ceremonial act, pouring red wine on the
    earth, which Old Juan tells him about. During the fi-
    esta, Old Juan keeps the musicians' cups full of whis-
    key so that when the dancing starts they might be one
    passionate instrument (TGU).

JUAN THOMAS See THOMAS, JUAN (P)

JUANA. Patient, fragile, but durable wife of Kino; mother
    of Coyotito. Her dark eyes are like "reflected stars"
    to Kino. With Kino, she lives a semi-primitive exist-
    ence. She grinds corn with a stone and repeats ancient
    incantations to guard her family from evil. She urges
    Kino to throw away the pearl (P).

JUANITO. An Indian teamster who claims that he is Castil-
    ian. Joseph Wayne believes him and accepts him as

his first vaquero even before he has any cattle. Juanito works for him as a friend and accepts presents
rather than pay for his labors. He courts Alice Garcia
in the traditional Spanish manner and wins her hand in
marriage. He catches Benjamin Wayne in the act of
making love to Alice and stabs him to death. He tells
Joseph Wayne what he has done, but also explains that
he did not know it was Benjy until after he had acted.
He wants Joseph to kill him, but when Joseph refuses,
Juanito goes into exile until the sharp and painful memory of the deed has faded. He returns during the
drought and finds Joseph at the sacred place in the
pines. He tells him about his son and about the death
of Willie Roams, and stays to help Joseph take care of
the stream and the rock. He convinces Joseph to visit
Father Angelo, and afterwards brings him to dinner at
Nuestra Señora. When Joseph departs, Juanito fears
his going and calls to him to take care (TGU).

JUANITO'S MOTHER. An Indian woman. She is remem-
    bered by Juanito as a woman who taught him that the
    earth is the mother and that she gives life and receives
    the dead. She once took Juanito to the sacred place in
    the pine grove (TGU).

JULE VITELA See VITELA, JULE (GW)

JULIUS EUSKADI See EUSKADI, JULIUS (EE)

JUNIUS MALTBY See MALTBY, JUNIUS (PH)

K

KATE See AMES, CATHY (EE)

KATHERINE MULLOCK WICKS See WICKS, KATHERINE
    MULLOCK (PH)

KATO, TAKASHI. A schoolmate of Robbie Maltby. Takashi
    is spied upon regularly by the Boy's Auxiliary Secret
    Service for Espionage against the Japanese until he be-
    comes a member of the group (PH).

KATY ("Saint Katy the Virgin"). A very bad pig who ate her
    brother and sister as well as her first litter, and she
    attacked two monks collecting tithes. Believing her to
    be possessed, Brother Paul attempted exorcism. When

the shadow of the cross fell across Katy's face, she experienced salvation. Katy went to the monastery where
she ministered to the sick and performed many miracles.
Fifty years after her death she was added to the Calendar of the Elect as Saint Katy the Virgin, determined
by committee to have been "a virgin by intent" (LV).

KEE, CHIN. Chin Kee is four times mentioned as the proprietor of a squid-packing plant. When extraordinary
circumstances compel the paisanos to consider working
for wages, their thoughts turn to Chin Kee. The apocalyptic occasion of Danny's party finally persuades the
brethren that their time has come for supreme sacrifice, and they troop down to the waterfront to spend one
day at menial labor. All Tortilla Flat burns with curiosity to learn what epic turn of events is in the wind.
It is probably significant of the paisanos' inverted scale
of values that they would rather work for an employer
with Oriental origins, a man no doubt the object of casual discrimination in contemporary California, than for
an Anglo. Then too, it is a worthwhile footnote on the
paisanos' preferred hand-to-mouth way of life to know
that even in hard times, paid jobs are always available
(TF).

KEEPER OF THE LIGHTHOUSE. A figure from Elizabeth's
childhood past. She was a lean, stern woman who kept
the lighthouse at Point Joe (TGU).

KELLING, RUDOLFO. At the start of Chapter V, the paisanos improvise outlandish syllogisms to justify their
feigned concern for Danny's health. Pablo's contribution to the unfolding tissue of rationalizations is the recent, melancholy example of Rudolfo Kelling, who
dropped dead despite his self-confident assurances to
his friends that he was "all right." The ever-vigilant
Pilon finds this too much to swallow: "Pilon's realism
arose mildly to the surface. 'Rudolfo fell into the
quarry above Pacific Grove,' he observed in mild re-
proof." As elsewhere, Steinbeck's irony is complex.
Rudolfo's death is, in fact, a portent of Danny's catas-
trophe at the end of the novel. Pilon's glib "realism"
ultimately fails to account for the irrational element
that makes a shambles of superficial predictions. At
the time, however, the reader is coaxed to side with
Pilon and thus overlook the serious import of an apparently negligible detail (TF).

KELLY, KISS OF DEATH. Welterweight fighter managed one
    time by Fauna Flood (ST).

KEMP, CORPORAL. Sergeant Axel Dane's subordinate at
    the San Jose recruiting office. He has learned to "Get
    along with the topkick and avoid all officers when pos-
    sible," and goes along with signing up Aron Trask,
    even though he is under age (EE).

KILPATRICK. In Chapter IX, Pilon shows off his knowledge
    of current affairs: " 'Cornelia Ruiz got a new man
    this morning,' Pilon observed. 'He has a bald head.
    His name is Kilpatrick.' " The paisanos are stung by
    Cornelia's preference for Anglo admirers (TF).

KING'S MISTRESS, THE See MISTRESS, THE KING'S
    (SRP)

KINO. The fisherman husband of Juana and father of Coyo-
    tito. He is devoted to his family and to the traditional
    ways of his people. His life is patterned by ritual and
    the harmonious rhythm he envisions in nature--all of
    which is interrupted when he finds "The Pearl of the
    World." He must kill four men before he realizes the
    extent of the trouble the pearl has brought (P).

KISS OF DEATH KELLY See KELLY, KISS OF DEATH
    (ST)

KNOWLES, FLOYD. A young man at the Hooverville govern-
    ment camp where the Joads spend their first night in
    California. He tells Tom Joad how the farmers arrest
    spokesmen for the migrants and how they blacklist pro-
    testers and murder rebellious farm workers who fight
    back. He has been in California six months and ex-
    plains how there is no steady work. When a contractor
    arrives to tell about fruit picking in Tulare County,
    Floyd asks to see his license and demands a contract,
    whereupon the contractor has a deputy try to arrest him
    on trumped-up charges. Floyd strikes the deputy and
    makes a break for it, whereupon Casy knocks the depu-
    ty out and goes to prison instead of Floyd (GW).

KROUPOFF, ALEXIS. Russian journalist. In an article pub-
    lished in Pravda, he proves that Lenin foresaw the re-
    turn of the French monarchy and approved it as a ma-
    jor step in the direction of eventual socialization (SRP).

LA SANTA ROJA (YSOBEL). The Red Saint of Panama who
is the dream of every man who had ever sailed the
Main. She is a delirium in the minds of the pirates,
a virgin for their prayers. Captured by Morgan, this
strange woman with black opaque eyes and straight,
black hair sees through Morgan's vain dreams. She
tells him that he will take no more cups of gold. Initially, the sensuous La Santa Roja thought that Morgan
might provide force and love for "the white fetish of my
body." But while she hoped he would be her brazen
figure of the night, she comes to regard him as a bab-
bler and a fop (CG).

LADY MODDYFORD See MODDYFORD, LADY (CG)

LAKE, JAKE. "In the night, in Monterey, a policeman patrols the streets on a motorcycle to see that good things
come to no evil." The ironical thing about Steinbeck's
lenient sentence is not so much that he is out of sympathy with the paisanos' ingenuous views on peace officers.
Rather, he is too jaundiced by experience to share the
paisano faith that broad-minded men like Jake Lake are
easy to come by. For Steinbeck, Jake is clearly a remarkable exception to the harsh rule of authority.
Jake's reaction to Big Joe Portagee's roadside romance
is characteristic of his live-and-let-live style: " 'You
get out of the street,' he said. 'Somebody'll come
along and run over you.' " On the day of Danny's funeral, Jake "arrested a roadster from Del Monte and
turned it loose and bought a cigar." Steinbeck often intimates that subordinates in a faceless system act hu-
manely when left to their own devices (TF).

LANSER, COLONEL. The commanding officer of the invading army who is a perceptive and generally humane man.
Although he comes to realize the futility of the invading
army's position against an occupied people whose will is
strong, he follows the orders given to him as he knows
he must. Although he occupies the town and inhabits
the mayor's house, he cannot control the villagers. He
is committed to the rules of war, but he learns that he
cannot long subdue a free people (MID).

LAPIERRE, MR. Bartender at the Abbott House in Salinas.
When Adam Trask goes there after Samuel Hamilton's
funeral, Mr. Lapierre serves him several hot rum tod-
dies, drinks with him, and gives him directions to

Kate's brothel, while advising him to go to Jenny's instead (EE).

LEADER, THE. Never referred to by name, the Leader is
a thinly disguised Hitler. Reflected in Lieutenant
Prackle, the fanaticism of the Leader has a special
poignancy (MID).

LEE. Adam Trask's Chinese cook. Though he was born in
the United States, Lee first wears a pigtail and speaks
pidgin English to strangers; but he is not only fluent in
English but is a cultured, widely-read person of philosophical bent. When he knows someone well enough to
let down his guard, he speaks in formal, dialect-free
English. As times change and he no longer has to be
defensive about his origins, he cuts off his pigtail and
drops his pidgin altogether. Lee and Samuel Hamilton
find that they have similar literary, artistic, and philosophical interests and become friends. Gradually Lee
becomes a mentor to Adam Trask. When the twins are
born, Lee becomes father and mother to them and supervises their upbringing. He also becomes more of a
father to Abra than her own parents. Lee often functions as spokesman for the author's moral and philosophical statements, including the exegesis of Genesis
and the understanding of the Hebrew word Timshel as
"Thou mayest."* Lee is a humanist whose wisdom,
tolerance, kindness, and patience express many of the
novel's positive values (EE).
[*See Joseph Fontenrose, "Another View of James
Gray's John Steinbeck," Steinbeck Quarterly, 8 (Winter
1975), 19.]

LEE CHONG See CHONG, LEE (ST)

LENNIE SMALL See SMALL, LENNIE (OMM)

LESCAULT, SUZANNE (SISTER HYACINTHE). An old friend
of Marie Héristal. They were childhood friends and
schoolmates together. She was a pretty and talented
child with a true singing voice and natural ability as a
dancer. When her father's business manipulations were
discovered and he committed suicide, she turned by
necessity to a career on the stage. She spent years
with the Folies Bergère and became ballet mistress.
Her bosom remained high, but she grew tired and her
arches had fallen. She turned to religious orders to

rest her feet. Her friendship with Marie continues throughout the years. When Pippin Héristal becomes King of France, she becomes a companion to the queen. She becomes an important force for the peace and security of France by advising the queen on domestic matters and by becoming a frequent confidante of the king. She comes to love and respect Pippin IV and tells him after his fall that he has shown courage and wisdom in his short reign as King of France (SRP).

LIEBHOLTZ, DR. HORACE. Mr. Pritchard's dentist in Chicago. Pritchard mentions Liebholtz as part of his fumbling effort to reconstruct his previous confrontation with Camille Oaks (WB).

LT. EMILE DE SAMOTHRACE See SAMOTHRACE, LT. EMILE DE (SRP)

LIEUTENANT PRACKLE See PRACKLE, LIEUTENANT (MID)

LIEUTENANT TONDER See TONDER, LIEUTENANT (MID)

LIPPO, LOUIS. A neighbor who drives Adam Trask in his buckboard to the Hamilton ranch. On the way, Louis explains the Hamilton family to Adam. His own father was an Italian immigrant who left him a small farm. Louis is a friend of Samuel's and advises Adam not to think that Samuel is strange and unreliable (EE).

LISA. London's daughter. Her cries during labor give Mac an idea for gaining acceptance by the migrants. Mac successfully delivers her child and in the process unites the migrants and wins approval for himself. Later in the novel, Lisa speaks freely to Jim because he was present during the delivery and she trusts him (IDB).

LISBETH SANDRY See SANDRY, LISBETH (GW)

LITTLEFIELD, ANNIE. A member of the Ladies' Committee of Sanitary Unit Number Four at the Weedpatch government camp. She is small and plump, with curly gray hair and a small mouth (GW).

LIZA HAMILTON See HAMILTON, LIZA (EE)

LIZZIE HAMILTON See HAMILTON, LIZZIE (EE)

LOFT, CAPTAIN. Although young, Loft is the total military
man. He knows and lives military regulations so fully
that his presence tends to intimidate his fellow officers.
Loft, the true professional, provokes Alex Morden.
Morden kills Captain Bentick, who attempted to inter-
vene, and Loft is the prosecutor of Morden at the military trial which follows. Loft is the only member of
the invading army who seems to have no humanity
(MID).

L'OLLONAIS. A vicious pirate with a love of cruelty. On
one occasion he cuts off eighty-seven heads with his
own hand. On another, he invades the Yucatan and destroys the country (CG).

LONDON. The leader of a group of migrant families who is
eventually elected to head the strike. London has great
physical strength and is a natural leader of men. Mac
successfully delivers London's daughter's baby and
thereafter London trusts Mac and often saves the strike
from collapse (IDB).

LOPEZ, MARIA. Lives with her sister, Rosa, in a white-
washed clapboard shack. She and her sister make the
best tortillas in the valley yet must also sell themselves to enhance their new restaurant business (PH).

LOPEZ, ROSA. Like her sister, Maria, Rosa decides to
encourage the customers to buy more tortillas by selling herself along with the food. When the sheriff
closes the restaurant, she and Maria go off to San
Francisco, bent on becoming "bad women" (PH).

LORAINE. Sometime prostitute, sometime soul-mate of
Camille Oaks, "she didn't love anyone ... so she had
nothing to be taken away, nothing to lose." Loraine
was currently living with an advertising man who con-
tracted venereal disease from her and later lost his
job. Like Camille, Loraine survives by submitting to
the flood of events, rather than by contending vainly
against the destructive element. She is opportunistic,
schooled in the tactics of social warfare, but sympathetic to the predicament of fellow drifters. Early in
life, she struck a bad bargain with fate, but she pays
her debts, if she has her price, too, and remains
self-possessed in a possessive, predatory demi-monde.
She is one of the many "capable victims" who people
Steinbeck's fiction (WB).

LOU. Cook at the Bear Flag Restaurant. Lou is a Greek
with dark eyes who witnessed William's suicide (CR).

LOUIE. Louie drives the Greyhound bus that brings Camille
Oaks from San Ysidro to Rebel Corners. Literally a
transitional figure between the automated, stationary
world of San Ysidro and the impassioned, turbulent pan-
orama that unfolds west of Rebel Corners, his primary
function is to register the initial glimpse of the novel's
femme fatale. For the task, Steinbeck nominates a
man with some strength of character. Louie is keenly
observant, even reflective. He is a proficient teamster,
the master of his rig, and performs his routine with
disdainful ease and authority. He is a trendsetter
whose reputation for finesse is not entirely undeserved.
Cautious but not craven, Louie negotiates the system
effectively and, with a shrewd capacity for self-analysis,
rarely overreaches himself.
    But he is an "operator" in a far less prepossess-
ing sense, too. Especially in contrast to Chicoy, his
liabilities all but outweigh his assets and render him
negligible as a person, if not as a pivotal minor figure
in the novel. He takes his cues from meretricious
self-help manuals and sleazy Hollywood styles. He is
wolfish and ruthless with women, whom he calls "pigs."
There is no inner reservoir of unpolluted manhood for
him to draw on, and his obscene, leering sexuality is
less a foil to Juan Chicoy's virile masculinity than a
bankrupt caricature of it. Louie forces his attentions
on Camille, but her superior aplomb and display of supreme indifference deftly parry his heavy-handed verbal
foreplay. The journeyman manipulator is no match for
the spontaneous artist of allure, and she brings the dis-
comfited bus driver to a standstill (WB).

LOUIS LIPPO See LIPPO, LOUIS (EE)

                       M

MA JOAD See JOAD, MA (GW)

MABEL. One of the regular girls at the Bear Flag. She
seems to be the most sentimental of the girls, but she
also is a natural-born hustler. She gives Fauna a beautiful wedding gown and crown that has been passed down
in her family from past generations for Suzy to wear as
Snow White at the masquerade. When she appears, it

is usually in the company of Agnes and Becky (ST).

MAC. An experienced Communist labor agitator who takes
Jim Nolan under his wing as the two of them attempt
to organize the apple pickers of the Torgas Valley.
Mac attempts to remain personally detached from the
laborers, and although he is not fully successful, he
does stress the welfare of the group over that of the
individual. The novel ends with Mac's using Jim's
mutilated corpse as a symbol to unify the workers
(IDB).

McELROY. When McElroy's prize black Angus bull perishes
in the deluge, Breed observes that "McElroy didn't have
that kind of money to throw away. He didn't see any
of the rest of the herd come down, but the bull would
be enough. Mac had put a lot of faith in that bull."
This brief but memorable image proposes an alternative
to the cutthroat urban economy. Breed's language reflects the sympathetic community of country people who
contend with nature, not with each other, in their
ceaseless effort to eke out an existence. "Mac" is one
of Steinbeck's favorite names for "the working stiff"
(WB).

McGREGGOR, ELIZABETH See WAYNE, ELIZABETH (TGU)

McGREGGOR, MR. Father of Elizabeth McGreggor. He is
a harness-maker and saddler by profession but a furi-
ous Marxist for the sake of argument. He is a sullen
man who sues his neighbor and browbeats his daughter,
but he miserably fails in both attempts. He feels his
daughter was filled with stories of fairies by his wife
before she died. He tells his daughter that women
should learn a trade, but he is shocked when Elizabeth
becomes a schoolteacher. He is wistful at Elizabeth's
wedding and tells Joseph he hates him because Joseph
is the stronger man. He confesses that he is a weak
man and that he hated his wife and daughter because
they knew. He refuses an invitation to visit Joseph and
Elizabeth and bristles when Joseph suggests that he will
come anyway (TGU).

McGREGGOR, MRS. Mother of Elizabeth McGreggor. She
was a highland woman. Her husband remembers her as
a stubborn woman without a single shred of reason.
Like her own parents, she believed in fairies, but when

her husband mentioned it, she would tell him that sometimes things are true even if they cannot stand up to
reason. Her husband believes that she filled her daughter with fairies before she died. Elizabeth remembers
picnics on Huckleberry Hill and picking berries with
her mother (TGU).

MACHADO, HUGO. At the start of the novel and again on
the day of Danny's funeral, "Hugo Machado, the tailor,
put a sign in his shop door. 'Back in Five Minutes,'
and went home for the day." Like Thoreau, Steinbeck
sees the tailor as the trendsetter, literally the signpost
of habit, in a community. Machado's two easy-come,
easy-go appearances express the leisurely silhouette of
Monterey life and the prevailing informality of Steinbeck's literary fashion (TF).

MACK. The leader and mentor of a group of vagabonds on
Cannery Row. He is a man who came to the Row to
escape the complexities of life where everything he had
ever done had turned sour. On the Row, Mack just
tries to enjoy life. He is the prime force behind the
party for Doc. Steinbeck refers to Mack and the boys
as "the Virtues, the Graces and the Beauties" (CR).

MACK. An alter ego for Steinbeck in the Prologue and the
leader of the inhabitants of the Palace Flophouse (see
Cannery Row). He stayed around and kept things in
order during the war. After a brief adventure seeking
uranium deposits with a secondhand Geiger counter, he
returned to Monterey and cleaned up the Palace Flophouse for the returning heroes. He is the recorder of
the changes that have taken place in Monterey and Cannery Row during the war. He is deeply concerned
about Doc and believes that he needs a woman to cure
his restlessness and melancholy. With Hazel's urging
he decided to help Doc by picking out a woman for him.
This problem is complicated by Mack's discovery that
Lee Chong may have sold the Palace Flophouse to Joseph and Mary Rivas. If true, Mack believes that their
home could be taken away from them. When he finds
out on Sweet Thursday that Joseph and Mary do not
know that he may own the Palace Flophouse, Mack de-
vises a plan to raffle the place to buy a four hundred
dollar microscope for Doc. The raffle is fixed so that
Doc becomes the ostensible owner of the Palace Flophouse. The masquerade planned by Mack and Fauna is

designed to secure the Palace Flophouse for the boys
and Suzy for Doc. At the Masquerade, however, Mack
finds out that he is the actual owner of the Palace Flophouse. When the planned union of Suzy and Doc fails,
Mack becomes lifeless and depressed and takes to his
bed. He springs to life again after Hazel breaks Doc's
right arm. He teaches Suzy how to drive in a mock-
up car and presents Doc with the promised gift, which
turns out to be a telescope rather than a microscope
(ST).

MACMINIMUM, MR. Regular customer at the Golden Poppy.
Suzy becomes so distraught when she hears of Doc's
broken right arm that she calls him Mr. Gross (EE).

MADAME PASMOUCHES See PASMOUCHES, MADAME
(SRP).

MADAME RUMORGUE See RUMORGUE, MADAME (SRP)

MAE. Works behind the counter at a lunch stand on Route
66. She is a composite character, typical of Minne or
Susy or other middle-aging employees taking orders and
calling them to the cook. She jokes with the truck
drivers and calls the wealthy travelers "shitheels."
Mae talks tough and has harsh, screeching laughter but
is a soft touch who sells a 15-cent loaf of bread to a
hungry migrant for a dime and sells his kids nickel
candy two-for-a-penny (GW).

MAE MUNROE See MUNROE, MAE (PH)

MAE, PHYLLIS. One of Dora Flood's girls who, on one occasion, suffers an infected arm after a drunk whom she
hit in the mouth got a tooth in her fist. Phyllis Mae
is among the celebrants at Doc's party (CR).

MAE ROMERO See ROMERO, MAE (LV)

MAGOT, M. Member of the National Assembly. He is asked
by M. Sonnet, former president of the republic, to form
a coalition government to replace the collapsed monarchy (SRP).

MAHLER, HAL. He runs Hal's poolroom in Santa Cruz.
When Joe Valery asks him about Ethel, he tells how she
was drowned, probably by "some crazy bohunk bastards

in the sardine fleet." Joe gives him $25.00 for this information. Hal has "large pale eyes made huge by thick glasses." He wears a green eyeshade and black alpaca sleeve guards. Hal says little unless he is eating and rarely speaks unless his mouth is full (EE).

MAJOR HUNTER See HUNTER, MAJOR (MID)

MALLOY, MR. AND MRS. SAM. A couple who in 1935 moved into an old boiler on Cannery Row which had been discarded by the owners of the Hediondo Cannery after it blew a tube for the third time. Mr. Malloy does a small but steady business renting the larger boiler pipes as sleeping quarters, and the couple lives happily until Mrs. Malloy, feeling the need to behave like a landlord, assembles useless material goods. A crisis between the couple occurs when Mrs. Malloy buys lace curtains and rods for the windowless boiler (CR).

MALLOY, MRS. SAM. Wife of Sam Malloy (see Cannery Row). Her nagging about the need for curtains in the old boiler eventually drove her husband out. While he serves his time as a trusty in the county jail, she is slinging hash in Salinas. She is waiting for him to get out (ST).

MALLOY, SAM. Former resident of the old boiler (see Cannery Row). Grew disgruntled with his home because of his nagging wife. He is a trusty now in the county jail. Agnes mentions that he was a nice person and a high Elk (ST).

MALTBY, JUNIUS. Small young man with a good education who comes from a cultural family. He spends his evenings reading R. L. Stevenson's Travels with a Donkey. He lives on the Widow Quaker's farm and eventually marries her. She nags him about his laziness. She dies and he attempts to raise their son, Robbie. Eventually he and Robbie leave for San Francisco where he will find work (PH).

MALTBY, MRS. QUAKER. A widow who rents a room to Junius Maltby. Because she is nervous about having a single man living in the house, she confesses her fears to Junius who promptly marries her (PH).

MALTBY, ROBERT LOUIS. Junius' son, called "Robbie," born as his mother dies. He grows up gravely, being treated always like an adult. When he goes to school, the younger boys imitate his slovenliness. Eventually he and his father move to San Francisco (PH).

MAMA TORRES See TORRES, MAMA (LV)

MAN WITH A TELESCOPE. Runs a small business on the beach. He asks five cents for the opportunity to see the moon. Juanito and Willie Romas look through the telescope, but when Willie sees the place of his nightmare he hangs himself from a tree limb that night (TGU).

MANAGER OF THE SAFEWAY. He allows the seer to steal one Baby Ruth at a time, but stops him when he tries to steal three. On the second Sweet Thursday of the spring he recommends to Judge Albertson that the charges be dropped (ST).

MANFRED MUNROE See MUNROE, MANFRED (PH)

MANSVELDT, EDWARD. In bravery and in soldiery, the most eminent of all the pirate brotherhood. He had once captured St. Augustine in Florida as well as Granada and St. Catherine's Isle. Consumed by the power of dream, Mansveldt wanted to create a new nation in America. Eventually, when his ship was wrecked near Havana, he was captured (CG).

MANUEL GOMEZ See GOMEZ, MANUEL (TGU)

MANUEL THE GUITARIST. Old Juan's son-in-law. He is a smiling, shiftless Mexican boy who imitates Old Juan's actions. He plays the guitar and when the musicians arrive for the New Year's fiesta he comes to life. At the height of the wild dancing, he sheds his previous shy embarrassment and howls a shrill minor bar with meaningless words (TGU).

MANUEL THE RIDER. One of the ranch workers. He and Jose are to dig a grave for Elizabeth Wayne. He reports to Joseph Wayne that over one hundred cows are dead because of the drought. He also tells him that they will lose more cows on the trip to San Joaquin. When Joseph tells him that they will start when the hay is gone, he reports the hay will be gone by the next day (TGU).

MARGIE YOUNG-HUNT See YOUNG-HUNT, MARGIE (WOD)

MARIA LOPEZ See LOPEZ, MARIA (PH)

MARIE HERISTAL See HERISTAL, MARIE (SRP)

MARINE, GEORGES DE. The Comte de Marine. A listless seventeen-year-old who takes Clotilde Héristal to the Les Ambassadeurs where she meets Tod Johnson (SRP).

MARN, DR. ("The Harness"). The Randall's doctor. He leaves sedatives for Peter after Emma's death (LV).

MARSH, CHARLIE. Charlie is occasionally mentioned as the town derelict. His usual role is to serve as the ultimate yardstick of alcoholic excess, not as an outcast target of parochial derision. Thus the superlative insult to Torrelli's wine is that "lately it is so bad that Charlie Marsh even would not drink it." On the day of Danny's funeral, it is not Danny's fraternity but the voice of the public that asks, "How can Charlie Marsh be as dirtily drunk as usual? It is sacrilege. It is outrage." Even as the paisanos themselves drift in a spiritual morass, they steer clear from the hazard of such sanctimonious judgment (TF).

MARTEL, CHARLES. Uncle and friend of Pippin Héristal. Proprietor of a small but prosperous art gallery and antique store. He is in his late sixties and is described as a worldly man, gentle but inflexible, of impeccable carriage and dress. At the rear of his gallery is the most comfortable and discreet bachelor's quarters in Paris where he still entertains selected young ladies. He knows that the choice of Pippin as King of France is a political move to set up a patsy as the head of government. He retires into semi-privacy once Pippin becomes king to avoid various nobles asking favors, but he still retains an interest in business by trying to sell Tod Johnson some dubiously authentic paintings by Boucher. He warns Pippin not to become active in the affairs of state because it will bring about his fall. When Pippin rejects his advice, he decides to leave for America. He does one last favor for the king by removing his wife and daughter to the country during

the coming political crisis. When Pippin is deposed,
he heads south for Portugal (SRP).

MARTHA WAYNE See WAYNE, MARTHA (TGU)

MARTIN, MISS. Tularecito's teacher who recognizes his
artistic genius. Her schoolroom is wrecked by the
young boy (PH).

MARTIN, ROSA. In Chapter IV, Pablo reports that "Danny
is with Rosa Martin, that Portagee girl." Pilon is
alarmed: "Maybe that girl will want to marry Danny.
Those Portagees always want to marry, and they love
money. Maybe when they are married Danny will both-
er us about the rent. That Rosa will want new dresses. All women do. I know them." When put to the
test, Pilon's extravagant theory proves defective.
Danny is currently more interested in Mrs. Morales
than in Rosa. The principal target of Steinbeck's satire is probably not Pilon's male chauvinism or even his
scandalous suspicion of a "Portagee" (Big Joe's subsequent treachery notwithstanding). Rather, Steinbeck
once again takes aim at Pilon's own breathtaking leaps
of logic, the superficially entertaining but ultimately
sinister plot of his metaphysical imagination (TF).

MARULLO, ALFIO. After Ethan's grocery business failed,
Alfio Marullo bought the establishment and he presently
employs Ethan as his clerk and general factotum. When
Ethan spurns the lucrative but shady scheme of Bigger's
syndicate, Marullo rewards the act of fidelity, first with
a symbolic gift of candy Easter eggs, then more tangib-
ly with $60 and the loan of his Pontiac so that Ethan
and Mary can enjoy a July 4th respite. Ethan has already betrayed Marullo's rough generosity. Acting on
Joey Morphy's tip, he has anonymously informed a government agent, Richard Walder, that Marullo is an il-
legal immigrant. Ethan knows that his boss will either
flee in panic or face deportation. Banking on Marullo's
unsuspecting good will and Baker's covert cooperation,
Ethan withdraws Mary's money from their joint account
and cold-bloodedly waits to repurchase the store for a
fraction of its worth. On Independence Day weekend,
Walder arrives with the stunning news that Marullo is
returning to his native Italy and has given the store to
his honest American friend, Ethan Hawley.
       Marullo epitomizes the rags-to-riches success

story of countless European refugees who entered the
United States in the wake of World War I. It is a
story of disillusionment: "He'd memorized the Decla-
ration of Independence in dialect. The Bill of Rights
was words of fire. And then he couldn't get in. So
he came anyway. A nice man helped him--took everything he had and dropped him in the surf to wade
ashore. It was quite a while before he understood the
American way, but he learned--he learned. 'A guy got
to make a buck! Look out for number one!' " During
the era of the Sacco and Vanzetti trial, Marullo learned
that "money got no friends but more money" and became
a "one man Mafia." Tapping the resource of his three
thousand year old name, Marullo thrived in the rich
soil of his adopted land. In repayment, he has opened
Ethan's eyes to the hard, often cruel facts of American
life. Two centuries of Hawley history have much to
absorb from three transplanted millennia of Mediterran-
ean wisdom.

The key to Marullo is his integrity. As man and
as character, he is all of a piece and a source of
strength. He informs the texture of the novel, rather
than leans on it for support, and educates Ethan and
Steinbeck's audience about the ground rules of their re-
spective worldly and literary experience. Accustomed
to pigeon-holing Marullo as "a Catholic and a wop," as
a sinister yet negligible stereotype, Ethan is brought up
short by his initial perception that his employer is a
sensitive, suffering human being: "It was the shocking
discovery that makes a man wonder: If I've missed
this, what else have I failed to see?" Correspondingly,
the reader recognizes that Marullo is one of Steinbeck's
elect characters. He is the vehicle for symbolic, often
biblical refinements, but he also fosters the unpreten-
tious, journeyman imagery that typically links Steinbeck's
plots to his universal themes. Marullo represents Roman practicality, the imperative compromise with the
world of Caesar, and his remark to Ethan that "you give
service" is notable for its ironic religious overtones.

But the reader comes to appreciate, too, that triv-
ial details like Marullo's "gleaming" and "gold-capped
teeth" establish his credentials as a leading participant
in Steinbeck's major text. At the end of the novel,
Walder explains to Ethan that Marullo "wants to make
you a kind of monument to something he believed in
once"; "You're his down payment, kind of, so the light
won't go out." From the start, Steinbeck has carefully

prepared Marullo as one of the few bright spots illuminating an otherwise desolated wasteland, as a ray of hope. At the end, the man who rummages in garbage to learn about society is himself a dying and discarded remnant; but his collapse is less the sign of failure than of his unstinting contribution to the novel. He retains a lingering attachment to Thoreau, who similarly accorded July 4th a prominent place on his calendar and discovered the secret springs of rebirth in the "groceries" of social intercourse and the rubbish of human neglect (WOD).

(MARY) ELLEN HAWLEY See HAWLEY, (MARY) ELLEN (WOD)

MARY HAWLEY See HAWLEY, MARY (WOD)

MARY RIVAS See RIVAS, MARY (ST)

MARY STEINBECK See STEINBECK, MARY (EE)

MARY TELLER See TELLER, MARY (LV)

MAY ("The Murder"). A blond prostitute in Monterey to whom Jim Moore would go every Saturday. Jim found no companionship in his Slavic wife, and after a year of marriage he seeks May as one of his own kind (LV).

MAY NOLAN See NOLAN, MAY (IDB)

MAYOR CLOUGH See CLOUGH, MAYOR (TF)

MAYOR CRISTY See CRISTY, MAYOR (ST)

MAYOR ORDEN See ORDEN, MAYOR (MID)

MAYOR PRO TEM. Interim successor to Mayor Cristy of Pacific Grove. He writes a proclamation for the paper when the butterflies finally arrive on the second Sweet Thursday of the spring (ST).

MAYOR, THE. A resident of the first shack at the Hooverville near Bakersfield. He is a bearded man in shirt sleeves who is "bull-simple" from having been beaten too much by the police (GW).

MECHANT, PERE. The little Pastor of the Pediment (SRP).

Clotilde Héristal meets him during her association with
lower class workers. She is so impressed that she
almost joins an order of nuns devoted to silence, black
bread, and pedicures for the poor (SRP).

MEEK, TOM. The Salinas constable. When he learns that
Cal Trask made $15,000 in beans, he considers him a
young punk who is getting too smart (EE).

MEELER, CHARLIE. Early in the novel, Charlie is identified as a casual purveyor of community gossip. In
Chapter XIV, Charlie figures prominently in the incident of Tall Bob Smoke's putative suicide. Having
vainly waited for days for someone to drop by and talk
him out of shooting himself, Tall Bob finally admits
Charlie to his room: "But he did not shout; no, Charlie Meeler jumped and grabbed that gun and that gun
went off and shot away the end of Bob's nose." This
ludicrous dramatization of the man who cut off his nose
to spite his face is a slapstick overture to the bizarre
anecdote of the Ravannos, father and son (TF).

MEER, MRS. Jim Nolan's landlady before he joins the Communist Party (IDB).

MERLIN. A strange old man with a long white beard who
lives high on a hill near the Morgan home in Wales.
Merlin resembles an ancient Druid priest with farseeing
eyes that watched the heavens. Henry explains his
dreams to Merlin before he leaves home. And Merlin
understand Henry's quest to "capture the moon," and
tells him he may even succeed if only he remains a
child (CG).

MIKE ("The Vigilante"). After helping lynch a black man,
Mike realizes that the experience gave him a feeling
akin to sexual satisfaction (LV).

MILDRED PRITCHARD See PRITCHARD, MILDRED (WB)

MILTON, GEORGE. Small and quick with restless eyes and
sharp features. He protects Lennie, his idiot companion, from harm. After promising Lennie that together
they will buy a ranch, he is forced to shoot him to
keep him from being subjected to the cruel wrath of
Curley, whose wife Lennie accidentally kills. George
feels ashamed for getting angry so frequently with

Lennie. George expresses his wish to be free of Lennie but realizes that there is no place for him to go (OMM).

MINISTER OF NATIONAL MONUMENTS. Presents a bill for three hundred thousand francs to Pippin IV after Princess Clotilde turns on the fountains and floodlights at Versailles to celebrate the return of the monarchy (SRP).

MISS ALMA ALVAREZ See ALVAREZ, MISS ALMA (TF)

MISS JACK See JACK, MISS (LV)

MISS MARTIN See MARTIN, MISS (PH)

MISS MORGAN See MORGAN, MISS (PH)

MISS WINCH See WINCH, MISS (ST)

MR. ALFRED CORTEZ See CORTEZ, MR. ALFRED (TF)

MR. ALFRED WONG See WONG, MR. ALFRED (ST)

MR. AND MRS. MUSTROVIC See MUSTROVIC, MR. AND MRS. (PH)

MR. AND MRS. TOM TALBOT See TALBOT, MR. AND MRS. TOM (CR)

MR. ANDERSON See ANDERSON, MR. (IDB)

MR. BACON See BACON, MR. (EE)

MR. BAKER See BAKER, MR. (WOD)

MR. EDWARDS See EDWARDS, MR. (EE)

MR. FENCHEL See FENCHEL, MR. (EE)

MR. LAPIERRE See LAPIERRE, MR. (EE)

MR. ROLF See ROLF, MR. (EE)

MR. SEPIC See SEPIC, MR. (LV)

MR. SIMON See SIMON, MR. (TF)

MR. THOMAS See THOMAS, MR. (GW)

MR. WAINWRIGHT See WAINWRIGHT, MR. (GW)

MR. WEBB See WEBB, MR. (IDB)

MRS. AMES See AMES, MRS. (EE)

MRS. BACON See BACON, MRS. (EE)

MRS. BANKS See BANKS, MRS. (PH)

MRS. BRUNO See BRUNO, MRS. (TF)

MRS. CHAPPELL See CHAPPELL, MRS. (LV)

MRS. EDWARDS See EDWARDS, MRS. (EE)

MRS. GUITTIEREZ See GUITTIEREZ, MRS. (TF)

MRS. MEER See MEER, MRS. (IDB)

MRS. MORALES See MORALES, MRS. (TF)

MRS. MORGAN See MORGAN, MRS. (PH)

MRS. MORIT See MORIT, MRS. (PH)

MRS. MUNROE See MUNROE, MRS. (PH)

MRS. PALOCHICO See PALOCHICO, MRS. (TF)

MRS. PASTANO See PASTANO, MRS. (TF)

MRS. QUAKER MALTBY See MALTBY, MRS. QUAKER (PH)

MRS. RATZ See RATZ, MRS. (LV)

MRS. RODRIGUEZ See RODRIGUEZ, MRS. (LV)

MRS. SATO See SATO, MRS. (TF)

MRS. SCHMIDT See SCHMIDT, MRS. (IDB)

MRS. TRASK See TRASK, MRS. (EE)

MRS. WAINWRIGHT See WAINWRIGHT, MRS. (GW)

MRS. WILLA WHITESIDE See WHITESIDE, MRS. WILLA
(PH)

MISTRESS, THE KING'S.   The grand-niece of Sister Hyacinthe's Superior.   She is quiet, well-bred, a little
stocky, but does beautiful needlework.   She becomes
the public mistress of Pippin IV, but privately she
never meets him (SRP).

MODDYFORD, LADY.   Wife of Sir Charles Moddyford who
has taken care of Sir Edward Morgan's daughter Elizabeth since Sir Edward's death.   Lady Moddyford urges
Elizabeth to marry Henry Morgan (CG).

MODDYFORD, SIR CHARLES.   British Governor of Port
Royal who receives Morgan upon his return from the
conquest of Panama.   Governor Moddyford discusses
what he hopes will be Morgan's willingness to buy his
pardon from the British king (CG).

MOLLIE HAMILTON See HAMILTON, MOLLIE (EE)

MOLLY MORDEN See MORDEN, MOLLY (MID)

MOLLY MORGAN See MORGAN, MOLLY (PH)

MONTEZ, GRACIE.   In Chapter XIV, the novel turns the
corner from farce to the grotesque with the story of
Petey Ravanno, his father Old Ravanno, and the two
Montez sisters.   Steinbeck based his fictionalized account on a true incident that had become a celebrated
nugget in Monterey lore.   Gracie "was not a very good
girl.   When she was only twelve years old the fleet
came to Monterey, and Gracie had her first baby, so
young as that.   She was pretty, you see, and quick,
and her tongue was sharp.   Always she seemed to run
away from men, and men ran fast after her.   And
sometimes they caught her.   But you could not get close
to her.   Always that Gracie seemed to have something
nice that she did not give to you, something in back of
her eyes that said, 'If I really wanted to, I would be
different to you from any woman you ever knew.' "
        Petey became hopelessly infatuated with this elus-
ive charmer.   The stronger his feelings, the more
Gracie teased and laughed.   At last, Petey faked suicide

to win sympathy, and his ruse triumphed. Overcome
by such a flattering gesture of devotion, the former
Lorelei consented to marriage and renounced her will-
o'-the-wisp caprice. Now, "She is a good woman. She
never misses mass, and she goes once a month to con-
fession." After the wedding, Old Ravanno followed in
his son's footsteps and hungered for Gracie's sister,
'Tonia. But when he attempted to imitate Petey's strat-
agem in order to consummate his own December and
May passion, he accidentally hanged himself.

    The friends appreciate the first part of this tale,
the part about Petey and Gracie, "for they liked a story
with a meaning." Presumably, they respond to the tidy
ending, not the preliminary phase that seems to fasci-
nate Steinbeck. In the two preceding chapters, the
paisanos have rejoiced when the Pirate finally bought his
precious candle and have then magnanimously assisted
Teresina and her family. With the adventure of Petey
and Gracie, Steinbeck probes the lure of the unattain-
able objective and the mad extravagance of the pursuit
of beauty. Gracie may confer grace on Petey, but the
anecdote is as much a premonitory foil for the conclud-
ing nightmare of Old Ravanno as an epilogue to earlier
events. It is possible to detect Arthurian overtones and
the like, but the linking function of this manic overture
to the novel's denouement should not be minimized.
Danny's death, the end of the novel, and the end of the
paisanos' dream of unity all follow a frenzied carnival
of love-making. In retrospect, the meaning of the young
woman's flirtatiousness is harder to grasp than the
young woman herself. Petey's quest for matrimonial
possession of Gracie objectifies Steinbeck's authorial
wooing of high-spirited literary resources. Both men
struggle for a supremacy that will not crush out excitement and liveliness. Both men risk failure rather than
capitulate to fate (TF).

(MONTEZ) 'TONIA See 'TONIA (MONTEZ) (TF)

MOORE, JIM ("The Murder"). A Monterey County farmer.
    Married to a Slavic girl, he treats her more as a do-
mesticated farm animal than a human being and wife.
For companionship Jim goes to a prostitute in Monterey,
but returning home early one Saturday he finds his wife
in bed with her cousin. Jim kills the man and savagely
whips Jelka, realizing Jelka's father's admonition: "Slav
girl! He's not like a man that don't beat hell out of
him" (LV).

MORALES, ARTHUR. At the start of the novel, Danny wax-
es sentimental in the mode of ubi sunt: " 'Where is
Arthur Morales.' Danny asked, turning his palms up
and thrusting his arms forward. 'Dead in France,'
he answered himself, turning the palms down and drop-
ping his arms in despair. 'Dead for his country.
Dead in a foreign land. Strangers walk near his grave
and they do not know Arthur Morales lies there.' "
The histrionic posturing continues: " 'Where is Pablo,
that good man?' " But the rasping note of realism in-
trudes: " 'In jail,' said Pilon. 'Pablo stole a goose
and hid in the brush; and that goose bit Pablo and Pablo cried out and so was caught. Now he lies in jail for
six months.' " Already, the question of who lies where
has dramatized a fundamental dynamic of the novel, the
collision of pretentious literary mannerism and prosaic
common sense. Furthermore, Steinbeck lays a firm
foundation for his tricky irony. Danny's facade discred-
its the name "Arthur" and the use of a conventional
form, elegy, to evoke the grim character of modern
warfare; yet the novel to follow will persistently busy
itself with the Arthurian and other traditional structures.
     The dialogue proceeds with a rare aside on the
theory of language: "Danny sighed and changed the subject, for he realized that he had prodigally used up the
only acquaintance in any way fit for oratory. But the
loneliness was still on him and demanded an outlet.
'Here we sit,' he began at last. '--broken-hearted,'
Pilon added rhythmically. 'No, this is not a poem,'
Danny said. 'Here we sit, homeless. We gave our
lives for our country, and now we have no roof over
our head.' 'We never did have,' Pilon added helpfully."
The comedy is a vehicle for a key debate. The mer-
its of the Romantic view that poetry springs from a
non-renewable resource of inspiration vies with the
pragmatic but perhaps equally moral contention that human experience is an inexhaustible fund of material for
the self-effacing craftsman prepared to capitalize on it.
For the moment, Danny's lyricism is put to flight. Pilon demonstrates that to dissect a formulaic celebration
of death is to murder it, but Steinbeck cultivates the
tough-minded irony that arises from the grave. The
onset of the novel does not, however, vitiate the spectacular ending. In retrospect, Pilon's criticisms seem
sterile and parasitic in comparison to Danny's flourish-
ing life-force and flamboyant death (TF).

MORALES, MRS. Danny's backyard neighbor, Mrs. Morales, is a troubling reminder of his unsought responsibilities as a man of property. Routine exploitation is simple enough, and a glint comes to Pilon's eye when he first savors the spectacle of Mrs. Morales's chickens. But until the momentous night that his rental house burns down, Danny is burdened by the obligation to court the wealthy widow. For once, there are substantial grounds to the apprehensions of Danny's friends. Sex as an adjunct to a rise in fortunes becomes a coercive, irksome task, and Danny's response to the loss of real estate is the relief of the enfranchised bond-servant: "He could not explain to his friends the coolness that had come to his relationship with Mrs. Morales since he was the owner of only one house; nor could he, in courtesy to Mrs. Morales, describe his own pleasure at that coolness." Steinbeck uses Mrs. Morales to scrutinize distinctions between false and true freedom and to set the stage for the greater conflict of freedom and liberty (TF).

MORDEEN. Joe Saul's young and very attractive wife. Mordeen loves Joe Saul very much, and, sensing his distress about his probable impotency, gives herself to Victor to provide Saul with the child he so badly wants. Mordeen is a kind, generous woman, who is even kind to Victor whom she dislikes. She is deeply hurt when Saul rejects her and moves, and grateful when he returns (BB).

MORDEN, ALEXANDER. A young miner whose argument with Captain Loft resulted in Morden's killing Captain Bentick. Condemned to be shot, Alex admits his fear. Mayor Orden tells him that he can go to his death in the knowledge that his action made the people one. As the first indication of the public anger at the occupation, Alex's killing of Bentick is a unifying action of the type Steinbeck often shows as necessary in the formation of group man (MID).

MORDEN, MOLLY. When her husband is killed by the invaders, Molly apparently takes her grief quietly. She is a beautiful woman, and Lieutenant Tonder gives her a poem expressing his love for her. Molly seems to encourage the Lieutenant, much to Annie's chagrin, but when Tonder calls at night Molly meets him with concealed shears (MID).

MORGAN, ELIZABETH. Henry's cousin and later his wife;
daughter of Sir Edward Morgan. She is not at all beautiful, but proudly pretty. She dresses well, but is
pale. In every way, she seems Sir Edward's echo.
She is sure and safe, and Henry marries her because
she represents the security he is seeking (CG).

MORGAN, GEORGE. Molly's father; he was a traveling
salesman. One day he left and never returned (PH).

MORGAN, GWENLIANA. Henry Morgan's paternal grandmother. Gwenliana is an old, wrinkled woman who
makes strange prophecies, but whose shrewdness has
declined so that everyone takes them for poor guesses.
Like Henry and Robert, she is a dreamer. When she
learns of Henry's plan to sail for the Indies, she
prophesies greatness for him (CG).

MORGAN, HENRY. The novel's central character is loosely
patterned on the infamous buccaneer. As a young man,
Morgan goes to sea, hoping to become a great adventurer. He is betrayed and sold to a West Indies planter
as an indentured servant, but he manages to use his
position to accumulate wealth and power. Later he organizes a pirate brotherhood and becomes a daring and
feared buccaneer. His greatest conquest is the city of
Panama and the beautiful woman known throughout the
Indies as La Santa Roja. Ultimately, the self-serving
Morgan finds that his conquests give him little pleasure.
He deserts his companions, gains a pardon from the
British king, marries a woman of high society, and retires to Jamaica where he serves as Lieutenant-Governor until his death. Despite his conquests, Morgan remains forever a boy. He is an unintelligent and unhappy person who never really grows to manhood (CG).

MORGAN, JIMMIE. Seventeen-year-old son of Bert and Mrs.
Munroe. He is enormously cynical, sullen and secre-
tive. He mistrusts his parents. He dreams of being
a scientist. "Shark" Wicks fears the influence that Jimmie may have over his daughter, Alice, and warns him
to stay away. When Jimmie does not, "Shark" comes
"gunning" for him (PH).

MORGAN, MISS. Takes over as teacher when Miss Martin
quits. Miss Morgan is young and pretty and successfully deals with Tularecito. She first tells him about

the gnomes that he will later spend his evenings search-
ing for. She also takes an interest in the precocious-
ness of Robbie Maltby (PH).

MORGAN, MOLLY. A nineteen-year-old, highly romantic
young woman who is interviewed for a school teaching
position by John Whiteside. She comes from a poor
family; her father, a traveling salesman, was admired
tremendously by her for his adventurous life (PH).

MORGAN, MRS. Molly's mother, a sensitive, tired woman
who tries her best amidst poverty to keep the family
together (PH).

MORGAN, MOTHER. Henry Morgan's mother. A woman of
common sense who does not want Henry to go to sea.
For years she had controlled Robert's wild thoughts
with her common sense approach to life, but she cannot stop young Henry from leaving home (CG).

MORGAN, ROBERT. Henry Morgan's father who understands
and even shares his son's dreams. Robert is an old
and tired man whose youth "went out of me sticking to
coins." Robert also knows that his son will be a great
man because he is not very intelligent and cannot realize any thought or reason but his own (CG).

MORGAN, SENATOR. Coming from a movie one night, Jim
Nolan sees a crowd and climbs on the pedestal of the
statue of Senator Morgan so that he can see what is oc-
curring. When the police raid the gathering, Jim is
given thirty days in jail for vagrancy (IDB).

MORGAN, SIR EDWARD. Robert Morgan's wealthy brother
who is Lieutenant-Governor of Jamaica when young Henry first arrives on that island. Edward is a vain man,
an actor cast in a foolish role. He wears a purple
coat with lace at the neck and wrists, and carries a
long rapier. He has a daughter, Elizabeth, whom Henry eventually marries. Edward is killed in a battle
with Indians (CG).

MORGAN, TOM. Molly's brother; he kills her puppy (PH).

MORIT, MRS. A nagging, critical woman for whom Molly
Morgan works (PH).

MORPHY, JOSEPH PATRICK ("JOEY"). A teller at Baker's
First National Bank, Joey is the unwitting instigator of
Ethan's anomalous plot to commit the perfect robbery.
As a person, he is a scrupulous and proficient account-
ant, an engaging raconteur of thinly-disguised personal
narratives, and a sympathetic receptacle for his friends'
confessions. The characterization is plausible and di-
verting and amply justifies Morphy's more important
function as an indispensable structural element.

In the first place, Joey is a foil and interlocutor
for Ethan, the yardstick that takes the measure of
Ethan's point of view; and like so many of the characters, he chips in here and there to the swelling biblical overtones of the narration. But his prime fascination is his role as self-effacing "teller," as the hidden
mainspring of inevitable sequence. Outwardly, Joey is
a natty dresser, a protean master of stylistic modula-
tion who deftly adjusts to varying occasions in order to
resurrect the past, comment on the present, and augur
good or ill for the future. His curious surname may
suggest the narcotic effect of uncut gossip--he has "the
inside dope on everything--and everybody"--but just as
likely, Steinbeck has in mind the notion of a plastic,
amorphous "sleeper" in the mix of his fictive ingredients. Joey's initial stimulus for Ethan's nascent crime
surges up from its resting place in Ethan's unconscious-
ness in much the same way that the cumulative effect
of Steinbeck's imagery gradually proceeds to the fore-
front of his readers' notice. The novel consistently re-
enacts this drama of the dream scenario that eventually
conditions and shapes reality.

The immediate particulars of Ethan's scheme to
outwit the First National do not eclipse Steinbeck's
broader inference that any plot, felonious or literary,
is a dictatorial subterfuge that imposes order only by
suppressing free options. Two formal eccentricities of
The Winter of Our Discontent testify to Steinbeck's not
necessarily successful, but certainly intriguing impa-
tience with the fetters of orthodoxy: the shift, after
the first two chapters of each of the novel's major
parts, from third to first person narration; and the
robbery episode itself, which springs from the slender-
est of psychological pretexts and casually vanishes on
the brink of consummation. Like Conrad's Lord Jim,
the novel must "jump" to escape the unbearable "trap"
of premeditated fortune.

Even the fanatically systematic Joey concedes that

"everybody's a little out of synch," and the comment
paves the way for the clash between metaphysical ra-
tiocination and scattered irrationality that furnishes the
novel's momentum with a stabilizing dialectic. Whereas Aunt Deborah clings to the notion of plot as the har-
binger of meaning, Joey seems to represent plot for
the sake of plot, tyrannical, autonomous, and completely gripping. In Steinbeck's fiction, plot often masquer-
ades as a bumbling ne'er-do-well and technical embarrassment, but beneath the surface it retains the driving
energy of Poe's obsessive exercise in literary detection
and the diabolical urgencies of Dostoevski's massive
analysis of secret guilt and spectacular self-exposure.
From the omniscient control deck of his saintly bach-
elorhood, Joey circulates the life blood of literary effect, the irrepressible insinuations of strong plot (WOD).

MOTHER MORGAN See MORGAN, MOTHER (CG)

MULE-TAIL BUCK See BUCK, MULE-TAIL (LV)

MULEY GRAVES See GRAVES, MULEY (GW)

MUNROE, BERT. Moves into the Battle farm after it has
been deserted by the Mustrovics. Bert completely reno-
vates the house. He is only fifty-five, but he is tired
and views the farm as a place where he can rest. He
believes he lives under a curse. He wants to go with
Raymond Banks to watch an execution at San Quentin
but "turns yellow" and stays home (PH).

MUNROE, MAE. The nineteen-year-old daughter of Bert
and Mrs. Munroe; she is a pretty girl with a voluptu-
ous figure. She resembles her mother. She has little
conception of ideals. She marries Bill Whiteside and
breaks Pat Humbert's heart (PH).

MUNROE, MANFRED. The serious but subnormal seven-
year-old son of Bert and Mrs. Munroe. His face is
pinched and drawn by adenoids. At times, he beats
his forehead on the floor until the blood runs into his
eyes (PH).

MUNROE, MRS. Wife of Bert Munroe, a plump woman who
wears a rimless pince-nez on a ribbon (PH).

MURIETTA, EMILIO. In Chapter XIV, Emilio Murietta is

mentioned in passing as one of Cornelia Ruiz' many admirers: " 'This Emilio is a great talker. He said to
Cornelia, 'There is nothing nicer to have than a pig.
He will eat anything. He is a nice pet. You get to
love that little pig. But then that pig grows up and his
character changes. That pig becomes mean and evil
tempered, so that you do not love him any more. Then
one day that pig bites you, and you are angry. And so
you kill that pig and eat him.' " This thumbnail sketch,
along with Murietta's name, prompts conjecture. Joaquin Murrieta was a notorious bandit in 19th century
California, alternately reviled as a bloodthirsty killer
and romanticized as a champion of the downtrodden
Hispaño minority. Correspondingly, Emiliano Zapata
was a Mexican man of the earth who led an abortive revolt against an oppressive government. Both men were
brutally executed. Steinbeck's scenario for the movie
Viva Zapata! is an unqualified success and a major contribution to the art of cinema (TF).

MURPHY, DR. H. C. A physician with whom Lee discusses
the anatomy of the brain and the pathology of cerebral
hemorrhage. He is called in to attend Adam Trask after his stroke (EE).

MURPHY, FATHER. A young and understanding priest. He
taught Joseph and Mary Rivas the theory of honest labor.
He secured a city job for his protégé as a gardener at
the Plaza in Los Angeles where Joseph and Mary secretly grew marijuana plants (ST).

MURPHY, FATHER. In Chapter IV, Father Murphy is the
topic of Pilon's slighting irreverence: "And where a
mass comes from is of no interest to God. He just
likes them, the same as you like wine. Father Murphy
used to go fishing all the time, and for months the
Holy Sacrament tasted like mackerel, but that did not
make it less holy. These things are for priests to explain." Steinbeck shares his characters' suspicion of
organized religion, especially when an Irish priest administers the Sacrament to paisanos. Father Ramon is
the priest of the people, and even Danny's reprobates
show him some measure of respect when he shows a
willingness to go fishing for souls (TF).

MURPHY, LIEUTENANT-COLONEL. Legendary figure killed
by a troop of sad Yaquis on their way home to Mexico.

Alice tells the children the story of how he rode
through the valley holding his breast open to show he
had no heart. She believes that the Yaquis had eaten
it.   There is a place down the road from the Wayne
ranch where he is supposed to ride once every three
months (TGU).

MUSTROVIC, MR. AND MRS. They take possession of the
Battle farm along with their son in 1921. They are
skeleton people with tight skin. They disappear mys-
teriously two years later (PH).

MUSTROVIC, YOUNG. Son of the old couple who take over
the Battle farm in 1921. He is tall, with coarse black
hair. He works the farm for two years before he disappears (PH).

MUTT, DOUBLETREE ("The Red Pony"). Jody's dog,
Doubletree Mutt has that canine ability to sense human
emotions (LV).

MYRTLE CAMERON BATTLE See BATTLE, MYRTLE
CAMERON (PH)

N

NELLIE ("The Red Pony"). Bred to a stallion so Jody can
have a colt, Nellie is killed in an attempt to save the
foal (LV).

NICHELSON, ALF. Alf is a jack-of-all-trades who works
hard as a carpenter, tinsmith, blacksmith, electrician,
plasterer, scissors grinder, and cobbler, but who is
a financial failure. He knows everything about everyone in Salinas and is "a vicious male gossip, insatiably
curious and vindictive without malice." He tells Joe
Valery about Faye, Faye's death, and Kate and Adam
Trask (EE).

NILSON, HARRY. Harry interviews Jim Nolan for Party
membership. When he determines the validity of Jim's
motives, he accepts his membership and assigns him to
work under Mac's direction (IDB).

NOAH JOAD See JOAD, NOAH (GW)

NOBLE, OSCAR. A sheriff's officer in Salinas. He has

pale gray eyes and stubble whiskers and wears a gray
hat and red mackinaw. After Kate's suicide, he picks
up Joe Valery to take him to the sheriff's office for a
checkup. When Joe tries to run for it, Oscar shoots
and kills him (EE).

NOLAN, JIM. A young recruit to the Communist Party who
helps organize a strike of migrant workers in California's Torgas Valley. Although inexperienced in labor
organization, he learns rapidly and gradually takes increasing leadership. Throughout the novel he complains that he is not being given anything to do, but his
final role is a dramatic one. Jim is hit in the face by
a blast from a vigilante shotgun, and Mac carries the
body back into the strikers' camp. He props up the
corpse so the light will fall on the bloody, faceless
head and utilizes Jim as a symbol to encourage renewed
unity and militancy among the strikers (IDB).

NOLAN, MAY. Jim Nolan's older sister. She disappears and
is never again heard from (IDB).

NOLAN, THEODORE. A mechanic who is the uncle of Jim
Nolan and is apparently Jim's only living relative (IDB).

NORMA. Norma is the latest in a succession of working
girls, "gawky and romantic and homely," hired by Alice
Chicoy. In the past she has been inconsequential drab
flotsam, caught in the sluggish cycles of daily survival.
Juan Chicoy offers no threat to her primness, and she
keeps herself intact against the likes of Pimples by
pulling down her shades at night. She adopts clever
stratagems to frustrate Alice's rummaging curiosity, for
Norma has vowed to "keep my secret inviolate." In her
daydreams, she consecrates herself to the cult of Hollywood, an acolyte at the shrine of the king, Clark
Gable. Her hero is epic in his dimensions, the fount
of chivalrous courtship, of manly gentility, of paternal
concern. Norma writes Clark Gable letters and ac-
cumulates a nest egg to finance her pilgrimage to the
holy city where he reigns. Meanwhile, his image
obligingly frequents her chaste fantasies, undisturbed
that Norma "would be an old-looking woman long before
she was old."
  For Norma, the day of the flood is full of event
and crisis. Ernest Horton kindly receives her tale
that she is Clark Gable's cousin and is gaining experi-

ence at Rebel Corners for her promised film career.
Horton rewards Norma's attentiveness with a charm,
a new-fangled portrait of her idol. Alice bursts upon
the two and accuses them of immorality. Still reeling
from this shock, Norma later surprises Alice as she
is reading one of Norma's gushing letters. Boldly, the
scullery maid determines to set forth on her Cinder-
ella journey.

Norma "ached for love" and starts "pouring out
her life" when Camille Oaks befriends her on the bus.
Seizing a casual remark dropped by her glamorous
benefactor, Norma envisions a radiant future, when she
and Camille, respectable and independent, will live together in one of those lavish apartments pictured in the
magazines. With practiced expertness, Camille recommends a few, brief strokes that immensely improve
Norma's appearance. Pimples moves in, first with
a soulful lament that thaws Norma's reserve, then with
an all-out, frontal assault. Norma rushes to Camille
in indignation and panic, only to be told that "everybody's a tramp."

Norma's crushing normality is not inconsistent
with her learning the constant refrain of the novel,
"We'll see how it goes," at the very end, but Steinbeck's
language discourages any further speculation about what
will become of her (WB).

NURSE, THE. She is "a strong, broad woman with heavy
    black eyebrows." Called in to nurse Adam Trask after
    his stroke, she is breezy and bossy, calling her patient
    her "darling" and "sugar pie" and addressing Cal and
    Lee as "sonny" and "Charley." She becomes so ob-
    noxious that Lee and Cal order her out of the sick-
    room (EE).

O

OAKS, CAMILLE. A stunning young woman who earns her
    living by taking off her clothes at stag parties, Camille
    Oaks is on her way to Los Angeles for a respite. She
    travels from San Ysidro to Rebel Corners on Louie's
    Greyhound bus and then heads for San Juan de la Cruz
    with Chicoy's entourage. Camille magnetizes the at-
    tention of every man she meets and so incites the envy
    of every woman, but she has mastered techniques to
    cope with any predicament. (The alias "Camille Oaks"
    is her impromptu coupling of a cigarette advertisement

with a tree she sees through a window.) During the
trip, she stymies Mildred Pritchard's jealousy as deftly
as she neutralizes Pimples' goatishness. She takes advantage of cooperative circumstances to protect herself
from Louie and Chicoy, but Mr. Pritchard and the
fawning Norma are more problematical. In roundabout
fashion, Pritchard opens negotiations to establish Camille as his mistress; correspondingly, Norma dreams
of becoming her roommate. Camille emphatically
freezes out the insinuating businessman and more
suavely but no less firmly cools Norma's misguided enthusiasm. At the end of the book and of the journey,
Camille is fatigued but unscathed. She has made a
tentative appointment to get together with Ernest Horton, the one man on the bus who harmonizes with her
poised, good-natured pragmatism.

Camille's resplendent sexuality is not just the effect of a body designed to please all mankind and a
face that is unique. Rather, she is a blend of ingredients that defies analysis: "in some subtle way this
girl smelled of sex." Ironically, and in pronounced
contrast to Mildred Pritchard, Camille is only moderately interested in physical love-making. Her real en-
thusiasms are preeminently commonplace, as homely
as they are irreproachable. She would happily settle
for placid domesticity, a tidy home with children.
Preferably, her husband would be an older man, experienced, contented with himself, who had matured beyond the passions that agitate younger men and render
them unfit. In lieu of achieving this unlikely goal, Camille enjoys the unaffected society of other women like
herself, women such as her former roommate Lor-
raine, whose comprehensive disillusionment has re-
placed sentimentality with courage, candor, and cheer-
fulness. By herself, Camille takes hikes through the
countryside and reads Saroyan.

As a teenager, Camille for the first time "knew
she was different from other girls, but she didn't quite
know why." The sign of her special destiny is a pair
of ugly forceps scars that she attempts to conceal with
her hairdo. The fertility goddess is marked from
birth. With time, she has learned to make the most
of her peculiar fate, trained herself in the role of the
outsider. She is keenly sensitized to the unconscious
scenarios of human behavior, the dramatic actions each
person shapes from the materials of life. Whereas
Mildred often complements Steinbeck's views with nu-

ances that he respects but is reluctant to endorse, Camille's level timbre is a colloquial descant that fortifies the resonating authorial voice. Within her personal silhouette she encodes mysterious rhythms of existence, but she remains an astutely critical observer
as she maneuvers the rapid pulse of events. Her motto, "we'll see how it goes," expresses, with the inci-
siveness of a mathematical constant, the core of Steinbeck's non-teleological philosophy (WB).

OLD JINGLEBALLICKS See JINGLEBALLICKS, OLD (ST)

OLD JUAN See JUAN, OLD (TGU)

OLD LADY SOMERS See SOMERS, OLD LADY (ST)

OLD MAN. One of those who pulls things out. An ancient
villager who rescues marble statues of Pan, Leda, a
baby with a shell, and a marble vase from a moat on
the two or three occasions during the year when vandals push them into the reedy water. When Pippin IV
asks him why he does it, he replies that he is one of
the people who pulls things out. On a later visit Pippin asks him what he thinks of the king. He replies
that the king does not exist because he has done nothing worthy or unworthy (SRP).

OLD MAN. An old white-bearded man who lives on a cliff
five hundred feet above the sea. He has lived there
for twenty years and claims that he is the last man in
the western world to see the sun. Thomas Wayne
fears him, but Joseph Wayne finds him interesting. He
shows Joseph his secret--how he sacrifices a small
animal every night as the sun sets. He does this because it make him glad and, through the beast, he becomes the sun. He refuses to think about his past and
hints that there are dangerous memories not to be
meddled with. Joseph thinks about the old man during
the drought and offers the blood of a calf in sacrifice.
He recognizes, however, that the old man's secret was
only for him and that it will not work for anyone else
(TGU).

OLD MAN, THE. A passenger on the sightseeing bus that
passes "The Pastures" at the end of the book. He
yearns for the peace of the valley (PH).

OLD PETE RAVANNO See RAVANNO, OLD PETE (TF)

("OLD RUIZ") RUIZ See RUIZ ("OLD RUIZ") (TF)

("OLD TOMAS") TOMAS See TOMAS ("OLD TOMAS")
   (TF)

OLIVE HAMILTON See HAMILTON, OLIVE (EE)

ONE-EYED MAN, THE. Works at a service station on
   Route 66. He is thin, with stringy muscles and dirty,
   oily skin. He wears greasy jeans and shirt. His
   heavy underlip hangs out in a sullen pout. One eye is
   missing, and the empty socket is uncovered, red and
   raw, with squirming muscles visible. He wallows in
   self-pity and hates his boss for mocking his deformity.
   He helps Tom and Al Joad repair the Wilsons' car with
   a used connecting rod bearing. Tom lectures him
   against feeling sorry for himself and urges him to cover his eye, clean himself, and start feeling some self-
   esteem (GW).

ORDEN, MAYOR. The political and intellectual leader of a
   small Scandinavian village which is quietly occupied
   during a war. Although allowed to continue his office,
   the mayor refuses to serve the interests of the invading army and encourages resistance by all his people.
   Embodying the rebellious spirit of all oppressed people,
   Mayor Orden secretly asks his allies for explosives to
   use in the war of treachery. When, at the end of the
   novel, the mayor is to be killed, he tells Col. Lanser
   that herd men may win battles but that free men will
   always win the wars (MID).

ORDEN, SARAH. As the wife of the mayor, Sarah Orden
   wears the title "Madame" as majestically as if it were
   an office, and perhaps it is. She seems totally concerned with her husband, primarily his appearance,
   and she is convinced that she created him. It is a
   comment on her character that she is only vaguely
   aware that the village has been occupied, and she
   speaks of the mayor's arrest at the end of the novel
   simply as "nonsense" (MID).

OSCAR NOBLE See NOBLE, OSCAR (EE)

OWNERS, THE. Owners of the Oklahoma farms, who evict

the tenants and replace them with tractors and with cotton farming. They are composite characters in Chapter Five. Some are kind and hate the necessity of eviction; some are angry because they hate to be cruel, and some are cold from the arrogance of ownership. They are in turn slaves to the Bank or the Company. They plan to make a quick profit and then sell the land (GW).

P

P_____, DUCHESS OF. One of the many boarders at Versailles. She is described by Marie Héristal as an insulting, insufferable slut (SRP).

PA JOAD See JOAD, PA (TOM JOAD, SR. or OLD TOM JOAD) (GW)

PABLO SANCHEZ See SANCHEZ, PABLO (TF)

PALOCHICO, MRS. Mrs. Palochico owns a peripatetic goat that is always ready to be of service and provide goods when occasion demands. Steinbeck almost sacrifices the goat in order to pave the way for Big Joe Portagee's perfidy, but Jesus Maria comes to the rescue: "When Mrs. Palochico lost the goat of her heart, the good goat of milk and cheese, it was Jesus Maria who traced the goat to Big Joe Portagee and halted the murder and made Big Joe give it back." Whenever the narrative shows signs of fatigue, Jesus Maria imitates the forthcoming goat and uncomplainingly replenishes the staple ingredients of incident and color (TF).

PANCHO. He finds the baby, Tularecito; he is Franklin Gomez's hired hand (PH).

PANCHO. A drunken companion of Benjamin Wayne. He plays the concertina while Benjy serenades Elizabeth McGreggor (TGU).

PARIS, COMTE DE. The Bourbon Pretender. Even though he is trained, available, and legitimate, the mention of his name at a closed meeting of the Royalists parties causes a near riot despite the parties' general agreement to restore the monarchy (SRP).

PASMOUCHES, CAPTAINE. Captain of the guard. Even though he is a spy for the French Minister of Police and several other parties and countries, he does not report the secret motorcycle rides of Pippin IV. He genuinely likes the king and he genuinely likes the Lucky Strikes the king gives him (SRP).

PASMOUCHES, MADAME. Wife of Captaine Pasmouches. Pippin IV delivers a note to her as a favor to her husband. He stays for a cup of coffee and an assortment of petits fours before assuming his motorcycle ride (SRP).

PASTANO, MRS. In Chapter III, Pilon bungles his role as Icarus: "Pilon's soul was not even proof against his own memories; for as he watched the birds, he remembered that Mrs. Pastano used sea gulls sometimes in her tamales, and that memory made him hungry, and hunger tumbled his soul out of the sky." Comically, Steinbeck traces the filament of naturalistic events that reels Pilon's soaring altruism back to earth and stiffens into his next rope of reasoning (TF).

PAT HUMBERT See HUMBERT, PAT (PH)

PAUL, BROTHER ("Saint Katy the Virgin"). After being attacked by Katy, Brother Paul is successful in converting her to Christianity, and he takes the repentant pig to the monastery (LV).

PAULETTE. A slave girl of mixed bloods whom Henry (representing Flower) buys at the slave dock at Port Royal. She is lithe and rounded with a sensuous, passionate beauty. Henry, who takes her to live with him, views her as a perfect "sexual contraption." After Morgan leaves James Flower's plantation, Paulette is assigned as a servant in Flower's home (CG).

PEDRO, DON. A citizen of Panama who fears the invasion of Morgan's brotherhood and who tells exaggerated stories of Morgan's prowess (CG).

PEDRONI, JAKE. One of the migrants' patrols. London asks him to see that Dan gets an enema (IDB).

PEPE TORRES See TORRES, PEPE (LV)

PERE MECHANT See MECHANT, PERE (SRP)

PETER RANDALL See RANDALL, PETER (LV)

PETEY RAVANNO See RAVANNO, PETEY (TF)

PHILLIPS, DR. Tells Helen Van Deventer that her daughter,
    Hilda, is mentally ill and in need of psychiatric help.
    He urges Helen to commit her (PH).

PHILLIPS, DR. ("The Snake"). One of the earliest of Stein-
    beck's fictional portraits of Ed Ricketts, Dr. Phillips
    operates a commercial laboratory on Cannery Row. A
    woman interrupts his work asking to buy a male rattle-
    snake. He sells her the snake as well as a white rat
    to feed the rattler. Phillips becomes annoyed with the
    woman's desire to see the snake kill and consume its
    victim, but he becomes ill when the woman begins to
    imitate the snake's movements (LV).

PHYLLIS MAE See MAE, PHYLLIS (CR)

PILON. Pilon so dominates Tortilla Flat that any crisp syn-
    opsis of his contributions to the plot would fail to do
    him justice and would certainly curtail his true scope.
    He is present from start to finish, stage manages many
    of the major episodes, and presides as resident genius
    of Danny's roundtable. To emphasize his deceitful ex-
    ploitation of the Pirate in Chapter VIII, when Saint An-
    drew's Eve occasions a precarious glimmer of altruism,
    would merely obscure a ubiquitous energy that is the
    very pulse of the novel's unsettling complexity. At the
    start, the narrator explains that, "Danny and his friend
    Pilon (Pilon, by the way, is something thrown in when
    a trade is conducted--a boot) had two gallons of wine
    when they heard about the war." To be sure, the ac-
    tivity of bartering is so pervasive as to clamor for the
    status of key metaphor, and Pilon the casuist always
    mounts the platform when a bargain is in the offing.
    But to imply with a parenthetical afterthought that Pilon
    is a mere gratuity, a stirrup-cup tossed off to ease
    possible friction and seal a trade, is extremely mis-
    leading. In actuality, Pilon is a dangerous con artist
    who spins specious logic out of thin air and hoodwinks
    his companions with fast-talking plausibility. At the
    rhetorical level of the book, his exasperating points of
    order plot the trajectory of seemingly random incident.
    His zany metaphysics, deliberately straying from com-
    mon sense if not indeed abandoning reality altogether,

nevertheless schematize an otherwise hopelessly tangled
skein of events. If Pilon is a pernicious nuisance, he
is also the closest approximation the novel has to offer
of the Machiavellian artificer, and no amount of burlesque overburden can disguise his formidable role as
self-anointed critic and foremost on-the-scenes instigator of Steinbeck's own crafty maneuvers. Like Pilon,
Steinbeck casts an informed eye for the ludicrous on
the unconscious rhythms of behavior.

Pilon is hard to pin down because he represents
a conflict of interest. His technical virtuosity, which
expertly quarantines contending clusters of irrationality
and then negotiates between them, is itself a principal
axis of Steinbeck's concern. Leslie Fiedler has remarked that "a vexing problem ... in the tradition of
the American novel" is a persistent "confusion of modes
and levels of credibility"; and Arthur L. Simpson has
similarly observed, in the specific instance of Tortilla
Flat, that "sympathy and satire make an uneasy mix."
The novel emphatically drives home the lesson that Pilon is the spokesman for satirical perceptions. He is
a "realist," but only in the idiomatic sense that he pro-
fesses skepticism towards human nature and orchestrates every opportunity to deflate rosy optimism and
expose frailty. He is not a realist in the sympathetic
sense that Steinbeck is. He has no reverence for can-
did impartiality, no patience with humanity as he finds
it. As a satirist, Pilon is a parasite who feeds on
human folly. His specialty is grandiose monuments of
rationalistic caprice. Their lack of integrity, their excess of artifice, topple these matchstick structures
time and again. But Pilon emerges unscathed, unen-
cumbered, and unchanged. The brunt of his collapsing
satire buries alive the gullible victims it maimed in the
first place.

In Chapter X, it is Pilon who prescribes diabolical punishment for the officer who seduced the Caporal's bride: " 'We should have been there,' Pilon cried.
'We would have made that capitan wish he had never
lived. My grandfather suffered at the hands of a priest,
and he tied that priest naked to a post in a corral and
turned a little calf in with him. Oh, there are ways.' "
Pilon and Danny stand at opposite horizons of the narrative, and this speech summarizes Pilon's at its
worst: mob psychology, the cruel grip of past prece-
dent, endemic blasphemy, arbitrary violence, and superfluous vengeance.

At times, <u>Tortilla Flat</u> threatens to become a static point around which concentric circles of experience accumulate, each new turn confirming Pilon's grim appraisal that mankind worships death. Pilon adumbrates the latent malice of the communal ethos run riot and bent on self-murder, the obscene sacrifice of life itself. His intellect is the hired servant of outrageousness. Danny, the soul of imagination, the libertarian, Promethean culture hero, attempts to break the cycle, but his final gesture of revolt is enigmatical, a destructive fall from grace as much as a soaring vault to immortality.

On the surface, Pilon is a pungent, entertaining spoof of the gift of the gab, the man who is too clever by half; but he also characterizes Steinbeck's alarmed speculations about the morality of fictive networks and the equivocal value of literary conservatism. More than once, Steinbeck seems to wince at the irrevocable tyranny of the plots he sets in motion and the deadly finality of the sentences he labors to perfect (<u>TF</u>).

PINEDALE. Breed's neighbor upstream, Pinedale exhibits the mutual concern of country folk in times of emergency (<u>WB</u>).

PIPPIN ARNULF HERISTAL <u>See</u> HERISTAL, PIPPIN ARNULF (<u>SRP</u>)

PIRATE, THE. <u>Tortilla Flat</u> spans three principal movements. The first (Introduction through Chapter VI) pieces together the staple ingredients of the book, and the last (Chapters XV through XVII) records the cataclysmic shattering of a critical mass grown too set in its ways to accommodate change. Danny's society is blown apart by the impact of the very same freedom it meant to preserve but eventually can neither suppress nor contain. The orderly, episodic center of the narrative (Chapter VII through XIV) enjoys the poised, inertial stability of an even keel, a temporarily sustained, synthetically produced equilibrium between the raw matter of the genesis and the mystical "translation" of the millennial conclusion.

The Pirate, introduced at the start of Chapter VII, combines the naked humility of a marginal existence and the ascetic vision of an Old Testament hermit. He thus personifies the union of contending opposites that permits the novel to build to an authentic climax before

the doomsday denouement.   The Pirate is an ingenuous
but mysterious soul, feeble-minded but elect, who ekes
out a scavenger's living by day and by night cowers
in an abandoned hovel, his only companions a pack of
five ferocious and devoted mongrels.   The relentless
logic of Pilon, who "knew everybody and everything
about everybody," leads him to the Pirate's cave to
sniff out the secret hoard that the Pirate, day by day,
quarter by quarter, must have amassed.   The Pirate's
initial suspicion and defiance further whet Pilon's curiosity and spur him to new exhibitions of sneaky insinua-
tion.   He overwhelms the tender-hearted ruffian with
the astonishing news that, "Thou art a worry to thy
friends."   Understandably, the hitherto friendless Pirate
welcomes Pilon's invitation to join Danny's entourage.

The Pirate makes himself at home and gratefully
rewards his benefactors with the choicest morsels he
collects each day from Monterey's back alleys.   Each
evening, the paisanos lubricate the Pirate with gothic
tales of misers whose fanatical self-reliance admitted
ruinous rays of oversight.   Frustrated in their efforts
to shadow the Pirate's nocturnal visits to his forest
hiding place, the paisanos reach the brink of despair
when, at the end of Chapter VII, the Pirate produces
his bulging sack of two-bitses for safe keeping and reveals his ambition of buying a candle for Saint Francis.
Once upon a time, Saint Francis answered his prayers
for a dying pet.   When the paisanos learn that the Pirate's dog has since been run over by a truck, they
concede defeat.   Henceforth, the Pirate's treasure will
be the inviolable talisman of their social compact.

In Chapter XII, Big Joe commits the unforgivable
sin and rifles the Pirate's cache, but the aftermath of
his treason is the discovery that there is already enough
money on hand to buy the long-awaited candle.   The Pirate, in borrowed finery and (eventually) joined by his
curs, attends church in rapture and triumph to hear
Father Ramon accept his gift.   Later, he sees a vision
of Saint Francis as he repeats the Father's sermon to
his canine retainers.

Chapter XII signals the beginning of the end for
the paisanos' idyllic life.   The Pirate subsides into the
background.   The weight of Big Joe's treachery throws
the story out of kilter.   The timebomb of Danny's restlessness continues its countdown to disaster.   The legend of Tortilla Flat has achieved a memorable apotheo-
sis, but it will not be reaffirmed.

In Steinbeck's fiction, simple, trusting folk live
a charmed life, "children, insane people, fools, and
mystics" who open the eyes of blind science that "dent-
ed existence to anything it could not measure or explain." The Pirate and his magic circle of hounds
momentarily stay the headlong course of Danny and his
followers and hold Big Joe's savagery at bay. From
this nucleus emanates the spectral luster that charac-
teristically illuminates Steinbeck's serene passages, an
intimate ambience of author and audience at peace with
each other (TF).

POITIN, ACADEMICIAN. Esteemed member of the Royal
Academy of Music. He presides over the pomp and
circumstances of the convention to deliberate the Code
Pippin. He accomplishes a brilliant piece of improvisa-
tion by signaling the trumpeters to play the traditional
hunting call while a page dashes off to find Pippin IV's
forgotten pince-nez (SRP).

POM-POM, JOHNNY. Johnny Pom-Pom is a denizen of Tortilla Flat, a hanger-on to Danny's coterie who circulates gossip as a kind of liaison with the community at
large. It is Johnny Pom-Pom who once stumbled on a
Geodetic Survey marker and thus educated Pilon about
the severe penalties of such serendipity. It is Johnny
Pom-Pom who carries the message of Torrelli's rage
when Sweets' vacuum cleaner proves engine-less. And
it is Johnny Pom-Pom who brings the news of Danny's
rambunctious jail break with Tito Ralph in Chapter XV
and who makes a willing accomplice when the paisanos
incinerate the deed Torrelli has obtained to their house
(TF).

PORTAGEE, BIG JOE. The introduction to Tortilla Flat
mentions as an afterthought that Big Joe Portagee spent
his entire Army hitch in jail. Big Joe resurfaces in
Chapter VIII, by which time the episodic, second leg of
the novel is well under way. He celebrates his freedom by launching a monumental binge and wallowing in
whatever filth Monterey has to offer: "It was not a
safe thing to lead Joe into temptation; he had no resistance to it at all." These antics earn him a month's
sojourn in the Monterey lockup, a comfortable stay that
enables Big Joe to renew friendships and retrim the
balance of form and content in his personal ecology:
"a man's days are rightly devoted half to sleeping and

half to waking, so a man's years are rightly spent half
in jail and half out."

Free again after thirty days, he looks up his
friend Pilon and accompanies him on a Saint Andrew's
Eve treasure hunt. After Pilon locates a promising
place to dig, the two paisanos stand guard throughout
the night. With notable lack of success, Pilon tries to
kindle in Big Joe the same pure flame of altruism that
has beaconed his own search to a fortunate conclusion.
Next day, Big Joe casually enlists in Danny's company
and promptly violates the order's first commandment
by filching Danny's blanket and trading it for a gallon
of Torrelli's wine. As penance, Big Joe provided the
labor when he and Pilon return to their site and begin
to excavate. Much to their chagrin, the prize turns
out to be a Geodetic Survey marker, quite out of commercial bounds, and they repair to the beach to salve
their disappointment with Joe's wine. When Joe follows his custom and falls asleep, Pilon steals his
pants and prevails on Senora Torrelli to give him wine
in exchange. The chapter ends when Pilon, having re-
possessed pants and blanket both, rejoins Big Joe on
the beach.

Big Joe next plays a prominent role in Chapter
XI, when he makes muddy love with Tia Ignacia. This
obscene episode amply sets the stage for Big Joe's ultimate perfidy in Chapter XI, when he makes off with the
Pirate's treasure and is thrashed, expertly, within an
inch of his life for his trouble. From evil comes
good: the paisanos retrieve the Pirate's sacred booty
and discover there is more than enough to buy a candle
for Saint Francis. Big Joe is pardoned from further
punishment, but for the remainder of the tale he is little more than tolerated as a weak link that bears constant watching. Like the paisanos, Steinbeck loses enthusiasm for Big Joe and sweeps him into a corner.

Big Joe is indispensable to the progress of the
novel, but he has no more dramatic depth than moral.
Curiously, he seems more the pre-lapsarian innocent,
the unregenerate natural man, than the sinister in-
triguer, contemptible rather than truly loathsome. He
is a tool, a necessary but unprepossessing foil to the
more complicated designs of the other paisanos, especially of Pilon and Danny. He is the waste product of
the lively episodes that find use for him. Sensibly contemplated, Big Joe's deliberately meager portrait de-
flects the argument that Steinbeck is much concerned

with primitivism. In fact, the portrait suggests that
primitive lumps of material make surprisingly little
contribution to Steinbeck's wide-ranging literary scheme
and thus further suggests that Steinbeck's reputed primitivism is at most an artistic effect, scarcely a cause
for critical condescension (TF).

PORTUGUES, BARTOLOMEO. A member of the pirate broth-
    erhood who once took a great prize but was captured
    near Campeche before he could get away with it. He
    was sentenced to hang, but stabbed his guard and es-
    caped. Eight days later, he returned to Campeche and
    stole his ship back (CG).

POT MENDER, A ("The Chrysanthemums"). An unnamed,
    traveling jack-of-all-trades who feigns an interest in
    Elisa Allen's chrysanthemums to get work. Given a
    pot of the flowers for "a lady down the road a piece,"
    he later discards the chrysanthemums in the middle of
    the road and drives on with the container (LV).

POTOIR, RAOUL DE. A musketeer of the Rear Guard.
    When a crazed critic of the monarchy attempts to shoot
    Pippin IV during the royal procession but kills a royal
    horse instead, he cuts the horse free and gallantly takes
    its place in harness. For this act, he demands and re-
    ceives a pension for life (SRP).

PRACKLE, LIEUTENANT. Naively romantic, Prackle seems
    more the aspiring Casanova than the soldier. Although
    preoccupied with women and impressed with his own
    talent, Prackle is the stuff out of which fanatics are
    made. He is such a supporter of the Leader that he
    has even copied his mannerisms (MID).

PRESIDENT SONNET See SONNET, PRESIDENT (SRP)

PRIEST, THE. He urges Kino to thank God for having found
    the pearl (P).

PRITCHARD, BERNICE. With her husband and college-age
    daughter, Mrs. Pritchard has embarked on a long-post-
    poned journey to Mexico, a "pleasure" trip that each of
    the Pritchards secretly resents. When the bus bogs
    down, the emotionally stranded husband and wife break
    into unprecedented public quarrel. Fearing the onset
    of a migraine headache, Mrs. Pritchard seeks shelter

and repose in a nearby cave. Mr. Pritchard, scalded
by Camille Oaks' disclosures, rushes upon his wife and
brutally attacks her, virtually rapes her. Alone again,
Mrs. Pritchard scratches her face to simulate bloody
abuse and then serenely contemplates the orchid house
she will exact from her husband as penitential tribute.

On the surface, Bernice Pritchard is the very personification of old-fashioned sweetness. Dainty, petted,
and perfumed, she cultivates her reputation as the ideal
wife, mother and companion. She is passionately attracted to well-groomed things, the miniature, the ex-
quisite, and dreams of owning a hothouse for precious
flowers. To her friends, Bernice appears frail, vic-
timized by an "acid condition" and recurrent illness,
but plucky and long-suffering in adversity.

In fact, Mrs. Pritchard is "ruthless" and full of
"delicate malice." She orchestrates her cloying submis-
siveness with the acute policy of a domestic queen. If
not feigned, her headaches are probably psychosomatic:
"they brought the family to heel." Her mind is immune
to ideas and her body is frigid, but the mousy exterior
conceals the rapaciousness of a shrike. She knows her
targets and her homing instinct is infallible. Mrs.
Pritchard will quash her husband's rebellion, if not her
daughter's, and perpetuate the tyranny of her artificial
charm.

Steinbeck's portrayal of a viperous, hysterical
housewife is not a chauvinistic condemnation of mother-
hood so much as a sweeping indictment of a social system that renders certain women superfluous. Economi-
cally, Mrs. Pritchard is an ornament, not a factor but
a grasping consumer; intellectually, she is a listless
cipher, a banality; and physically, she is an exhuasted
wasteland, a toxic mannequin (WB).

PRITCHARD, ELLIOTT. With his wife and daughter, Mr.
Pritchard is headed for a holiday in Mexico. The sequence of mishaps that befall Chicoy's caravan strips
Pritchard of an indispensable prop, the encouragement
and reinforcement of other prosperous businessmen who
think and behave precisely like himself. Thrown on his
own resources, Pritchard soon exhausts his shallow
fund of social capital. Inadvertently, he antagonizes
Ernest Horton and then must ingratiate himself with this
former footsoldier whom he would normally dismiss at
a glance. Next, he is dragged into a family squabble,
an unseemly spectacle that adds to his discomposure.

Later, as his wife naps and his daughter saunters off
in search of Chicoy, Pritchard astonishes himself by
cautiously propositioning Camille Oaks, whom he fails
to recognize as the star attraction at a stag party he
once attended. She promptly slices through his fastidi-
ous overtures. Rejecting his offer of a "position,"
Camille identifies herself and forces Pritchard to con-
front the mediocrity that underlies his brittle, super-
cilious mask. Rubbed raw by these failures, his pride
routed, Pritchard savagely attacks his wife, but the
aftermath of swashbuckling violence is not reinvigorated
self-esteem or even manly contrition. Pritchard merely suffers the furtive, unsatisfactory guilt of a naughty
boy who craves chastisement by a pure "lady."

With surgical dispatch, Steinbeck takes the measure of prevailing Babbittry. Pritchard and his cronies
blackball from their smug fraternity any element in conflict with their carefully preened image. They are the
American norm. Celebrating the rituals and raiment
of material pieties, they denounce as subversive any
challenge to their doctrine of conformity, any heresy of
imaginative, individualistic style. Success means affluence, power, and the unctuous aura of moral com-
placency and jingoism that mantles commercial domi-
nance.

Pritchard's self-deception is total. It is through
Chicoy that Steinbeck conserves the essential American, isolate, stoic, and commanding, whereas the im-
perious financier is less a self-made captain of enterprise than a plastic instrument. Put to the test of
self-reliance, his prefabricated shell of orthodoxies col-
lapses like a handful of thin clay (WB).

PRITCHARD, MILDRED. In presenting his version of the
pre-1960s American college girl, Steinbeck is often
ironical but never unsympathetic. Mildred is well
chested, athletic, nubile, fully aware of her "strong
sexual potential," but not given to brooding about it.
Her brief, ecstatic liaison with Chicoy at the novel's
denouement is the consummation of a groundswell that
is one of the narrative's principal rhythms. The spectacle of her parents' quarrel has been a dismaying
revelation, but the frictional collision with "a man of
complete manness" is less an illumination of consciousness than a wholesome confirmation of an already
blooming selfhood.

With youthful naiveté, Mildred assumes that her

satisfactory love affairs are synonymous with the entire wavelength of human experience. Nevertheless, she proves herself a sentient, compassionate person with strong intuitive perceptions. Her observations are always robust and often polished: she is tolerant of her father, skeptical of her mother, humorously outspoken with Van Brunt, and fascinated by the behavior of other women. Her views offer a valuable counterpoint to Steinbeck's own; they enrich and balance the novel's psychological mix.

Mildred's intellectual pretentions have the mark of the dilettante enthusiast. "She was studying Spanish in college, a language she was incapable of understanding, just as her instructors were." She devotes herself to fashionable liberal causes and condescends to the society that has molded her more than her self-centered vitality cares to admit. The pattern of a strident, militantly aggressive and emancipated girl who eventually succumbs to the attractions of a Juan Chicoy is clearly controversial. Like D. H. Lawrence, Steinbeck risks over-emphasis of the body at the expense of the mind. Yet his portrait is full of admiration for an unmistakable life force chafing within a chrysalis of superficial sophistication. When Mildred removes her glasses to view the world at first hand, the wry tone of the book gives way to unstinting affirmation. Union with the self-enfranchised bus-driver is the premier compliment the novel can bestow. The latest episode in Mildred's education sponsors newly fortified integrity and leaves no regrets (WB).

PROPRIETOR, THE. Runs a roadside camp on Route 66. He is lanky and sullen, demanding $0.50 per group of campers. When Tom refuses to pay because his family has already done so, the proprietor warns that deputies might arrest him as a vagrant for sleeping out. He labels the migrants shiftless and calls Tom a troublemaker (GW).

PROSPEROUS MAN, THE. A passenger on the sightseeing bus that passes "The Pastures" at the end of the book. He sees the valley as an investment opportunity (PH).

Q

QUINN, HORACE. When Adam Trask is shot, Horace Quinn is the new deputy sheriff for the King City district. He

wants to give up ranching and become sheriff. Horace
investigates the shooting and first thinks that Adam
murdered his wife, but the sheriff informs him that
Mrs. Trask has become the new girl at Faye's brothel.
In 1903, Quinn becomes sheriff at Salinas and remains
in that office until 1919. He has broad shoulders, a
broad and pink face, and a mustache "like the horns of
a longhorn steer" that turns white as he becomes portly
with age. He wears a Stetson hat and a Norfolk jacket.
As he puts on weight, he transfers his revolver from a
belt to a shoulder holster. After Kate's death, Quinn
burns the compromising pictures she has taken to blackmail prominent citizens of Salinas. When he has the
potential victims notified that the pictures have been destroyed, they force him out of office (EE).

                          R

RABBIT HOLMAN See HOLMAN, RABBIT (EE)

RAGGED MAN, THE. He spends the night with the Joads
     in a roadside camp on Route 66. His face is black
     with dust and lined with sweat, and he wears a ripped
     coat and dungarees with the knees missing. He has
     been to California and is going back home to starve.
     He explains to the Joads the method by which California
     farmers use handbills to lure surplus migrant labor to
     the fields in order to depress farm wages. His wife
     and two children have died of starvation (GW).

RALPH, TITO. Tito Ralph is the custodian of the Monterey
     jail. "He had a vast respect for the law." That is,
     during the day he fraternizes with the prisoners and at
     night he is faithful to his own, unwritten code that free-
     ly encourages keepers and inmates to frequent local
     saloons in each other's company. Regular guests like
     Danny would not think of breaking the rules, and it is
     the comic prelude to crisis when the game comes to an
     end. During Danny's final fling, he spends one night in
     jail. He gets Tito Ralph drunk, as usual, and all the
     captives escape: "They caught Tito Ralph this morning
     and told him he could not be jailer any more. He was
     so sad that he broke a window, and now he is in jail
     again." This Runyonesque ending participates in the
     "Catch-22" essence of the entire novel, the essence of
     a losing game played by shifting rules. Tito Ralph is
     free at the end (" 'I escaped again,' Tito Ralph said

wanly.   'I still had the keys!'') and watches over
Danny's death bed (TF).

RAMA WAYNE   See   WAYNE, RAMA (TGU)

RAMIREZ, DOLORES ENGRACIA ("SWEETS").   After Danny
    inherits property, it is only a matter of time before he
    becomes ensnared in the seductive web that Sweets Ra-
    mirez spins for him: "She was not pretty, this lean-
    faced paisana, but there was in her figure a certain
    voluptuousness of movement; there was in her voice a
    throatiness some men found indicative." Chapter IX
    chronicles the romance from its initial whirlwinds of
    humid passion, through the azure firmament of domes-
    tic tranquility, into the occluded gloom of tapering af-
    fections and disillusionment.
        In the opening scene, the unpredictable Sweets is
    full of disdain, but Danny penetrates this proud reserve
    and pledges his constancy with a magnificent, gleaming
    vacuum cleaner (two dollars, haggled down from four-
    teen). He moves in with Sweets, enjoys a fortnight of
    grace while she takes on airs and excites envy by punc-
    tuating her conversation with timely references to her
    marvelous machine. Danny's friends become increas-
    ingly alarmed by their leader's protracted absence.
    Sweets poses a mortal threat.   Like the heroic com-
    itatus of old, bent on rescuing a disarmed companion,
    they marshall all their magic to bring Danny to his
    senses: "Their campaign had called into play and taxed
    to the limit the pitiless logic of Pilon, the artistic in-
    genuousness of Pablo, and the gentleness and humanity
    of Jesus Maria Corcoran. Big Joe had contributed
    nothing." Meanwhile, the sub-plot of Susie Francisco
    and Charlie Guzman mutters warnings about the wiles
    of women.
        Pilon the wizard hatches a scheme of deliverance.
    First the friends assail Danny with remorseless accusa-
    tions: he has become the butt of ridicule. Yet more
    ominously, Sweets "has told some people that you have
    promised to put wires into her house so the sweeping-
    machine will work." Danny confesses the error of his
    ways and "sighed with relief that his problem was as-
    sumed by his good friends." Pilon scouts Sweets' daily
    movements, breaks into her house when she is gone to
    market, and absconds with the offending appliance, now
    cleverly disguised as a rose bush. Torrelli precipi-
    tates the uproarious denouement when, after purchasing

the vacuum cleaner for two gallons of wine, he discovers that it lacks a motor.

The episode is a contemporary fabliau. It achieves real texture because Steinbeck weaves together many threads of motif and mode. At mid-field, the dual encumbrances of material and sexual possession clash boisterously with the prior claims of Danny's clan and are routed (or at least forfended until the end of the novel). Steinbeck folds in his dramatic ingredients with great good taste, maintains amusing balance between meaty subject and saucy decor, proves every inch the connoisseur of a comic tour de force (TF).

RAMON, FATHER. The paisano priest earns Steinbeck's sympathetic respect when he embraces the spirit of the Pirate's offering to Saint Francis. " 'Do not be ashamed,' Father Ramon said. 'It is no sin to be loved by your dogs, and no sin to love them. See how Saint Francis loved the beasts.' Then he told more stories of that good saint." Later, the Pirate repeats Father Ramon's remarks to his own adoring (canine) congregation. Steinbeck was fond of dogs, and his normal anticlericalism might well be expected to crumble before a story-telling priest who detected the sources of ceremony and object lesson in the awkward gesture of a simple soul (TF).

RANDALL, EMMA ("The Harness"). Peter Randall's sickly but shrewd wife. Following Peter's San Francisco trips, Emma would become ill. Peter would feel guilt and remorse, and Emma would gain control for another fifty-one weeks. After her death, Emma's influence was as strong as it had been during her lifetime (LV).

RANDALL, PETER ("The Harness"). For over twenty years Peter Randall wore a web harness to hold back his shoulders and an elastic belt to keep in his stomach. His wife got him to wear these supports and she made him into a highly respected and conservative Monterey County farmer, save one week each year when he went to San Francisco, got drunk, and "... went to a fancy house every night." When his wife Emma died, Peter took off the harness and planted sweet peas, but at the customary time he was back in San Francisco. For Peter, Emma was still alive, worrying him all year about his sweet peas (LV).

RANDOLPH, WILLIAM.   Engineer, fireman, and president
of the Hediondo Cannery. He found a stripped engine
which he hauled to Monterey and improvised into the
company's first boiler. This boiler, eventually abandoned and stripped again, became the home of Mr. and
Mrs. Malloy (see Cannery Row). Suzy chooses it as
her home after she leaves the Bear Flag (ST).

RAOUL DE POTOIR See POTOIR, RAOUL DE (SRP)

RASMUSSEN, ALBERT.   In Chapter XIV, Rasmussen is men-
tioned as one of Cornelia Ruiz' swarm of suitors.
"What trouble that Cornelia has," Danny remarks.
"Every day some trouble" (TF).

RATZ, MRS. ("Johnny Bear").   Operator of a rooming house
in Loma, California, who rents the narrator of "Johnny
Bear" what he calls "... a furnished room, the most
dismal I have ever seen" (LV).

RATZ, TIMOTHY ("Johnny Bear").   While his wife keeps a
rooming house, Timothy keeps a vigil in the Buffalo
Bar playing solitaire, drinking only when he wins,
therefore constantly cheating (LV).

RAVANNO, OLD PETE.   Steinbeck more than once dramatizes the pathological cycle of the father who imitates
the son. After Petey Ravanno's tempestuous courtship
of Gracie Montez culminated in staid matrimony,
Petey's father, Old Pete, felt hopeless and lonely.
Soon he became enraptured by Gracie's younger sister,
'Tonia: "Tonia was fifteen, and she was prettier, even,
than Gracie. Half the soldiers from the Presidio followed her around like little dogs." Old Pete's en-
treaties went to no avail. In desperation, he decided
to try his son's trick: feign suicide to win 'Tonia's
heart. "The viejo could not stand it any more. But
he was not a man to invent anything. He was not like
Pilon." After finishing his preparations in a strategi-
cally convenient tool shed, Old Pete hanged to death
when the door closed shut on him.
    Pilon is scandalized by this macabre tale, not so
much because "old men should not run after babies"
as because the tale itself seems irrational: "It is not
a good story. There are too many meanings and too
many lessons in it. Some of those lessons are opposite. There is not a story to take into your head.

It proves nothing." The strong suspicion is that Pilon
has become the inadvertent spokesman for Steinbeck's
last word on Tortilla Flat. Only the note of disapproval is out of tune. The true-to-life origins of the anecdote merely compound the unconscious irony of Pilon's
myopic criticism. Implicitly, Steinbeck admonishes the
inflexible disciples of well-made realism. Realism
tidily collects the random data of human topography.
Another kind of fiction explores subterranean strata and
taps the secret currents that pressure "accidental" out-
bursts of seeming insanity. Such natural fiction may be
superior to Pilon's studied inventions (TF).

RAVANNO, PETEY. With the exception of Petey, the moth-
erless Ravanno children all came to bad ends. As a
youth, Petey himself was tutored in all manner of reckless behavior by his father, Old Pete. When he first
cast eyes on "La Belle Dame Sans Mercy" of Tortilla
Flat, Gracie Montez, Petey was already stripped of
self-restraint and was the ready victim of ungoverned
folly. Jesus Maria perceives that Petey "was different"
from the others drawn to Gracie's ineluctable flame:
" 'Petey wanted what Gracie had so much that he grew
thin, and his eyes were as wide and pained as the eyes
of one who smokes marihuana.' " Old Pete pleaded
with Gracie, and Petey cut squids for Chin Kee to buy
Gracie presents, but these unheard of proofs of devotion merely fueled Gracie's coquetry. Finally, Petey
"was crazy" and tried to hang himself. Old Pete res-
cued him in the nick of time and Gracie, no end pleased
by the spectacular commotion she had stirred up, married Petey and immediately reformed. The couple took
up housekeeping in respectable bliss and could only
stare with amazement and disapproval at the calamity
that soon befell Old Pete.
     The episode is the fulcrum on which the novel
pivots from sunshine to gloom, but Petey's story is important in its own right as a comment on the causes
and effects of melodramatic fits of passion. With clinical impartiality, Steinbeck maintains an objective middle course between Petey's opening extravagance and
closing reserve. The artist is an observer who syn-
thesizes cool moderation from the fire and ice of human nature (TF).

RAWLEY, JIM. Manager of the Weedpatch government camp.
He is a lean and little man with frayed white clothes,

"a thin, brown, lined face and merry eyes." His voice is warm and his manner kind and understanding. Ma Joad is at first suspicious of him, but he quickly wins her over by his unauthoritarian friendliness. The Jesus lovers call him the devil, because he is tolerant of human weaknesses. He says that sin is being cold and hungry, not in harmless pleasures (GW).

RAYMOND BANKS See BANKS, RAYMOND (PH)

RED. "That driver for the Red Arrow Line"--muscular, flirtatious candidate for one of Alice Chicoy's casual, typically vicarious love affairs. During Alice's solitary, drunken reverie, her attention rivets on Red's image, then continues, along the "red arrow line" of her erotic fantasy, to introduce scenes of sexual initiation with her earliest paramour, Bud (WB).

RED WILLIAMS See WILLIAMS, RED (CR)

RICHARD FROST See FROST, RICHARD (CR)

RICHARD WALDER See WALDER, RICHARD (WOD)

RICHARD WHITESIDE See WHITESIDE, RICHARD (PH)

RILEY ("The Red Pony"). In "The Leader of the People" Jody recalls a big boar, Riley, that ate a hole into a haystack and smothered himself (LV).

RILEY, BERTHA. Two years after May Nolan's disappearance, Bertha also dropped out of sight (IDB).

RITTAL, SHERIFF ("Johnny Bear"). Although Sheriff Rittal has been dead for seven years, his re-election poster still hangs in the Buffalo Bar (LV).

RIVAS, CACAHUETE. Nephew of Joseph and Mary Rivas and trumpet player for the Espaldas Mojadas. His trumpet-playing unnerves his uncle who makes him practice down on the beach where the waves and sea lions might drown him out. He causes problems, however, by aiming his trumpet into the sewer pipes for resonance. He notifies the guests of the beginning of the masquerade by playing "Whistle While You Work" (ST).

RIVAS, JOSEPH and MARY. New owners of what was for-

merly Lee Chong's grocery (see <u>Cannery Row</u>). Joseph
is the delicate opposite of Doc. His smartness is the
kind that cuts its own throat. Since his childhood, he
has done everything illegally or immorally. Among his
past experiences are those of the gang leader, pool
hustler, and burglar, but nearer to his ideals is the
con artist. After years of larceny and fraud, he buys
the grocery as a front for his wetback operation. This
venture, however, is complicated by a group of wet-
backs who form a musical group called Espaldas Mojadas. He is an admirer of Doc and Fauna Flood but
thinks Suzy is a bad risk. Mack and the boys believe
that he is the unknowing owner of the Palace Flophouse
and create the raffle scheme to shift its possessions to
Doc. After Suzy moves from the Bear Flag to the
boiler, Joseph and Mary take a new interest in her.
His desires are thwarted, however, by Doc, who almost
kills him for lurking about the boiler. Despite their
combat they remain friends (<u>ST</u>).

RIVERS, CONNIE. Husband of Rose of Sharon. He is nineteen years old, sharp-faced and lean. He has pale
blue eyes that are alternately dangerous, kindly, and
frightened. Connie does not altogether know what to
make of the change brought about in his wife by her
pregnancy. He does not boast, works hard, and is quiet in a group. At first, it is predicted that he will
make a good husband, but the hardships he encounters
en route and in California are too much for him. He
wishes he had stayed behind and driven a tractor, and
he talks about studying to be a radio repairman, but
he lacks the fortitude and endurance to see things
through and so deserts his pregnant wife and walks away
at the Hooverville camp near Bakersfield. His irre-
sponsibility is a foil to the Joad family loyalty and to
Tom's increasing sense of responsibility not only to the
Joads but to all oppressed farm workers (<u>GW</u>).

ROARK ("Saint Katy the Virgin"). Katy's original owner,
Roark was described as a very bad man who ridiculed
the church until he saw Katy's conversion. From that
moment on his life was changed (<u>LV</u>).

ROBERT LOUIS MALTBY <u>See</u> MATLBY, ROBERT LOUIS
(<u>PH</u>)

ROBERT MORGAN <u>See</u> MORGAN, ROBERT (<u>CG</u>)

RODRIGUEZ. A captain in the army of Panama whose
    troops are easily defeated by Henry Morgan's band of
    pirates (CG).

RODRIGUEZ, MRS. ("Flight"). A Monterey friend of Mama
    Torres with whom Pepé is to spend the night. Drink-
    ing in the Rodriguez kitchen, followed by a quarrel, re-
    sulted in Pepé's killing a man (LV).

ROLETTI, MR. Ninety-three years old, he develops senile
    satyriasis and has to be forcibly restrained from chasing
    high-school girls (ST).

ROLF, MR. Rector of St. Paul's Episcopal Church in Sa-
    linas. Unmarried, young and curly-haired, with simple
    tastes, he has closed up most of the rectory. Mr.
    Rolf is a high church clergyman who believes in celi-
    bacy and wishes to bring confession into the Episcopal
    Church as a sacrament. He is very fond of Aron Trask
    and has long conversations with him about the ministry,
    which Aron plans to enter (EE).

ROMAS. A middle-aged driver who leads the teams filled
    with the materials for the construction of Joseph Wayne's
    ranch. His son, Willie, is mentally disturbed. He
    warns Joseph not to build his house under a tree. He
    also tells him of the ten-year drought, the second in the
    memory of the elders, that dried the wells and killed
    the cattle. When the drought comes, Joseph rides to
    Nuestra Señora to question Romas about leading a cattle
    drive. He tells Joseph about the death of Willie, who
    hanged himself. He eventually leads the cattle to water
    and returns to tell Joseph of the terrible ordeal over
    the mountains (TGU).

ROMAS, WILLIE. Son of Romas, the driver. He is haunted
    by pains which shake his body and dark dreams that tor-
    ture him when he sleeps. He dreams that he is at a
    dead and dry place where people come out of holes and
    pull off his arms and legs. He likes to sleep near
    horses because he feels safe when the horses are near.
    When Willie looks into a telescope he discovers that the
    place of his dreams is real. He becomes sick and
    hangs himself from a tree limb that very night (TGU).

ROMERO, MAE ("Johnny Bear"). The narrator of "Johnny
    Bear" has a romantic interest in this "pretty half-Mexi-

can girl." The narrator is embarrassed when Johnny mimics their conversation so he can get whiskey (LV).

ROOT ("The Raid"). A young, inexperienced, socialist labor organizer. Although afraid he will run when confronted by a raiding party, Root endures a beating and forgives his attackers (LV).

ROSA LOPEZ See LOPEZ, ROSA (PH)

ROSA MARTIN See MARTIN, ROSA (TF)

ROSE. The cook in the Héristal household. She provides a means for Marie Héristal to vent her emotions through an occasional household squabble. In family matters she aligns herself with Madame against Pippin Héristal (SRP).

ROSE OF SHARON. Oldest daughter of Ma and Pa Joad and wife of Connie Rivers. Still in her teens, she has a soft and round face, and her body was plump and provocative until her pregnancy, which makes her intensely serious. She has ash-blond hair braided into a crown. As food and shelter become increasingly inadequate for the Joads, Rose of Sharon complains and worries that her unborn child may be endangered. She is sullen and self-pitying after her husband deserts her. A "Jesus lover" at the Weedpatch government camp terrifies her with predictions that her child will be born dead and damned. Her child's being stillborn during the flood represents the inhumane destructiveness of the special interest groups oppressing the migrants. But the experience converts Rose of Sharon in part from being a self-centered young woman to a person capable of understanding and compassion, and the novel closes with her feeding a starving migrant with her mother's milk (GW).

ROSENDALE, BULLET. In Chapter V, as Monterey pauses in preparation for the scenes of evening, "At El Paseo dancing pavilion, Bullet Rosendale opened a carton of pretzels and arranged them like coarse brown lace on the big courtesy plates." Steinbeck might have chosen satire, but his sibilant diction breathes life into Rosendale's spontaneous composition (TF).

ROSY TORRES See TORRES, ROSY (LV)

ROY. A mechanic whom Will Hamilton sends to deliver the
new Ford that Adam Trask buys. He wears box-toed
shoes, Duchess trousers, and a coat that comes nearly
to his knees. He is nineteen years old and has studied
for three months in automobile school. Roy chews to-
bacco and sneers contemptuously at people who are not
experts in automotive mechanics. With his mechanic's
knowledge, he considers college graduates to be ignor-
amuses. "Just call me Joe," he informs everyone (EE).

RUDOLFO KELLING See KELLING, RUDOLFO (TF)

RUIZ, CORNELIA. The serialized affairs of Cornelia Ruiz
are an unfailing source of gossip and food for thought:
"it was a rare day and night during which Cornelia had
not some curious and interesting adventure. And it was
an unusual adventure from which no moral lesson could
be drawn." Cornelia is a notorious whore, and occasionally Danny's paisanos patronized her liberal display
of wares, but more often they celebrate her as the supreme example of feminine culture and technique. Similarly, Steinbeck is vaguely noncommittal about Cornelia's
moral profile but openly relishes her adroit management
of situations that call for utmost tact and practiced
aplomb. (To discourage one overenthusiastic admirer,
"She just cut him up a little bit on the arms. Cornelia
was not angry. She just didn't want the black one to
come in.")
        Thus Cornelia comes to represent the acute angles
of Steinbeck's own vision at the same instant that she
mirrors the paisanos' fatally shortsighted focus. Pilon
articulates the paisanos' carpe diem creed when he says,
of Cornelia, "Give peace to that Cornelia, and she will
die. Love and fighting, and a little wine. Then you
are always young, always happy. What happened to
Cornelia yesterday?" It would be erroneous to conclude
that Steinbeck endorses Pilon's sentiments. Tortilla
Flat is sometimes too clever not to verge on literary
exploitation--of women, of an audience struggling toward
enlightened response--but seldom lapses into slothful
acquiescence (TF).

RUIZ ("Old Ruiz"). "When Old Ruiz was dying the priest
came to give him solace, and Ruiz confessed. Cornelia
says the priest was white as buckskin when he came
out of the sick-room. But afterward that priest said
he didn't believe half what Ruiz confessed." In Chapter

IV, Old Ruiz is cited as the object of his daughter's
sometimes surprising piety. Cornelia's earnings as a
whore purchase masses in his memory. Later, however, Pablo curses father and daughter in the same
breath: "Two of one blood. 'Know the breed and know
the dog,' Pilon quoted virtuously." Perhaps Steinbeck
casts a grain of skepticism on all fanciful confessions.
The theme of inherited traits of character is one of his
favorites, but one that arouses his curiosity more than
it gains his partisanship. Pilon's airtight epigrams
must be greeted with extraordinary caution (TF).

RUMORGUE, M. Premier of France and titular leader of the
Proto-Communist Party. His government fails on the
issue of Monaco. He is a reluctant leader whose main
interest lies in psycho-botany and in his experiments
concerning pain in plants. He is the author of Tenden-
cies and Symptoms of Hysteria in Red Clover, and after
his willing departure from politics, works quietly on
"Inherited Schizophrenia in Legumes" (SRP).

RUMORGUE, MADAME. Wife of M. Rumorgue. She sends
him a telegram saying that the Poland China sow,
named Anxious, had farrowed. He departs immediately
from the meeting to form a new French government and
returns home (SRP).

RUPERT HOGAN See HOGAN, RUPERT (TF)

RUTH TIFLIN See TIFLIN, RUTH (LV)

RUTHIE JOAD See JOAD, RUTHIE (GW)

S

ST. ALBERT See ALBERT, ST. (MID)

SAIRY WILSON See WILSON, SAIRY (GW)

SALESGIRL. Employed at J. C. Penney's. She sells Suzy a
tomato-colored dress and matching shoes. She appears
only as a voice in a department store (ST).

SAM. A fiery migrant who travels with London. Sam cannot forget "Bloody Thursday" in San Francisco and is
knocked down by London when Sam starts to attack
Bolter. Sam finally gains his vengeance. When Ander-

son's barn is burned, Sam retaliates by burning down
Hunter's house in Torgas (IDB).

SAMOTHRACE, LIEUTENANT EMILE DE. Life Guard at
Versailles. He is on duty at the palace gate when Pippin IV and Tod Johnson appear in a state of drunkenness. His report on the altercation caused by a man
calling himself the Crown Prince of Petaluma and another muttering "Baa! Baa!" is removed from the book
by the next evening (SRP).

SAMUEL HAMILTON See HAMILTON, SAMUEL (EE)

SANCHEZ, PABLO. It is the appropriate sign of his respect
for convention that Pablo commences the novel in
shackles: " 'Pablo stole a goose and hid in the brush;
and that goose bit Pablo and Pablo cried out and so was
caught. Now he lies in jail for six months.' " Pablo
remains filed away until Chapter III, when he re-
emerges at the moment auspicious for Pilon. Pilon has
just agreed to rent Danny's spare house, and the obligations of the man of property that burden Danny are prov-
ing contagious. When Pablo affably consents to sublet,
Pilon sighs with relief. He had not realized how the
debt to Danny rode on his shoulders. The only stipula-
tion is that Pablo will "use all the house except my
bed." Danny later declares his own bed off limits.
Evidently, the "debt" of real responsibility weighs on
several phases of behavior.
      Henceforth, Pablo is the adhesive that endows the
narrative with the loose continuity of a wild goose chase.
During the preliminary section, prior to Chapter VII,
he is always at hand, egging on Pilon and Danny and
serving Pilon, especially, in the role of echoing interlocutor. Of all Danny's retinue, Pablo is the only member, even during the scrupulously proportioned body of
the book, who does not dominate some particular episode. Rather, he is omniscient but retiring, like a cat
in ambush: "Pablo, with cat-like stroke, killed a fly
that landed on his knee"; "Then Pablo took the bottle
from him, and Pablo played with it as a cat plays with
a feather." Such feline gestures enact in pantomime a
critique of Pablo's dramatic function. His is the dynamic of feint, pounce, and recoil. "The artistic in-
genuousness of Pablo" is a clue to Steinbeck's otherwise
puzzling strategy. It is Pablo who buys a candle for
Saint Francis that presently burns down the rented house.

He is thus the unconscious, absent-minded spark that ignites ensuing events. Moreover, his insouciance mirrors the studied casualness with which Steinbeck fashions an atmosphere of symbolic melodrama from a base of earthy realism and a more lofty superstructure of allegory and allusion. Pablo prefigures the stylish irony of literalness passing into literary elegance.

Pablo personifies the novel's surfaces, the visible mosaic of cruelty and concern that takes shape as the paisanos' ruling usage. He is the custodian of sophisticated manners and is quick to denounce departures from established custom. His parochial assessment of Cornelia Ruiz (" 'I am not one to cast stones but sometimes I think Cornelia is a little too lively. Two things only occur to Cornelia, love and fighting.' ") becomes the cornerstone of Pilon's definitive pronouncement on the paisano ethic: " 'Love and fighting, and a little wine. Then you are always young, always happy.' "

Pablo keeps things going: " 'There is more to this story,' he said. 'Let Jesus Maria tell the rest.' " He loyally travels the strand of Steinbeck's narrative like a debonair passenger on a train to oblivion. His receptivity to the tale of Ravanno summarizes the appeal of the novel itself: " 'I like it because it hasn't any meaning you can see, and still it does seem to mean something, I can't tell what.' " The comment, like Pablo, is rudimentary, even contemptible, but Steinbeck is probably mapping out the furthest limits of the broad-based audience he included within the sweep of his catholic vision (TF).

SANDRY, LISBETH. Spokesman for the "Jesus lovers" at the Weedpatch government camp. She is a stocky woman with suntanned face and intense black eyes. Over her gingham dress, she wears an apron made from a cotton bag. Mrs. Sandry terrifies Rose of Sharon with sermons on the sinfulness of dancing and theatre, and predicts hellfire and damnation for people indulging in idle pleasures. When she says that Rose of Sharon's unborn child will be damned, Ma Joad tells her to get out, whereupon she has a case of howling convulsions (GW).

SANTA ROJA, LA (YSOBEL) See LA SANTA ROJA (YSOBEL) (CG)

SAONE, CHILDERIC DE. Merovingian participant in the
    closed meeting of Royalist parties. He suggests that
    the Royalists turn to the holy blood of Charlemagne for
    the throne of France. He points that living in Paris is
    Pippin Arnulf Héristal, a descendant from the legitimate
    branch of Charlemagne. He proposes as new King of
    France His Gracious Majesty Pippin of Héristal and
    Arnulf of the line of Charlemagne. The nobility agree
    and carry the name to the National Assembly where it
    is approved (<u>SRP</u>).

SARAH ORDEN <u>See</u> ORDEN, SARAH (<u>MID</u>)

SAUL, JOE. A lithe, middle-aged man, Joe Saul is first an
    acrobat, then a farmer, and finally a sailor. His face
    is rough and pock-marked, and he has large, dark eyes.
    Joe Saul is tortured by a fear that he is impotent--that
    he cannot father a child by his beautiful wife, Mordeen.
    Saul is furious when he learns that Mordeen (whom he
    loves very much) has had relations with another man
    (Victor) because of her desire to give Saul the child he
    wants so badly. Joe Saul finally renounces his "crawl-
    ing, whining ego," finds the courage and courtesy to re-
    ceive the product of Mordeen's adultery, and accepts
    the child Mordeen has given him (<u>BB</u>).

SAWKINS, CAPTAIN. A pirate whose eyes burned with a
    Puritan fire. He expresses concern over Morgan's de-
    cision to attack Panama (<u>CG</u>).

SCHMIDT, MRS. A migrant woman who is a friend of Mrs.
    Dakin. Dakin sends his wife to call on Mrs. Schmidt
    when London suggests a private talk with Dakin (<u>IDB</u>).

SCOTTY ("The Chrysanthemums"). Henry Allen's hired hand.
    He has no apparent role in the story (<u>LV</u>).

SEER, THE. Big, bearded stranger that Doc meets on a
    lonely stretch of the beach. His eyes have the inno-
    cence of a wise baby, and his face seems chiseled out
    of the material of prophets. He invites Doc to dinner,
    which he serves in his make-shift home in one of the
    deep little creases created by pines that have stood
    against the moving sand. A man of visions as he is,
    he possesses an iron simplicity and a monolith of logic.
    He advises Doc that there are some things a man can-
    not do without love. His weakness is a love of Baby

Ruths which he steals one at a time from the Safeway. He is arrested when he recklessly steals three Baby Ruths from the store. When Doc sends Hazel to the Monterey Jail to seek his release, he advises Hazel that a man's friend should do anything to help him, even if it causes pain (ST).

SENATOR MORGAN See MORGAN, SENATOR (IDB)

SENATOR VEAUVACHE See VEAUVACHE, SENATOR (SRP)

SENOR CAPORAL See CAPORAL, SENOR (TF)

SENORA TORRELLI See TORRELLI, SENORA (TF)

SEPIC, JELKA ("The Murder"). Raised in a traditional Slavic environment, Jelka cannot relate to her Anglo husband, Jim Moore. Outwardly submissive, Jelka signals her cousin when Jim leaves for Monterey. Jelka accepts her cousin's death and her own beating, apparently believing that Jim's cruelty indicates his concern for her and his acceptance of her in the traditional Slavic sense (LV).

SEPIC, MR. Jelka's father, who told Jim Moore on his wedding day to be sure to beat Jelka. "Slav girl! He's not like a man that don't beat hell out of him" (LV).

SERGEANT AXEL DANE See DANE, SERGEANT AXEL (EE)

SERGEANT VAUTIN See VAUTIN, SERGEANT (SRP)

"SHARK" See WICKS, EDWARD ("SHARK") (PH)

SHERIFF RITTAL See RITTAL, SHERIFF (LV)

SHERIFF, THE. Horace Quinn's predecessor as sheriff of Monterey County. He is slow but thorough. He knows that Cathy has become a whore at Kate's place and threatens to run her out of the county unless she keeps a pseudonym, dyes her hair, and conceals her past so that the Trasks do not learn where and what she is (EE).

SHIP'S COOK. A sea-weary man, with sad brown eyes like

a dog's.   There was something of the priest about him,
and he took it as his duty to instruct Henry in the ways
of the world.   There was also something of the thug
about him, and he was as insincere as he was kind and
gentle.   He tells Henry that buccaneers generally fail
in their quests because they are little children who
"fight like hell and die very nicely..."   (CG).

SIMON, MR.   Mr. Simon owns the establishment, presumably a pawnshop, where Danny negotiates the purchase
of a vacuum cleaner for Sweets Ramirez in Chapter IX.
When Simon undertakes to cheat Danny, he merely follows the time-honored practice of all Monterey mer-
chants with their paisano customers.   Danny "laid his
two dollars on the counter and waited while the explosion took place; the fury, the rage, the sadness, the
poverty, the ruin, the cheating.   The polish was in-
voked, the color of the bag, the extra long cord, the
value of the metal alone.   And when it was all over,
Danny went out carrying the vacuum cleaner."   Two
dollars is less than the fourteen asking price, but then
the machine is missing an engine (TF).

SIR CHARLES MODDYFORD   See   MODDYFORD, SIR
CHARLES (CG)

SIR EDWARD MORGAN   See   MORGAN, SIR EDWARD (CG)

SISTER HYACINTHE   See   LESCAULT, SUZANNE (SRP)

SLIM.   The quietly grave leader of the ranch hands.   He
wears a Stetson; his long black hair is combed straight
back.   His skill with the bullwhip is legendary.   His
talk is backed by a quiet dignity which commands without obvious effort.   He is the one man in camp in
whom George confides (OMM).

SMALL, LENNIE.   A huge man with a shapeless face and
large, pale eyes, with wide sloping shoulders.   His
arms hang, ape-like, at his sides.   He is a hard
worker.   In his idiocy, Lennie accidentally kills Curley's wife.   George, his companion and loyal friend,
is forced to kill him.   Lennie loves soft, furry things
and desires only to live on a ranch with George and
tend rabbits (OMM).

SMASHER ("The Red Pony").   A shepherd dog belonging to

the Tiflin family (LV).

SMITH, STONEWALL JACKSON. Ethan's sympathetic portrait locates New Baytown's chief of police in the sus-
taining tradition of the leathery Western lawman:
"Stoney Smith is a man who wouldn't give away what
day it is unless he were on the stand under oath. Chief
Smith runs the police work of the town and he's dedicated, studies the latest methods, and has taken the
F.B.I. training in Washington. I guess he's as good a
policeman as you are likely to find, tall and quiet and
with eyes like little gleams of metal. If you were going in for crime, the chief would be a man to avoid."
Through Stoney, Steinbeck demonstrates that literary
conservatism, a deferential appreciation for the forms
of the past, need not signify flagging inventiveness.
The Chief stands for the common sense justice of the
American frontier, a law and order stance tempered
by philosophical compassion for human foibles. He
possesses the cool technical impartiality of a combat-
tested veteran, and he is wryly reconciled to the isola-
tions of his profession.
    Unobtrusively, Stoney punctuates the narrative with
reminders of his official presence. Ironically, however, Ethan's criminal plans do not "avoid" Stoney but
count heavily on his unsuspecting good nature for their
success; and as if in fulfillment of Ethan's unconscious
prophecy, Stoney's crisis of conscience comes late in
the book when he is summoned before a secretly im-
paneled grand jury and is compelled to testify against
his friends in the city administration. Loyalty to the
law comes in agonizing conflict with loyalty to the un-
written but equally insistent codifications of social duty.
Stoney acquits himself as a reliable public servant, but
his subsequent bitterness suggests that the path of rec-
titude is never comfortable and perhaps that an honest
man in a fallen world is a futile anachronism. "Ethan,"
he said fiercely, "do you think I'm a good cop?"
    "The best."
    "I aim to be. I want to be. Eth--do you think
it's right to make a man tell on his friends to save
himself?"
    "No, I don't."
    "Neither do I. I can't admire such a government.
What scares me, Eth, is--I won't be such a good cop
any more because I won't admire what I'm doing." In
Margie's words, Stoney is "a tough, male man." What

is the place of such a man, Steinbeck seems to ask, in a moral climate that makes "stonewall" synonymous with perjury? (WOD).

SMOKE, TALL BOB. Tall Bob Smoke is a Saroyanesque fig- ure manqué, a caricature of the typical American's obsession to stand at the head of the parade, to project a personable image, to be loved. Tall Bob is a latter- day cowboy who never quite lives up to his own expec- tations. Somehow, his best laid plans, his fool-proof exhibitions of courage and prowess, always collapse in fiasco. His horse faints at the critical moment. His skill fails him when, as poundmaster, he tries to lasso a dog before a large crowd. So he decides in despera- tion to stage a suicide and make the people sorry for laughing at his repeated mishaps. With rare poetic justice, everyone takes pity on Bob when he bungles even this stab at greatness and shoots his nose off. Henceforth, "they let Tall Bob carry the flag in every parade there is. And the city bought him a net to catch dogs with."

The sentimental Jesus Maria finds a bitter sweet- ness in the account of Tall Bob: "That story of Tall Bob is funny; but when you open your mouth to laugh, something like a hand squeezes your heart." By con- trast, he proceeds to tell the tale of Old Ravanno: "And there is a funny story too, but it is not pleasant to laugh at." Steinbeck is probably content with both verdicts, even though Jesus Maria tends to overlook the satirical side of Tall Bob's saga. Structurally, the an- ecdote is an early link in the chain leading to Danny's death, a kind of negative example. Tall Bob is in truth a follower. His vicarious vision of a celebrity is the mere derivative of society's meretricious advertise- ments of itself, an other-directed political facade. The thrust of his promotions is an escape from freedom, a flight into the comfortable refuge of "adjustment." He lacks a center. Danny, on the contrary, is radically liberated, a self-propelling centrifugal force, oblivious to social guidance, that finally flies out of any human orbit whatsoever. For most of the novel, freedom from responsibility and unconstrained liberty play off against each other in dynamic equilibrium. Total eva- sion of choice and complete acceptance of choice look like twins for some time but finally split apart like a fractured atom of experience. Correspondingly, Stein- beck's formal literary apparatus and free-wheeling tone

manage to live in temporary harmony until, with the
shock of Danny's farewell plunge, the paisanos dissi-
pate like a puff of smoke (TF).

SOCRATES. Before he is taken to be executed, Mayor Orden tries to recall some of the words of Socrates related to living a life which would bring him to an un-
timely end. With Doctor Winter's help, he repeats the
words to give himself strength as the time for his
death approaches (MID).

SOMERS, OLD LADY. One of the many residents of Cannery Row whose toilets resound with "Stormy Weather"
when Cacahuete aims his trumpet at the sewer pipe.
She is taking an enema at the time (ST).

SONNET, PRESIDENT. French President. He calls the his-
toric conference of the leaders of all parties to form
a new government. After Pippin IV is declared deposed and outlawed, he asks M. Magot to form a coalition government (SRP).

SONNY BOY. Operator of a good restaurant and bar on the
wharf in Monterey. He is the only Greek born in
America named Sonny Boy. He probably knows more
secrets than any man in the community because his
martinis act like truth serum. He fixes the dinner
scenario for Doc and Suzy according to Fauna Flood's
instructions (ST).

SOTO, MRS. When Pilon takes up residence in Danny's
"other house" in Chapter III, he is delighted to discover
that it resembles Danny's own home in every particular: "It had its pink rose of Castile over the porch,
its weed-grown yard, its ancient, barren fruit trees,
its red geraniums--and Mrs. Soto's chicken yard was
next door." Pilon hopes that Mrs. Soto's chickens will
prove as accommodating as Mrs. Morales' have been
for Danny, despite its promising attributes, the new
house turns out to be a sorry duplicate for the original.
The spirit of a symbol cannot survive transplantation
(TF).

STARVING MAN. When the Joads flee the flood and take
refuge in a barn at the end of the novel, they encounter
a boy with a man who has not eaten for six days. He
is about fifty, with a gaunt face covered by a stubble

beard; his eyes are vague and staring. Without milk, he will starve to death. In the novel's final scene, Rose of Sharon, who has just lost a stillborn baby, feeds him mother's milk from her breast, an act symbolic of the milk of human kindness (GW).

STEINBECK, ERNST. Husband of Olive Hamilton and father of John Steinbeck. After moving to Paso Robles and to King City, he settles in Salinas at 130 Central Avenue (EE).

STEINBECK, JOHN. Author and narrator of the book, Steinbeck is also a minor character in it, when Tom Hamilton and later Adam Trask visit the Steinbeck house in Salinas. As narrator, he is a middle-aged adult looking back on his mother's family, the Hamiltons, and philosophizing on the meaning of events in the novel. As a boy at the time of the later events, he is simply a curious observer (EE).

STEINBECK, MARY. Daughter of Olive Hamilton and Ernst Steinbeck and sister of John Steinbeck. As a child, she does not want to be a girl and asks her uncle, Tom Hamilton, to tell her how she can get to be a boy. Mary is a tomboy who likes athletics and despises killing and dolls. Her hair is so light that it is almost white, and she usually wears it braided so it will be out of the way of her activities (EE).

STONEWALL JACKSON SMITH See SMITH, STONEWALL JACKSON (WOD)

STOUT MAN, THE. He is a pearl dealer, "a ceremonious shaker of hands," who rolls a coin back and forth over his knuckles. He informs Kino that his great pearl is of no value because it is too large (P).

STUTZ, JAKOB. Junius Maltby's hired man. He and Junius conduct erudite discussions together and do as little work as possible (PH).

SUMMER, ELLA. A member of the Ladies' Committee of Sanitary Unit Number Four at the Weedpatch government camp. She was the chairperson the week before the Joads arrive, and she keeps interrupting chairperson Jessie Bullitt (GW).

SUNDOG ("The Red Pony"). Jess Taylor's stallion who is
the sire of Jody's colt in "The Promise" (LV).

SUSIE FRANCISCO See FRANCISCO, SUSIE (TF)

SUZANNE (SISTER HYACINTHE) LESCAULT See LES-
CAULT, SUZANNE (SISTER HYACINTHE) (SRP)

SUZY. A pretty girl with a flat nose and a wide mouth.
She is twenty-one, five-foot-five, has a good figure
and probably brown (dyed blond) hair. Doc calls her
the only completely honest human being he has ever
met. She had a poor family life and was deserted by
her first lover. She takes a job at the Bear Flag even
though Fauna Flood and Joseph and Mary Rivas believe
that she is not a good hustler. She has many of the
same qualities as Doc, and when they meet he finds
her interesting. Mack and the boys want to find a
good woman for Doc, and Fauna wants to marry off
Suzy to a good man--the inevitable result is a match-
making effort by the Palace Flophouse and the Bear
Flag. Their efforts are complicated by the hostility
that she creates when she talks to Doc. She likes
him, but her honesty is too painful. At Fauna's urging, Doc asks Suzy to dinner at Sonny Boy's and, at
Fauna's urging, Suzy accepts. She is coached and
dressed by Fauna for the occasion; and, on Sweet
Thursday, she is able to act maidenly on their date.
She is dressed for the masquerade as a bridal Snow
White, but she rejects Doc's offer to be his girl because she realizes that she loves him and will not trap
him. She leaves the Bear Flag and, after talking Ella
into giving her a job at the Golden Poppy, she sets up
her home in the boiler which she remodels with the
money loaned her by Joe Blaikey. She becomes a good
waitress and an independent home owner, but she sets
her own destiny when she tells Hazel that if Doc was
in real trouble, she would help him. Even though she
tells Doc that she would only spoil the life he has,
she comes to him when she hears about his broken
right arm. She tells him that she will drive him to
La Jolla for the spring tides if he needs her, and when
he tells her that he loves her, she responds by saying,
"you got yourself a girl." She spends the rest of the
day learning how to drive in Mack's mock-up car and
that evening drives off with Doc after the car climbs
the curve and rips off the stairs of Western Biological (ST).

"SWEETS" RAMIREZ See RAMIREZ, DOLORES ENGRACIA
   ("SWEETS") (TF)

T

TAKASHI KATO See KATO, TAKASHI (PH)

TALBOT, MR. and MRS. TOM. Cannery Row residents.
   The Talbots are poor people. Tom is a writer and
   cartoonist whose stories and cartoons are regularly rejected by New York publishers. Mrs. Talbot, who is
   certain that Tom will one day be successful, tries to
   assuage her husband's depression by giving parties
   (CR).

TALL BOB SMOKE See SMOKE, TALL BOB (TF)

TARPEY. A figure from Elizabeth's childhood past. She
   remembers how he shot a squatter and was hanged from
   the limb of a tree on the fish flats (TGU).

TAYLOR, DANNY. After his disgraceful expulsion from the
   Naval Academy, Ethan's inseparable boyhood companion
   became the town drunk. His one remaining prop, Taylor Meadow, assumes strategic importance as the only
   feasible location for a New Baytown airport. Baker
   hopes to seize control of the tract by having Danny declared incompetent, but Ethan beats the banker to the
   punch by giving Danny $1,000. Ostensibly, there are
   no strings attached and the money will enable the all
   but hopeless alcoholic to attempt a cure. But Danny
   runs true to form. As collateral, he deeds his estate
   to Ethan, then uses the cash to drink himself to death
   in the cellar hole that is all that survives of the fallen
   house of Taylor. Ethan's appalling plan is a glorious
   success.
        Danny functions as Ethan's ghostly alter ego and
   the shadow of his dissolving conscience. Like Lazarus
   returned from a past that is dead, he wanders through
   Ethan's troubled dreams and points a spectral, melancholy finger of accusation. "You're as blind as I am,"
   Danny tells his one-time "brother," "only it's a different kind of blindness." From the white inferno of his
   damnation, the man with nothing more to lose but his
   name itself pronounces the last syllables of unanswer-
   able truth. Danny compares Ethan's maneuvers to a
   poker game, and Ethan's final gesture of farewell to

his friend is a nightmare kiss of Judas, but the possible implication that Danny is a card cheat or a homo-
sexual yields in the face of Steinbeck's wise decision
to leave his background a source of mystery. What
we know about Danny and Ethan is more horrible than
anything we might not know.

   Danny's haunting presence dramatizes a fundamental assumption of Steinbeck's fiction. It is not the
novelist, the artificer, who appoints Danny the other
half of Ethan's split personality and who places Danny
in circumstances that parallel Ethan's own. Parallel-
ism is a literary term for a trick of stagecraft, but its
source is human nature. The symmetrical relationship between Ethan and Danny prefigures the implicit
symbiosis of Steinbeck and his readers. As Ethan puts
it, "A man who tells secrets or stories must think of
who is hearing or reading, for a story has as many
versions as it has readers. Everyone takes what he
wants or can from it and thus changes it to his measure." Projecting from a dream world of ambiguous
associations, Danny is one of those enigmas in Steinbeck's fiction whose meanings are limited only by the
ingenuity of the reader (WOD).

TAYLOR, JESS ("The Red Pony"). Jody Tiflin takes a mare
   to be bred to Jess Taylor's stallion. The stud fee is
   five dollars, and Jody spends all summer working it
   out (LV).

TAYLOR, WILLIAM, IV. Pacific Grove first grader who
   brought his crayons home wrapped in the dust cover of
   the Kinsey report. When confronted, he says he got
   it from his teacher Miss Bucke (ST).

TELLER, HARRY E. ("The White Quail"). Isolated from
   his passive wife who has identified with the white
   quail in her garden, Henry kills the fowl and then suffers additional pain: " 'I'm lonely,' he said. 'Oh,
   Lord, I'm so lonely!' " (LV).

TELLER, MARY ("The White Quail"). Characterized by her
   husband as "kind of untouchable," Mary is totally preoccupied with her immaculate garden. Mary sees herself in a white quail which appears in the garden:
   "She's like the essence of me, an essence boiled down
   to utter purity." The reader knows that Mary will
   withdraw farther from reality if she discovers that her

husband's loneliness led him to destroy the quail (L<u>V</u>).

TENANT, THE.   A composite character in Chapter Five.
When the tractor driver moves onto his farm, he accuses him of working against his own people.   The
tenant man argues that owning a little property makes
the property part of him and makes him a more significant person as long as he works it himself, whereas the absentee landlord of large holdings is small.
The tenant wants to shoot the person responsible for
driving him off the land, but the driver tells him that
he does not know who is ultimately to blame.   The tenant insists that people are responsible, and that he is
going to work for change (<u>GW</u>).

TERESINA (MRS. ALFRED) CORTEZ   <u>See</u>   CORTEZ, TERE-
SINA (MRS. ALFRED) (<u>TF</u>)

TERREFRANQUE, COMTE DE.   Member of the Royalist party.   He announces to the conference of parties to select a new French government that the Royalist group
had joined forces.   He introduces the Duc des Troisfronts who delivers the Royalist proposal for solving
the conference's deadlock (<u>SRP</u>).

THELMA.   One of the girls at Kate's brothel.   She has
"dark, handsome, brooding eyes."   Kate works her
over for drinking vanilla extract (<u>EE</u>).

THEODORE NOLAN   <u>See</u>   NOLAN, THEODORE (<u>IDB</u>)

THOMAS, MR.   A small farmer near the Weedpatch camp
who is sympathetic towards migrant workers.   He is a
stocky, sunburned man wearing a paper sun helmet.
He wants to pay the migrants a fair day's wage, but
explains to them in anger that the Farmers' Association forces him to lower wages, or else the Bank of
the West will refuse him a crop loan.   He warns Tom
Joad and Timothy Wallace of the Association's plan to
instigate a fight at the Saturday night dance so that
deputies can clean out the camp (<u>GW</u>).

THOMAS WAYNE   <u>See</u>   WAYNE, THOMAS (<u>TGU</u>)

TIA IGNACIA   <u>See</u>   IGNACIA, TIA (<u>TF</u>)

TIFLIN, CARL ("The Red Pony").   A strong disciplinarian,

Carl is unable to give his son the understanding a young boy needs. In "The Gift" Carl's criticism of Jody is contrasted with Billy Buck's natural ability to love and teach the boy. Carl seems to believe that a man or a horse, regardless of his past usefulness, should be discarded, a fact that in "The Great Mountains" fills Jody with "a nameless sorrow." In "The Leader of the People" Carl's intolerance with his father-in-law stands in sharp contrast to Jody's sympathetic understanding (LV).

TIFLIN, JODY ("The Red Pony"). Jody is the central character in all four sections of "The Red Pony." Jody matures as he faces and learns to accept death as a part of life. In "The Gift" the red pony dies, and in "The Promise" Jody learns that sometimes new life comes out of death. "The Great Mountains" provides a counterpoint to "The Gift" in that Jody is confronted with a human death, that of an old man who has come home to die. In the final section, "The Leader of the People," Jody's grandfather lives in a past that is dead. Jody has matured, however, and he recognizes his grandfather's deepest needs and makes an appropriate response (LV).

TIFLIN, RUTH ("The Red Pony"). A sensitive and warm woman, Jody's mother is assigned a stereotyped role in "The Red Pony." In "The Leader of the People" she is individualized in her defense of her father in the face of her husband's cruel remarks (LV).

TILSON, DR. A King City physician who examines Cathy after she tries to abort herself with a knitting needle. When he lectures her against destroying life, she deceives him by pretending to be an epileptic and persuades him not to tell her husband what she did (EE).

TIM. A sailor from Cork who is responsible for Henry's being sold as an indentured servant. Actually, Tim is a goodhearted man who forms a genuine liking for Henry and who sobs like a small, whipped child when Henry is sold (CG).

TIMOTHY RATZ   See   RATZ, TIMOTHY (LV)

TIMOTHY WALLACE   See   WALLACE, TIMOTHY (GW)

TITO RALPH See RALPH, TITO (TF)

TOD JOHNSON See JOHNSON, TOD (SRP)

TOM ANDERS See ANDERS, TOM (MID)

TOM, BLIND ("Johnny Bear"). A Negro piano player who
    is compared to Johnny in that Blind Tom could perfect-
    ly imitate anything he heard on the piano (LV).

TOM BREMAN See BREMAN, TOM (PH)

TOM HAMILTON See HAMILTON, TOM (EE)

TOM JOAD See JOAD, TOM (GW)

TOM MEEK See MEEK, TOM (EE)

TOM MORGAN See MORGAN, TOM (PH)

TOMAS, APOLONIA. The fat wife of Juan Tomas, Kino's
    brother (P).

TOMAS, JUAN. Elder brother of Kino who cautions him
    that he must not be cheated when he sells the pearl.
    Kino looks to him for wisdom (P).

TOMAS ("OLD TOMAS"). In Chapter XIV, Jesus Maria
    broods about the cruel ridicule that Tall Bob Smoke
    suffered: "It is worse than whipping to be laughed at.
    Old Tomas, the rag sucker, was laughed into his
    grave. And afterward the people were sorry they
    laughed." Like most satirists, Steinbeck knew the
    sharpness of the literary weapons he wielded; but he
    was determined to avoid the promiscuous blood-letting
    of irresponsible, arrogant criticism. Whereas Jesus
    Maria sounds sentimental, Steinbeck was inclined to
    tough-mindedness, but the backbone of both attitudes
    is a steadfast insistence on fair play, whatever the ex-
    pense in terms of rigorous orthodoxy (TF).

TONDER, LIEUTENANT. Tonder is a romantic, but unlike
    Lieutenant Prackle. Whereas Prackle dreams of seduc-
    ing a woman, Tonder dreams of his own death acted
    out on a Wagnerian stage. Bitterly cynical, Tonder
    becomes almost someone else when he is captured by
    the beauty of Molly Morden, but he fails to grasp the

extent of Molly's desire to revenge her husband's
death.   Tonder is no match for Molly's shears (MID).

'TONIA (MONTEZ).   " 'Tonia was like Gracie, with that funny thing that she kept away from men.   Old Man Ravanno could not help it.   He said, 'Come to me, little
girl.'   But 'Tonia was not a little girl.   She knew.
So she laughed and ran out of the room."   Unlike her
older sister, Gracie, 'Tonia did not reform.   After
Old Ravanno's feined suicide became an all too tragic
reality, 'Tonia promptly turned her sorceress's eyes
on her brother-in-law, Petey.   Steinbeck more than
once portrays the anarchic eroticism of adolescent
girls as a uniquely subversive agency in the human
scheme.   His view of Danny's crew expands into a
critical appraisal of a special culture found wanting,
but he seems to echo the grave reservations paisano
men harbor towards the entire universe of the opposite
gender.   'Tonia no doubt signifies some malign allure,
some deceptive tonic of impossible rejuvenation, but
the naturalistic details that flesh out her characterization are too frankly sexual for her to be dismissed as
a neutral vehicle for abstraction.   Here, as elsewhere,
laughter is the tormenting note of a manifestly feminine witchery.   Here, as elsewhere, machismo sexuality seems a death wish in disguise (TF).

TONY.   Piano player at Sonny Boy's restaurant.   He is sick
the night Doc and Suzy dine at the restaurant (ST).

TORRELLI.   Torrelli's bootlegging operation is a kind of
flea market where the paisanos barter extraneous flotsam, most often at usurious discount, in return for
the vin ordinaire that is the lifeblood of their existence.   He is a character required by the mechanics of
the narrative, and the trick is to mask his architec-
tural function by making him seem organically real and
inevitable.   Steinbeck meets the challenge with remarkable success.   In the first place, Torrelli's Corsican
ancestry sets him up as the logical medium of exchange
between the Hispano minority and the Anglo majority.
His wine shop is an outpost of progress, a metaphor
of confrontation between the pure ethic of commercial
enterprise and an unruly nest of barbarians.   Then
too, Steinbeck skillfully negotiates the tightrope between Torrelli's sweeping mean-mindedness and the
epic duplicity of his paisano clientele.   In the contest

to exhaust all sympathies, two memorable mediocrities
struggle to a sickening draw.

Steinbeck carefully lays the groundwork for Torrelli's supreme act of treachery at the end of the novel.
Thus Pilon takes the measure of his implaccable an-
tagonist: "Torrelli was a forceful man to whom expla-
nations, no matter how carefully considered nor how
beautifully phrased, were as chaff. Moreover, Torrelli had, Pilon knew, the Italian's exaggerated and wholly
quixotic ideal of marital relations." The irreconcilable
hostility between two clashing cultures could not be cut
more clearly. Much of the narrative is concerned with
the paisanos' frequently productive skirmishes against
Torrelli's gullibility, his pocketbook, and his wife's
accident-prone virtue. Matters reach a climax during
Danny's terrible season of rampage. Confident that
"sooner or later Danny will go to Torrelli's," the com-
rades descend in a horde on the evil one's fortifica-
tions. Through the barred door, he recites his bill of
accumulated grievances: "What did that devil do then?
My wife he insulted and me he called bad names. My
baby he spanked, my dog he kicked! He stole the hammock from my porch." Torrelli gasped with emotion.
"I chased him to get my hammock back, and when I
returned, he was with my wife! Seducer, thief,
drunkard! That is your friend Danny! I myself will
see that he goes to penitentiary." Reassured that Danny has indeed paid Torrelli a visit, the friends depart
as Torrelli "trembled with rage and fear."

Next day, wearing a ferocious smile of pleasure
and anticipation, Torrelli ventures forth, striking terror into the soul of the community because "Seldom did
the face of Torrelli show any emotions but suspicion
and anger. In his capacity as bootlegger, and in his
dealings with the people of Tortilla Flat, those two
emotions were often called into his heart, and their
line was written on his face." He proclaims himself
owner of the paisanos' mansion and gloatingly produces
in proof the deed the mad Danny has signed. In a
flash, the friends lure away the offending document
from their jubilant foe, deposit it in their blazing
stove, and send the crushed rogue packing.

Like "The Miller's Tale" in Chaucer, the episodes involving Torrelli apply a thin layer of comedy
over a violent and squalid base, but unlike Chaucer's
fable, there is little trace of redemptive, earthy
wholesomeness. Torrelli is a repugnant scamp, un-

worthy of a moment's reprieve, but the paisanos, with their epithets, are scarcely better. It is the inexcusably underhanded Danny, not the predictably villainous Torrelli, who signs the dirty deed and sends establishment and anti-establishment crashing down together (TF).

TORRELLI, SENORA. Torrelli's spouse is the embattled citadel of her husband's reputation and the focal point of many paisano stratagems. Chapter V dramatizes a typical incident. Pablo and Pilon, assured of Torrelli's absence, enter his house and, "with conscious knowledge of their art, cozened their supper out of Mrs. Torrelli. They slapped her on the buttocks and called her a 'Butter Duck' and took little courteous liberties with her person, and finally left her, flattered and slightly tousled." Later, Pilon resumes the visit on his own and for undisclosed purposes. He returns to Danny's house, "nodded his head in the dark and spoke with a quiet philosophy. 'It is seldom that one finds all things at one market--wine, food, love, and firewood. We must remember Torrelli, Pablo, my friend. There is a man to know. We must take him a little present sometime.' " This and similar occurrences do little to relieve the novel's disparaging opinion of womanhood or to modify the image of the paisanos as exploitive scoundrels (TF).

TORRES, EMILIO ("Flight"). A small, twelve-year-old boy who helps maintain the family by fishing off the rocks. Emilio yearns for the day when he, like Pepé, will be sent to Monterey for medicine, a task which he believes will confer manhood on him (LV).

TORRES, MAMA ("Flight"). A widow with three children struggling to eke out an existence on a coastal farm south of Monterey. She sends her eldest son to Monterey for medicine, only to have him return a hunted murderer. Equipping Pepé for his flight into the mountains and warning him to avoid "the dark watching men," she realizes that he will never return (LV).

TORRES, PEPE ("Flight"). A nineteen-year-old boy whose preoccupation with his deceased father's switchblade knife is his sole concern. Sent to Monterey for medidine, he becomes involved in a quarrel and instinctively kills a man. His flight from the posse is on one

level a journey into manhood. On another level Pepé
becomes more like a wild animal as he loses the articles which represent civilization during his journey
into the mountains. He learns that manhood carries
with it concomitant responsibilities for one's actions
(LV).

TORRES, ROSY ("Flight"). Though only a child, fourteen-
year-old Rosy realizes that her brother's trip into the
mountains is one from which he will never return. She
intuitively knows Pepé will soon die (LV).

TRACTOR DIVER (JOE DAVIS'S BOY), THE. A composite
character in Chapter Five. When the owners evict the
tenant farmers, the tractor driver moves in. Wearing
goggles, a rubber dust mask, and gloves, he looks
more like a robot than a man. He has no love for the
land or its fertility, but he is proud of the power of
the tractor and its straight furrows. For $3.00 a day,
he is working against his own people, but he says he
has to think of his own family and can't worry about
anything else. He follows orders without question (GW).

TRASK. According to Van Brunt, Trask was a "crook" who
lined his pockets with public money when he served as
roadmaster of the county. The bridges he engineered
are probably jerry-built and unreliable. Details such
as Trask's two college-age sons suggest a trial run for
Adam Trask in East of Eden (WB).

TRASK, ADAM. Son of Cyrus Trask and half-brother of
Charles Trask. He is born in Connecticut in 1862
while his father is away at war. As a child, he is
quiet and obedient, avoiding violence and contention by
retiring into secretness. His younger brother Charles
protects him in fights but twice beats him brutally in a
jealous rage. Adam is Abel to his brother's Cain;
later he is Adam to his sons' roles as Abel and Cain.
Adam is his father's favorite but does not love his father and fears his father's intention of enlisting him in
the Army. Nevertheless, he spends five years soldier-
ing in the West during the Indian wars. As a soldier,
he develops an obsession with nonviolence and risks his
life rescuing wounded men. Mustered out in 1885, he
wanders around the country aimlessly and then re-en-
lists for another five years. In 1890, he is discharged
in San Franciso as a sergeant. Instead of returning

home, he wanders for three years as a hobo and spends
a year on a chain gang for vagrancy.

Returning home, he lives off and on with his
brother for several years but thinks of California.
While in the Army, he lived for a while with an Indian
woman who died of smallpox. When Cathy Ames
crawls to his doorstep after being almost killed by Mr.
Edwards, Adam nurses her back to health, falls intensely and idealistically in love with her, marries her,
and takes her against her will to the Salinas Valley of
California, where he buys a well-watered ranch in
choice bottom land. After giving birth to his twin sons,
his wife shoots him in the shoulder with a .44 Colt and
deserts him and the children. The shock makes him
an embittered recluse who ignores his sons until after
the death of Samuel Hamilton. Samuel and the Chinese
servant Lee manage to give Adam a new hold on life;
and after Samuel's funeral, Adam calls on his wife at
her brothel in Salinas. The encounter frees him from
her domination. Thereafter he takes an interest in his
children and leads a fairly normal life. He is tall,
gaunt, with a tight mouth and a faraway look and carries his wounded shoulder lower than the other.

Adam loses much of his inherited fortune on an
experiment with shipping refrigerated lettuce, but he is
still comfortably off. As his sons Aron and Caleb grow
up, they become rivals for his affection, as he and
Charles were rivals for their father's love. When Aron
is killed during the first World War, Adam suffers a
stroke that may prove fatal, but he summons the
strength to absolve Caleb of his sense of guilt for
Aron's death (<u>EE</u>).

TRASK, ALICE. Second wife of Cyrus Trask, mother of
Charles Trask and stepmother of Adam Trask. Not
very pretty, she has pale eyes, a sallow complexion,
and crooked teeth. Her husband thinks her greatest
virtue is the fact that she never says anything unless
asked and spends all her time diligently at housework.
As her husband becomes increasingly military in his
manner and demands, she shrinks more into the background and makes herself almost unnoticeable. She is
tubercular but keeps her husband ignorant of the fact.
While Adam is away in the army, she chokes to death
from consumption (<u>EE</u>).

TRASK, ARON. Son of Adam Trask and Cathy Ames, twin

brother to Caleb Trask. Aron is a handsome, even
beautiful boy whom people instantly like, by contrast to
his darker brother, who has to fight for love and acceptance. Reenacting the conflict between Adam and
Charles Trask, Aron is Abel to his brother's Cain. He
has wide blue eyes, fine and golden hair, a beautiful
soft mouth, and an expression of angelic innocence.
His prettiness makes other boys at first consider him
a sissy, but he proves himself a determined and fearless fighter. As soon as he meets her, Aron falls in
love with Abra Bacon. They plan to marry; but in his
teens, he sublimates romance to religion and becomes
a zealous high-church Episcopalian, planning to become
an ordained minister and considering celibacy. Abra
gradually falls out of love with him and comes to favor
the more earthly and realistic Cal. But Aron is his
father's favorite; and Cal, bitter over feeling rejected,
takes his idealistic brother to meet their mother in her
brothel. Unable to cope with the shock, Aron joins the
Army and is killed during World War I (EE).

TRASK, CALEB. Son of Adam Trask and Cathy Ames and
twin brother to Aron Trask. Unlike his golden, beautiful brother, Cal is dark, sharp, and brooding. He
is larger than his brother, with big bones, heavy
shoulders, and a square jaw. He is dark-skinned, with
dark brown hair and eyes. Whereas his brother is instantly and universally liked, Cal has to fight for acceptance and often nurses a sense of rejection. He is
the Cain to his brother's Abel. When people prefer
Aron, Cal finds compensation in destructiveness and revenge. His schoolmates mistakenly think he is thick-
skinned and insensitive, and he has no friends. He
does not wish to be mean but is sometimes in response
to loneliness. He craves affection, especially from his
father, but is often blamed for doing exactly what his
brother is praised for. When his father loses a large
investment in refrigerated lettuce, Cal speculates in
beans and earns $15,000 from inflated prices during
the war. He gives this money to his father, who rejects it as blood money. Cal has earlier investigated
rumors about his mother and discovers her running a
brothel in Salinas. Now he reveals their mother to Aron, whose idealism is shattered. In horrified reaction,
Aron gets drunk, joins the Army, and is killed. Cal
feels guilty of his brother's murder and the stroke Adam
suffers when learning of Aron's death. But Abra falls

in love with him, and his father's last words are a kind
of forgiveness (EE).

TRASK, CHARLES. Son of Cyrus and Alice Trask and half-
brother of Adam Trask. He is assertive, athletic,
muscular, and competitive. As a teenager, he is subject to fits of violence and uncontrollable rage. He
cannot bear to lose and tries to kill anyone who wins
over him. Bitterly resentful because their father prefers Adam, he nearly murders his brother. Charles
feels no remorse after such events; he fulfills himself
and never feels sorry. He is to Adam as Cain to Abel.
When digging out rocks, he injures himself with an iron
bar and receives a scar on his forehead that is the
mark of Cain. When he takes over the farm from his
father, Charles runs it extremely well but lives with
one slovenly woman after another and withdraws from
the life of the village as a misanthropic recluse. When
Cathy Ames turns up at the farm, Charles instantly dislikes her and tries to drive her away; but she recognizes him as a kindred spirit and seduces him after
agreeing to marry his brother Adam. In middle age,
Charles dies alone of a lung ailment (EE).

TRASK, CYRUS. Father of Adam and Charles Trask. In his
youth, he is wild and devilish. As a young recruit in
the Union army during the Civil War, he enjoys drinking, gambling, and whoring until he is shot in the right
leg, which is amputated at the knee. Recovering, he
gets gonorrhea from a Negro girl and passes it on to
his wife. As a wooden-legged veteran, he develops a
career as a professional soldier. He begins by invent-
ing stories about his campaigns but gradually makes
himself an expert on war in general and the Civil War
in particular. He never promotes himself above the
rank of private but exerts considerable influence in military circles, publishing letters to the War Department
in newspapers and articles in magazines. An organizer of the G.A.R., he becomes a paid secretary for
life. He favors his son Adam and insists that Adam
go into the Army, even though he has no desire or in-
clination for military service. Cyrus becomes famous
as a Civil War expert and is invited to dinner at the
White House. Eventually he moves to Washington.
When he dies of pneumonia, the Vice-President attends
his military funeral, and the President sends a wreath
(EE).

TRASK, MRS.   First wife of Cyrus Trask and mother of
Adam Trask.   She is a pale, introverted woman without joy or laughter.   A psychological masochist, she
seeks unhappiness and invents religious justifications
for it.   When her husband infects her with gonorrhea,
she decides that the deity requires that she be punished
for erotic dreams she had during her husband's absence.   After writing a suicide letter confessing crimes
she could not have committed, she dresses in a shroud
and drowns herself in a shallow pond (EE).

TRIFLET, M.   Radical Conservative and member of the conference of parties to select a new French government.
He delivers an impassioned but ineffective address
against the Royalist party (SRP).

TROISFRONTS, DUC DES.   Member of the Royalist party.
He proposes to the conference of parties to select a
new French Government that the monarchy be restored
in France.   His speech is well received by the party
leaders despite his split palate and lack of self-confi-
dence.   At the convention to deliberate the Code Pippin,
he is given the honor of introducing Pippin IV because
of his demand for the return of the monarchy (SRP).

TROISFRONTS, DUCHESSE DES.   The wife of the Duc des
Troisfronts.   She breaks into applause when her husband, despite his handicap of a split palate, introduces
the king at the beginning of the convention to deliberate
the Code Pippin (SRP).

TRUCK DRIVER.   Gives Tom Joad a lift just after he is released from the penitentiary.   He drives a red truck
for the Oklahoma City Transport.   He is a heavy man,
"broad in the shoulders, thick in the stomach."   He has
a red face and long squinting blue eyes.   He wears
army trousers and high laced boots.   As he talks to
Tom, he sounds like a snooping and insinuating investi-
gator, until Tom finally tells him that he was impris-
oned for homicide (GW).

TULARECITO.   A misshapen little boy, believed to have a
diabolical origin, who is found and raised by Pancho
and Franklin Gomez.   He resembles a frog and thinks
he is a gnome.   After his fifth year, his brain stops
growing, but he draws and carves remarkably well.
He spends his evenings looking for gnomes (PH).

TURTLE, THE. A land turtle crossing a highway. The turtle, the only character in Chapter 3, becomes symbolic of the migrants in their exodus to the southwest. Like them, he has "fierce humorous eyes." He is stubborn and persistent in pursuing his route. He crushes a red ant that crawls into his shell, just as Granma Joad later reaches up with "little wrinkled claws" to remove a red ant that runs over "the folds of loose skin" on her neck. Like the migrant farmers the turtle carries seeds with him, clamped into the shell. He escapes a trucker's attempt to kill him. Tom Joad picks him up and carries him with him to give to one of the children, but Tom finally releases him, and the turtle resumes his southwestern course (GW).

U

UNA HAMILTON See HAMILTON, UNA (EE)

UNCLE JOHN JOAD See JOAD, UNCLE JOHN (GW)

USED CAR SALESMAN. A composite character in Chapter Seven. He is taking advantage of the dispossessed farmers' desperation to sell them defective jalopies at exorbitant prices. Though he is the dishonest party, he calls his customers "bastards" and "sons-of-bitches" if they ask for reasonable treatment. At the same time that he sells wrecks with dead cells for batteries and with sawdust in the gears, he cheats customers who want to trade possessions such as a pair of mules; thus he makes a corrupt profit on both ends. He believes that people are basically decent, and so he takes advantage of their innocence and honesty to make a killing for himself. He represents the business man out to gouge the public for all the traffic will bear (GW).

V

VALDEZ, GREAT-GREAT GRANDMOTHER. Alice tells the story of the time the Valdez family was visited on All Souls' Eve by a great-great grandmother with a cough in her chest (TGU).

VALERY, JOE. Bouncer and pimp and hatchet man at Kate's brothel in Salinas. His real name is Joseph Venuta, and he is wanted for escaping from a San Quentin road gang where he was serving time for robbery. Neglected

and beaten as a child, he has developed a hatred for
the whole world. Everyone is a bastard except himself. Joe therefore trusts no one and will betray anyone. The only person he respects is Kate, because he
fears her and thinks she is more clever than anyone.
He carries out Kate's orders to frame Ethel, but when
he learns that Ethel may have evidence to convict Kate
of murdering Faye, he uses this to terrorize Kate as
part of some unformulated plan to blackmail her or take
over her operation. Finally catching him up, Kate advises the sheriff's office to check on Joe's fingerprints
and past record. When the sheriff sends an officer for
him, Joe tries to escape and is shot dead. His schem-
ing, however, is one factor leading to Kate's suicide
(EE).

VAN BRUNT. One of the original party headed for San Juan,
Van Brunt is a waspish, misanthropic man in his sixties who opposes even his own scheme that Juan take
the "old road" along the river. At the end of the novel,
Van Brunt suffers a near-fatal stroke. This event helps
lift the curse that has prevented Chicoy and his pil-
grims from completing their journey. Steinbeck's portrait is impartial as much as condemnatory. On the
surface, Van Brunt is thoroughly disagreeable, a med-
dling jail-house lawyer and garrulous purveyor of rumor
and innuendo. He relishes his self-proclaimed role as
cassandra and empirical soothsayer, as cruel testament
to past experience and prophetic voice of menacing
doom. But secretly he bears the "brunt" of human mis-
ery and anguish. His irrational rages are the uncontrollable symptom of two previous strokes and have im-
paired his vision, tormented him with humiliating sexual
impulses, and reduced him to a cringing state of terror,
envy, and wretchedness. The repulsive facade of a malicious nuisance who has outlived his own day conceals
a severely strained nerve tempted by suicide but finally
scornful of surrender. In dramatic terms, Van Brunt
is a crucial ingredient that precipitates the major action of Steinbeck's fable (WB).

VAN DEVENTER, HELEN. A tall and handsome woman. Her
life is characterized by a strong sense of tragedy, but
she thrives on it. Her daughter, Hilda, is hopelessly
insane (PH).

VAN DEVENTER, HILDA. Daughter of Hubert and Helen

Van Deventer.   She is insane (PH).

VAN DEVENTER, HUBERT.   Helen's husband.   She marries
him at twenty-five.   Three months after the wedding,
he accidentally shoots himself (PH).

VASQUEZ, ANGELICA.   In Chapter V, when Pablo buttresses
his arguments that Danny's health may be in unsuspected
jeopardy, he cites the recent sad case in point of Angelica Vasquez along with that of Rudolfo Kelling.   Pilon,
however, matter-of-factly reminds everyone present that
"Angelica ate a bad can of fish" and is not the most
telling example of death by undiagnosed disease (TF).

VAUTIN, SERGEANT.   The remaining guard on duty at Versailles.   The others have gone to Paris to participate
in riots against the monarchy.   When Vautin complains
to Pippin IV that he has been left behind, the king
grants him an immediate furlough of two weeks (SRP).

VEAUVACHE, SENATOR.   Socialist and a member of the
committee that carries word to Pippin Arnulf Héristal
of his election by proclamation as King of France.   He
holds the honorary title of Honnête Jean for refusing a
bribe.   He tells Pippin that a sampling of opinion indicates that Pippin has the support of the French people.
He later receives the title of Comte des Quatre Chats,
and at a meeting to plan a constitutional convention to
draft the Code Pippin he argues convincingly for the use
of royal costumes at the convention (SRP).

VENUTA, JOSEPH See VALERY, JOE (EE)

VICAR.   A clergyman who attempts to pray with Morgan as
Morgan is dying.   He is a Church pedant who is embarrassed by Morgan's refusal to pray, by his wish not
to go to heaven, and by his rambling comments on the
futility of his life (CG).

VICTOR.   Joe Saul's crude and insensitive, but virile assistant, who sleeps with Mordeen and by whom she becomes pregnant.   Victor is a thoroughly self-centered
man; he misunderstands and misjudges almost everything.   In the end, although he becomes increasingly
vicious and threatening, Victor is almost pitiable.   He
is pushed overboard by Friend Ed (BB).

VITELA, JULE. An assistant of Ezra Huston's at the Weed-
     patch government camp, who helps prevent the riot
     planned by the Associated Farmers. He is half Chero-
     kee, with a hawk nose, high cheek bones, and a slen-
     der receding chin. He and Tom Joad discuss bad con-
     ditions and hard times together (GW).

                            W

WAINWRIGHT, AGGIE. The girl Al Joad plans to marry.
     Her parents describe her as "a big girl--near sixteen
     ... a growed-up woman-girl." Al meets her in the
     boxcar camp, and her parents are afraid he will get
     her into trouble until he announces their marriage plans
     (GW).

WAINWRIGHT, MR. A neighbor of the Joads in the boxcar
     camp and father of Aggie Wainwright. He is an elderly
     man with deep eyes, blue-white hair, a silver stubble
     beard, and a delicately chiseled face. He is worried
     that Al Joad will get his daughter Aggie pregnant and
     shame the family. During the final flood, the Wain-
     wrights stay with the Joads and help them (GW).

WAINWRIGHT, MRS. A neighbor of the Joads in the boxcar
     camp and the mother of Aggie Wainwright, whom Al
     Joad intends to marry. She helps Ma deliver Rose of
     Sharon's stillborn baby (GW).

WALDER, RICHARD. Walder is the government agent as-
     signed to follow Ethan's anonymous tip and inquire
     about Marullo's background. Dramatically, he is more
     than a mere agent, a virtual deus ex machina who
     abruptly terminates Ethan's robbery plot and then pre-
     sents the astounding news that Marullo has turned him-
     self in to the authorities and given the store to Ethan.
     Walder is cut from plain cloth, reserved and conven-
     tional in manner and dress, settled in the routine of
     his unglamorous official duties. Almost to the extent
     that Marullo has been startled by Ethan's unparalleled
     "honesty," Walder has been jarred from his accus-
     tomed niche by Marullo's magnanimous response. He
     uses his day off to bring Ethan glad tidings. At the
     store, he drops his bureaucratic mask and slips into
     the familiar role of waiting on customers: "I used to
     have a job at Grand Union after school." Steinbeck
     selects this colorless but amiable courier to re-cement

the fragments of a shattered plot and to cast in boldest
possible relief the consequences of Ethan's reckless
double-dealing. With appropriate understatement, the
narrative contrasts the humble virtues of patient service to the frenzied machinations of a soul in jeopardy
(WOD).

WALLACE, TIMOTHY. A migrant at the Weedpatch government camp who goes out working with Tom Joad. He
has a white stubble beard and wears new blue dunga-
rees. He has a sharp face. Wallace is a member of
the Central Committee at the camp. He tells Tom
Joad Mr. Hines's definition that "A red is any son-of-
a-bitch that wants thirty cents an hour when we're pay-
in' twenty-five!" (GW).

WALLACE, WILKIE. Timothy Wallace's son. He looks
much like his father but has a dark stubble beard (GW).

WALTER DOGGEL See DOGGEL, WALTER (MID)

WALTER HASCHI See HASCHI, WALTER (SRP)

WATCHMAN, THE. He is gatekeeper at the Weedpatch government camp. When the Joads arrive, he assigns
them a place, signs them in, and explains to them the
cost, operation, and democratic government of the
camp (GW).

WATCHMAN, THE. His pacing tour of the rusting canneries
is the only sign of life at the once vital and active in-
dustry at Cannery Row (ST).

WAYNE, BENJAMIN. The youngest of the four Wayne brothers. When he begins his courting, Joseph Wayne decides to leave for the West. He becomes dissolute and
undependable, and, given the chance, he drinks himself
into a romantic haze and walks about the country, singing gloriously. His young wife, Jennie, knows that he
is in constant trouble with women, but her only fear is
that some night he may hurt himself. The family
knows that he lies and cheats, but, because he also
makes people happy, they love him and bring him West
to protect him. The Mexicans give him liquor and
teach him their songs; and when they are not watching,
he takes their women. He avoids his work on the
ranch when he can, and constantly runs off to Nuestra

Señora to drink and make love. His pleading voice
haunts Elizabeth and almost lures her into the streets.
She falls in love with his voice and fights the temptation to surrender to it by deciding to marry Joseph.
On the night of Elizabeth and Joseph's wedding, Benjy
is stabbed to death by Juanito when he discovers Benjy
making love to his wife, Alice. The Wayne brothers
believe that Juanito acted naturally and report Benjy's
death as accidental. He is buried on a side-hill a
quarter-mile from the ranch. Burton makes a cross
for the grave, and Thomas builds a white paling fence
around it. A short time later, Jennie returns to her
home in the East (TGU).

WAYNE, BURTON. One of the four Wayne brothers. He is
   physically and emotionally constituted for a religious
   life. He keeps himself from evil and finds evil in nearly all close human contacts. He had embraced his
   wife four times and has two children. His natural state
   is celibacy. His health is poor, but in his view it is
   a sign that God thinks enough of him to make him suffer. He rules his sickly wife with a firm and scriptural hand. He disapproved of his father's strange earthly ways and is dismayed to find Joseph Wayne acting
   in the same manner. His only joy seems to be contained in the occasional trips with his wife to religious
   meetings in Pacific Grove where he can find Christ
   again and recite sins before a gathering of people. He
   disapproves when Joseph allows Father Angelo to hold
   mass at the New Year's fiesta, and he is frightened by
   the wild emotion displayed by the dancers at the height
   of the celebration. It reminds him of witchcraft and
   the Black Sabbath. He warns Joseph against his pagan
   growth and his worship of the great oak tree. He becomes so enraged with Joseph's worship of the tree
   that he decides to leave the ranch, but before he departs he secretly girdles the tree. He decides to settle in Pacific Grove, and to turn to shopkeeping rather
   than farming. He believes his action against Joseph
   and the tree is right and he hints to Joseph what he has
   done by telling him that there is only one law and he
   has tried to live by that law (TGU).

WAYNE, ELIZABETH. Daughter of Mr. McGreggor and wife
   of Joseph Wayne. She is a lean, pretty young woman
   whose beauty lies in her deep grey eyes. She possesses a high spirit and at seventeen she becomes a

schoolteacher. She is the most eligible and desirable
young woman in Nuestra Señora because her education
would bring social elevation to her suitor. She is even
more widely educated than most teachers and has a
classical background. She is watched and finally courted by Joseph Wayne in an abrupt and direct way. She
is afraid of him, but, after being taunted in her soul
by the singing voice of Benjamin Wayne, she decides
to marry Joseph. At her wedding, she feels that Joseph's face resembles Christ's, and that her prayers
are to her husband. When she enters through the pass
leading to the Wayne ranch, she feels that an initiation
into the pain of womanhood has taken place. Her wedding night is disrupted by the news of Benjy's death,
and she is taken into the ranch by Rama, who becomes
her tactful and wise teacher. Her early days of marriage are happy ones and by the time winter comes she
is pregnant. During the first heat of summer, she
longs to smell the pines of her home in Monterey. She
travels into the pine grove near the Wayne ranch, and
penetrates its center where she finds Joseph's sacred
moss-covered rock. She is horrified by the sense of
something old and evil about it and flees back to the
familiar world of the ranch. She gives her husband a
son, and after resting, she tells him of her visit to
the pine grove and her desire to see the rock again.
She returns to the pine grove with Joseph to see that
the rock is nothing more than a physical thing, but
when she decides to climb up its back and tame it, she
slips and falls, breaking her neck. Thomas cries for
the first time in his life when he hears the news of her
death, and Joseph confesses to Rama that he loved
Elizabeth even though he did not know her as a person
(TGU).

WAYNE, HARRIET. Wife of Burton Wayne. She lives under
Burton's firm and scriptural rule. He parcels out his
thoughts to her and pares down her emotions. She has
some weak thing in her that cracks occasionally and
leaves her sick and delirious. She is sad when Burton
decides to move to Pacific Grove, but she tells everyone that it is a nice place and invites them to visit
(TGU).

WAYNE, JENNIE. Wife of Benjamin Wayne. She is mentioned by John Wayne as the Jenny (sic) Ramsey that
Benjy is courting in Pittsford. She knows about her

husband's infidelities, but she understands his strangeness and fears only that he might hurt himself on one
of his drunken adventures. She is grief-stricken by
Benjy's death, and every day for a while she places
some green thing on his grave. But she grows home-
sick for her own people and more fearful of living in a
new country without a husband. She decides to return
to her parent's home and leaves the valley without
much sadness. Her only dread is of the long train
trip ahead of her (TGU).

WAYNE, JOHN. Patriarch of the Wayne family. He is the
father of Burton, Thomas, Benjamin, and Joseph. His
flesh seems made of a stony substance. He gives Joseph permission to go to the West, and administers the
ancient blessing to his strongest son in spirit and character. His death is felt by Joseph even before he receives word of it. After he reads Burton's letter telling him of his father's final obsession with the new
land, he feels that John Wayne's spirit has entered the
huge oak tree under which he is building his ranch.
Burton grows to hate his father's paganism, but Joseph
admires his father's god-like loneliness and calm (TGU).

WAYNE, JOHN, II. Infant son of Elizabeth and Joseph
Wayne. His father believes that he is made out of the
strong stock of the Wayne family. He is called John
to continue the cycle of Josephs and Johns. His father
places him within the crotch of the sacred oak tree despite the protest of Burton. When Elizabeth dies,
Rama devotes herself to the infant. During the drought,
Joseph gives the child to Rama as a sacrifice for the
restoration of the land. He promises her that he will
never reclaim the child (TGU).

WAYNE, JOSEPH. One of the Wayne brothers and unquestioned lord of the Wayne clan. He resembles his father's stony appearance. His father regards him as
stronger and more sure and inward than his brothers.
When the farm in Pittsford, Vermont seems too crowd-
ed, he receives his father's permission and ancient
blessing to go to the West. He records his homestead
in the long valley called Nuestra Señora. He possesses
a physical, almost sexual, feeling for the land, and be-
builds his ranch under a great oak tree which he believes contains the spirit of his dead father. He accepts Juanito as his first vaquero and close friend and

eventually receives his brothers and their families as
members of the ranch. He feels like a great father
on the ranch and makes small offerings to his totem,
the giant oak. He also discovers a giant moss-covered
rock in a pine grove, and regards the rock and the
place as sacred.

He courts Elizabeth McGreggor and despite his
awkwardness and her fear of him they eventually marry.
When they travel through the pass to the Wayne ranch,
he tells Elizabeth that their marriage-sperm and -egg
is the same as their entry through the pass as a single
unit of pregnancy. His wedding night is disrupted by
the news that Juanito has killed his brother Benjamin.
He believes Juanito acted naturally as an enraged husband and tells Thomas to report Benjy's death as an
accident.

His pagan rites in worship of the tree are noticed
at the New Year's fiesta by Father Angelo and he is
warned against his ancient practices. His brother Burton also warns him against his offerings to the tree.
When he sees Joseph place his infant son in the crotch
of the tree, he secretly girdles it and the next day
takes his family to Pacific Grove. Joseph bears no
grudge against his brother because he acted according
to his nature. In the early weeks of the drought, he
decides to visit the pine grove to see if the spring that
flows from the giant rock has dried up. At her urging,
he takes Elizabeth with him, but when they are in the
grove, she falls from the rock and breaks her neck.
Her death makes him even more aware of the mysterious cycle of life and death.

When the drought continues, he decides to send
Thomas with the family and the remaining cattle to find
water and grazing land. He gives Rama his son to
keep and to raise. He returns to the pine grove and
bathes the green rock with the remaining water from
the stream as a final act of resistance to the drought.
He is joined by Juanito whom he tells that he now feels
responsible for the land. He goes to Nuestra Señora
with Juanito and talks with Father Angelo, but he returns to the grove to continue his struggle. He remembers the old man on the cliff-top and tries his way by
sacrificing a calf on the altar. He realizes, however,
that something more is required. He cuts his wrist
with a saddle buckle, and lies on his side and allows
his blood to flow upon the rock. As his life flows
from him, he feels the rain and sees the land grow

moist. He announces with his dying breath, "I am the
land ... and I am the rain" (TGU).

WAYNE, MARTHA. Oldest daughter of Thomas and Rama
Wayne. She is older than the other children and uses
her age and seriousness as a whip on the other children. She wins the prize for being the first one to
hear Elizabeth's baby cry because she knows to listen
for the slap. She diverts the children from the sadness of Burton's departure by telling them that her dog
had puppies though it has not had puppies at all. She
warns them not to talk to Joseph Wayne after Elizabeth's death. She cries bitterly when her family leaves
the valley because of the drought, but her tears are
shed because there is no one left to see her waving a
handkerchief (TGU).

WAYNE, RAMA. Wife of Thomas Wayne and mother of
three daughters. She is a strong, full-breasted woman
who is contemptuous of men's thoughts and actions.
She is an overpowering figure for the children, and she
is an efficient midwife and housekeeper. She understands her husband and treats him like an animal by
feeding, cleaning, and not frightening him. She is the
unquestioned authority on good and evil. When Elizabeth Wayne arrives at the ranch, Rama takes charge of
her and reveals her deeply instinctive knowledge of the
Wayne men and her worship of Joseph Wayne as more
than a man. She becomes a tactful and wise teacher
for Elizabeth, and prepares Elizabeth for the coming
birth and delivers the baby. After Elizabeth's death,
she takes care of the infant and gives herself to Joseph
to drain away his sorrow and to make him complete
again. When Rama and Thomas leave because of the
drought, Joseph gives her the baby so that he may be
alone with the land. She accepts the child, and confesses that she is glad to leave because she fears the
man (TGU).

WAYNE, THOMAS. Oldest of the four Wayne brothers. He
is a thick, strong man with golden hair and a long yellow mustache. He has a strong kinship with all kinds
of animals. He is not kind to them, but he acts with
a consistency that beasts can understand. Humans,
however, puzzle and frighten him. Joseph Wayne is
the only person he can talk to without fear. His wife,
Rama, understands him and treats him as if he were

an animal. They have three daughters. He is a constant companion to Joseph on the ranch, and often provides him with either a willing audience or a moderate
and natural voice of advice. He does not, however,
understand Joseph's pagan ways, though he senses their
link to natural things. He is afraid of Joseph's sacred
place in the pine grove and also fears the old man who
lives above the beach. He is the one who tells Joseph
of Benjamin's death, and when he hears of Elizabeth's
death he cries for the first time in his life. At the
fiesta, he goes to the barn when the dancing starts because he fears wild emotion. When the drought comes,
he grows anxious to leave the valley because he feels
that he cannot trust it any longer. He leads the cattle
and the remaining family out of the valley until they
find water (TGU).

WEBB, MR. The manager of Tulman's Department Store
where Jim Nolan worked. Informed that Jim had been
jailed for attending a radical meeting, Mr. Webb claims
that he has never heard of him (IDB).

WEE WILLIE See WILLIE, WEE (WOD)

WEELIE. In Chapter IV, Pilon cites "My Cousin Weelie" as
a source of authority on Mrs. Morales's age. Pilon is
given to polishing his reputation as a mine of informa-
tion with similar such references to conveniently unan-
swerable fact (TF).

WELCH ("The Vigilante"). A bartender fascinated with the
lynching. He purchases from Mike a fragment of the
lynched man's clothing to display in his bar (LV).

WHIT. A young laborer who calls Slim's attention to a letter
in a pulp magazine written by one of the ex-ranch
workers. He carefully places the magazine in safe-
keeping. He urges George to visit Susy's place, the
town brothel (OMM).

WHITESIDE, ALICIA. Richard's wife. She stares at a
bronze copy of Michelangelo's David before having her
baby, thoroughly convinced that her child will consequently look like the David. When he is born, she
names him John. She tries to have a second baby
against her doctor's orders and almost dies. She
spends the rest of her life as an invalid (PH).

WHITESIDE, BILL. John Whiteside's son, a big simple
young man who is attracted to Molly Morgan, the young
schoolteacher. He marries Mae Munroe (PH).

WHITESIDE, JOHN. He is one of the life-long residents of
the valley. A respected citizen, he is the clerk for the
local school board. He also owns a farm. He is the
son of Richard and Alicia Whiteside (PH).

WHITESIDE, RICHARD. He buys 250 acres in the valley and
builds a large house for his family and his descendants.
He believes he is founding a dynasty. His wife, Alicia,
will bear him only one son whom he will name John
(PH).

WHITESIDE, MRS. WILLA. John's wife. She tries to make
Molly Morgan, the new young schoolteacher, comfortable. She is a pleasant, gracious woman who truly
loves the valley (PH).

WHITEY. The regular bartender at La Ida who is "sick" as
often as he can get away with it. Whitey hired Eddie
as his substitute since he is convinced that Eddie is the
one person who would not try to keep his job permanently (CR).

WHITEY NO. 1. One of the inhabitants of the Palace Flophouse (see Cannery Row). During the war he took a
job at a war plant in Oakland, but broke his leg the
second day and spent three luxurious months in a hos-
pital bed. He attends all the meetings and parties, but
usually has very little to say. His one noticeable act
is to sell raffle tickets in the foreign and fancy pur-
lieus of Pebble Beach and Carmel and the Highlands (ST).

WHITEY NO. 2. One of the inhabitants of the Palace Flophouse. He is the new Whitey (see Whitey No. 1).
During the war he had fought with the marines and rumor has it that he earned a Bronze Star which he lost.
He never forgave the Marine Corps for taking away his
war prize, a quart jar of ears pickled in brandy. He
used to be a caddy at a country club, but he refused
to take a loyalty oath and was fired. He is no subversive, but he is strong-minded and independent. If
anyone refuses to buy a raffle ticket from him, he
throws a rock through his windshield. He teaches

Johnny Carriaga the art of palming so that the winning
raffle ticket may be drawn with dignity as well as deception. At the masquerade, he engages in a wild
wrestling match with Wide Ida. Mack tells him to stand
guard over Doc while he recuperates from his broken
arm. While on duty, he eavesdrops on Doc and Suzy's
reconciliation (ST).

WICK, DR. Removes a kidney stone shaped like a beagle's
head and big as a hand from Mrs. Gaston (ST).

WICKS, ALICE. Daughter of Katherine and "Shark" Wicks.
A truly beautiful baby, Alice becomes even a more
beautiful woman. "Shark" feels ferociously protective
toward her. She is worshipped by both of her parents,
even though she is actually a very stupid, dull and
backward girl (PH).

WICKS, EDWARD ("SHARK"). Called "Shark" by the people
in the village. He lives on the edge of town in a small
gloomy house. He has a blunt, brown face with small,
cold eyes. He is known as the trickiest man in the
valley. After losing out in a stock investment, he lies
about the loss. The townspeople think he is a financial
wizard. He loves his daughter, Alice, the way a miser
loves his money; he gloats over possessing the beautiful creature (PH).

WICKS, KATHERINE MULLOCK. Wife of "Shark." She is
not pretty but had "the firm freshness of a new weed,
and the bridling vigor of a young mare" before her
marriage to "Shark." After marriage, her face sags
and her hips broaden. "Shark" treats her as kindly as
he does his farm animals (PH).

WIDE IDA See IDA, WIDE (ST)

WILKIE WALLACE See WALLACE, WILKIE (GW)

WILKINS, DOC. Mentioned by Fauna as coming in the next
day after she hires Suzy as one of the regular girls at
the Bear Flag (ST).

WILL ("The Murder"). A deputy sheriff who, with the cor-
oner, removes the body of Jelka's cousin. Although
there will be a formal charge of murder against Jim
Moore, Will assures him that it will be dismissed,

and he urges Jim to "Go kind of light on your wife, Mr. Moore" (LV).

WILL ANDERS See ANDERS, WILL (MID)

WILL HAMILTON See HAMILTON, WILL (EE)

WILLARD AND JOEY See JOEY AND WILLARD (CR)

WILLIAM. A dark and lonesome-looking man who was once the watchman at the Bear Flag Restaurant. Tired by the company of Dora's girls, William longed to join Mack's group. Rejected by Mack as a pimp, William's heart broke. Always an introspective and self-accusing man, William concluded that no one loved or cared about him and so killed himself with an ice pick (CR).

WILLIAM. A Welsh road-mender with whom Henry talks before he leaves for the Indies. William is a suspicious man who nevertheless is filled with a longing when Henry tells him about his plans (CG).

WILLIAM AMES See AMES, WILLIAM (EE)

WILLIAM DEAL See DEAL, WILLIAM (MID)

WILLIAM RANDOLPH See RANDOLPH, WILLIAM (ST)

WILLIAM TAYLOR, IV See TAYLOR, WILLIAM, IV (ST)

WILLIAMS, DORA. Dora Williams is the madame of a Monterey brothel frequented by Big Joe Portagee. It is a latent mark of Big Joe's forthcoming ostracism from the paisanos' inner circle that he patronizes Dora's establishment, rather than paisanos like Cornelia Ruiz. His stormy liaison with Tia Ignacia does little to mend the unfavorable impression that he is disloyal and a potential outcast (TF).

WILLIAMS, RED. Operator of a filling station on Cannery Row who has developed an effective technique for dealing with the chicanery of Mack and the boys (CR).

WILLIE. "An Army friend" of Horton's, "a carpenter" at a movie studio, a scavenger amongst the refuse of people in high places. Willie earned favors in the service by procuring women for officers. As a civilian, he

lurks on the fringes of the world of decadent illusion
and panders to the carnal appetites of Hollywood hang-
ers-on. When he talks about Willie, Horton illuminates
the least attractive, corruptible phase of his own personality (WB).

WILLIE EATON See EATON, WILLIE (GW)

WILLIE ROMAS See ROMAS, WILLIE (TGU)

WILLIE, WEE. Ethan's vest-pocket introduction neatly ear-
marks the nocturnal division of New Baytown's two-
man constabulary: "Wee Willie gets lonesome and
loves to talk, and then later he talks about what he
talked about. Quite a few small but nasty scandals
have grown out of Willie's loneliness." Willie is the
voice of rumor. Spiced with suggestive overtones of
illicit sex, his malicious gossip is the antithesis of
Stoney Smith's wall of silence. But even in such a
minor character, there seems the note of personal distress and loneliness that Steinbeck seems to hear
(WOD).

WILSON, IVY. Meets the Joads on Route 66 and travels
with them to California. He is a lean, middle-aged
man with a furrowed face and sharp cheek bones. He
wears a blue shirt, jeans stiff with dirt, a black spotted vest, and a cheap straw sombrero. He stops at
Needles, knowing that his wife cannot cross the Mojave
Desert alive. He is friendly and hospitable, and becomes part of the Joads' extended family (GW).

WILSON, SAIRY. Wife of Ivy Wilson. She is a wizened
woman with a wrinkled face and skeletal arms and
hands covered with wrinkled skin. She is small and
shuddering, with blazing black eyes full of suffering,
but speaks with a beautiful low musical voice. Grampa Joad dies of a stroke in her tent. The Joads and
Wilsons travel as a unit to California. Sairy goes only as far as Needles and can go no further; she knows
she is dying and calls herself "jus' pain covered with
skin" (GW).

WINCH, MISS. Known for her foul disposition. She actually says good morning to the postman on Sweet Thursday (ST).

WINFIELD JOAD See JOAD, WINFIELD (GW)

WINTER, DOCTOR. Confidante of Mayor Orden and the
    philosophic spokesman in the novel. As he criticizes
    the characteristics of the collectivist state, he es-
    pouses a non-teleological theory of true leadership:
    "They think that just because they have only one leader
    and one head, we are all like that ... in a time of
    need leaders pop up among us like mushrooms." In
    this, as well as in his articulation of the non-teleologi-
    cal gospel of "breaking through," Doctor Winter is a
    fictionalized version of Edward F. Ricketts (MID).

WISTERIA. One of the regular girls at the Bear Flag. She
    does sixty days for a lady fight that is discussed with
    admiration in Cannery Row (ST).

WONG, MRS. ALFRED. Attends Fauna and Mack's mas-
    querade. She is struck between the shoulderblades by
    one of Johnny Carriaga's rubber-tipped arrows (ST).

WOODMAN OF THE WORLD. A former customer of Bear
    Flag. He is remembered because of his fight with
    Becky and the deep bite he inflicted on her shoulder
    (ST).

Y

YOUNG-HUNT, MARGIE. Twenty years ago, Margie divorced
    her cloyingly devoted first husband. He still sends ali-
    mony checks with the metronomic punctuality of a court-
    ly lover, but his health is failing and Margie's pros-
    pects for her encroaching middle age are bleak.
    Margie's second husband, a fortune hunter who soon
    died, was a trifling interlude. Her true métier has
    been service to lonely men. Either as Christian arche-
    type (Mary Magdelene? "O Daughter of Jerusalem"?)
    or pagan (Cleopatra? Ozma?), she has extended self-
    effacing, long-suffering solace to the impotent casual-
    ties of unrewarding domesticity.
        But Margie is no mere stereotype of the trollop
    with a heart of gold. Throughout the novel, she per-
    sonifies the uncertainty principle that animates human
    experience, the capricious twists of fortune that mock-
    ingly disrupt the tidy, linear prophecies of a Joey Mor-
    phy. In a narrative notably preoccupied with ancestry,
    she has inherited the gift of a great-grandmother who

"raised storms" and was punished for witchcraft. Like Madame Sosostris in T. S. Eliot's The Wasteland, Margie tells fortunes with a pack of tarot cards, and her uncanny accuracy disturbs even the skeptical Ethan, and she raises a hurricane of emotion within him.
Such happenings are less a polemical apology for the occult than Steinbeck's practical acknowledgment that with authors and with other men, stories have a way of telling themselves and of charting their own inscrutable loops and spirals.

At Easter time, Margie predicts a radical metamorphosis in Ethan's life: "Everything you touch will turn to gold--a leader of men." For the moment, Ethan resists the temptation of her body; but the electrifying challenge of her words is much harder to decipher and to ignore: "I dare you to live up to it and I dare you not to. So long, Savior!" During the remainder of the novel, Margie is still the most sensitive barometer of the change she has either caused or stimulated, and she alters the course of events to suit her convenience and sometimes Ethan's. She offers especially telling critiques of the cast of characters, and she appears before Ethan, in her dual capacity as seductress and sympathetic audience: "Artemis for pants" and "a kind of Andersen's Well--receptive, unjudging, and silent"--that is, a quiescent sounding-board for Ethan's malaise as well as a lawless spur to his "savage creativeness."

Margie is resilient and cautious, "mellow" with other women and impeccably manicured. She angles for Ethan as part of her campaign to secure a new lover before time runs out, but her fate is to preside with guarded curiosity over the mischievous greening of Ethan's consciousness, to pace the play of his unfolding fortune. Persistently, Ethan seeks to fathom her motives: "Is she an evil thing?" Is she up to some sort of game, "a kind of puzzle, a test"? Is she posing a question, "Can a man think out his life, or must he just tag along?" or is she demonstrating a truth, "A fake fortune was just as good as any and it is possible that all fortunes are a little fake?"

Ultimately, of course, Steinbeck assigns the wavelength of Ethan's destiny, but Margie, for all the grossness of her practiced sexuality, is the Delphic oracle pressuring Ethan to accept the franchise of the life force that sponsors him. Whether he will or not is a question that remains unanswered. Ethan is sometimes

in harmony with Margie and her "communications system that ran from her pointed patent-leather toe to her
curving soft chestnut hair"; and when she speaks as
"Pythoness," he concedes the aptness of her image of
him as a "snake changing its skin." But he can also
dismiss her hovering concern as the "cruelty that
comes to one when control of a situation is lost."
     Steinbeck may have lost control, too. The por-
trait of Margie struggles with superfluous detail and
misses its focus. Like Ethan, Steinbeck lavishes analysis on Margie but flounders in frustration and indecision. Margie has the last word, "You're a fake,
Ethan"; but her language is objectionable: "I'm betting
ten generations of Hawleys are going to kick your ass
around the block, and when they leave off you'll have
your own wet rope and salt to rub in the wounds."
Few readers quarrel with Steinbeck's earthiness, but
on this occasion the familiar idioms evade precision
and cheat the novel of its appropriate resolution. At
the end, Margie hedges on the obligations of her own
prescience. Like the novel itself, she represents a
major but unsatisfying literary effort (WOD).

YOUNG MUSTROVIC See MUSTROVIC, YOUNG (PH)

YOUNG PRIEST, THE. A passenger on the sightseeing bus
     that passes "The Pastures" at the end of the book.
     He thinks of building a church in the valley (PH).

YSOBEL See LA SANTA ROJA (CG)

Z

ZEIGLER, CAPTAIN. A pirate captain in Morgan's company
     whose nickname is "Tavern Keeper of the Sea" because
     of his habit of keeping his men at sea after a raid so
     that the men would spend their booty on liquor he sup-
     plies (CG).

APPENDICES

211

APPENDIX I

KEY TO ABBREVIATIONS

BB = Burning Bright (1950)

CG = Cup of Gold (1929)

CR = Cannery Row (1945)

EE = East of Eden (1952)

GW = The Grapes of Wrath (1939)

IDB = In Dubious Battle (1936)

LV = The Long Valley (1938)

MID = The Moon Is Down (1942)

OMM = Of Mice and Men (1937)

P = The Pearl (1947)

PH = The Pastures of Heaven (1932)

SMS = Steinbeck Monograph Series

SRP = The Short Reign of Pippin IV (1957)

ST = Sweet Thursday (1954)

TF = Tortilla Flat (1935)

TGU = To a God Unknown (1933)

WB = The Wayward Bus (1947)

WOD = The Winter of Our Discontent (1961)

APPENDIX II

A SELECTED BIBLIOGRAPHY

by Tetsumaro Hayashi

A. STEINBECK'S PUBLISHED WORKS

ALPHABETICAL CHECKLIST

America and Americans (1966)

Bombs Away (1942)

Burning Bright (1950)

Burning Bright (Play) (1951)

Cannery Row (1945)

Cup of Gold (1929)

East of Eden (1952)

The Forgotten Village (1941)

The Grapes of Wrath (1939)

In Dubious Battle (1936)

Journal of a Novel (Post-humous) (1969)

The Log from the Sea of Cortez (1951)

The Long Valley (1938)

The Moon Is Down (1942)

The Moon Is Down (Play) (1943)

Of Mice and Men (1937)

Of Mice and Men (Play) (1937)

Once There Was a War (1958)

The Pastures of Heaven (1932)

The Pearl (1947)

The Red Pony (1937)

A Russian Journal (1948)

Sea of Cortez (1941)

The Short Reign of Pippin IV (1957)

Sweet Thursday (1954)

Their Blood Is Strong (Pamph-let) (1938)

To a God Unknown (1933)

Tortilla Flat (1935)

Travels with Charley in Search of America (1962)

Vanderbilt Clinic (Pamphlet) (1947)

Viva Zapata! (Posthumous)
(1975)
The Wayward Bus (1947)

The Winter of Our Discontent
(1961)

CHRONOLOGICAL CHECKLIST

Cup of Gold (1929)

The Pastures of Heaven
(1932)

To a God Unknown (1933)

Tortilla Flat (1935)

In Dubious Battle (1936)

Of Mice and Men (1937)

Of Mice and Men (Play)
(1937)

The Red Pony (1937)

The Long Valley (1938)

Their Blood Is Strong
(Pamphlet) (1938)

The Grapes of Wrath (1939)

The Forgotten Village (1941)

Sea of Cortez (1941)

Bombs Away (1942)

The Moon Is Down (1942)

The Moon Is Down (Play)
(1943)

Cannery Row (1945)

The Pearl (1947)

Vanderbilt Clinic (Pamphlet)
(1947)

The Wayward Bus (1947)

A Russian Journal (1948)

Burning Bright (1950)

Burning Bright (Play) (1951)

The Log from the Sea of Cortez
(1951)

East of Eden (1952)

Sweet Thursday (1954)

The Short Reign of Pippin IV
(1957)

Once There Was a War (1958)

The Winter of Our Discontent
(1961)

Travels with Charley in Search
of America (1962)

America and Americans (1966)

Journal of a Novel (Posthumous)
(1969)

Viva Zapata! (Posthumous)
(1975)

GENRE CHECKLIST

NOVELS

Burning Bright (1950)

Cannery Row (1945)

Cup of Gold (1929)

East of Eden (1952)

The Grapes of Wrath (1939)

In Dubious Battle (1936)

The Long Valley (1938)

The Moon Is Down (1942)

Of Mice and Men (1937)

The Pastures of Heaven (1932)

The Pearl (1947)

The Red Pony (1937)

The Short Reign of Pippin IV (1957)

Sweet Thursday (1954)

To a God Unknown (1933)

Tortilla Flat (1935)

The Wayward Bus (1947)

The Winter of Our Discontent (1961)

PLAYS AND FILMSCRIPTS

Burning Bright (1951)

The Forgotten Village (1941)

The Moon Is Down (1943)

Of Mice and Men (1937)

Viva Zapata! (1975)

NON-FICTION

America and Americans (1966)

Bombs Away (1942)

Journal of a Novel (1969)

The Log from the Sea of Cortez (1951)

Once There Was a War (1958)

A Russian Journal (1948)

Sea of Cortez (1941)

Their Blood Is Strong (1938)

Travels with Charley in Search of America (1962)

Vanderbilt Clinic (1947)

B. RECENT BOOKS AND MONOGRAPHS OF JOHN STEINBECK (1972-76)

Books

Richard Astro. John Steinbeck and Edward F. Ricketts: The Shaping of a Novelist. Minneapolis: University of Minnesota Press, 1973.

_____ and Tetsumaro Hayashi, eds. Steinbeck: The Man and His Work. Corvallis: Oregon State Univ. Press, 1971.

Steve Crouch. Steinbeck Country. Palo Alto, Cal.: American West Publishing Co., 1973.

Warren French. John Steinbeck. Boston: Twayne, 1975 (revision of his 1961 book).

Adrian Goldstone and John Payne. John Steinbeck: A Biblio-
graphical Catalogue of the Adrian H. Goldstone Collection.
Austin: Humanities Research Center, University of Texas,
1974.

Tetsumaro Hayashi. A New Steinbeck Bibliography (1929-
1971). Metuchen, N.J.: Scarecrow Press, 1973.

_____, ed. Steinbeck's Literary Dimension: A Guide to
Comparative Studies. Metuchen, N.J.: Scarecrow Press,
1973.

_____, ed. A Study Guide to Steinbeck's "The Long Val-
ley." Ann Arbor, Mich.: Pierian Press, 1976.

Howard Levant. The Novels of John Steinbeck: A Critical
Study. Columbia: University of Missouri Press, 1974.

Peter Lisca, ed. John Steinbeck, "The Grapes of Wrath":
Text and Criticism. New York: Viking Press, 1972.

Nelson Valjean. John Steinbeck: The Errant Knight: An
Intimate Biography of His California Years. San Francisco:
Chronicle Books, 1975.

Tom Weber. All the Heroes Are Dead: The Ecology of
John Steinbeck's Cannery Row. San Francisco: Ramparts
Press, 1974.

Monographs

Richard Astro and Joel Hedgpeth. Steinbeck and the Sea,
Proceedings of a Conference Held at Marine Science Center
Auditorium, Newport, Oregon (May 4, 1974). Newport,
Ore.: Oregon State University Sea Grant College, 1975.

Reloy Garcia. Steinbeck and D. H. Lawrence: Fictive
Voices and the Ethical Imperative (SMS, No. 2). Muncie,
Ind.: Steinbeck Society, Ball State University, 1972.

Tetsumaro Hayashi, ed. Steinbeck Criticism: A Review of
Book-Length Studies (1939-1973) (SMS, No. 4). Muncie,
Ind.: Steinbeck Society, Ball State University, 1974.

_____, ed. Steinbeck and the Arthurian Theme (SMS,
No. 5). Muncie, Ind.: Steinbeck Society, Ball State Uni-

versity, 1975.

Lawrence W. Jones. John Steinbeck as Fabulist, edited by
Marston LaFrance (SMS, No. 3). Muncie, Ind.: Steinbeck
Society, Ball State University, 1973.

Roy S. Simmonds. Steinbeck's Literary Achievement (SMS,
No. 6). Muncie, Ind.: Steinbeck Society, Ball State University, 1976.

Other Items of Importance

The Steinbeck Quarterly (Special The Long Valley numbers:
Volume V, nos. 3-4, 1972 and Volume VI, no. 1, 1973),
edited by Tetsumaro Hayashi.

The University of Windsor Review (Special Steinbeck Issue,
Spring 1973), edited by John Ditsky; includes 4 papers which
were presented at the MLA Steinbeck Society Meeting, 1972.

C. RECENT DOCTORAL DISSERTATIONS ON JOHN STEIN-
BECK (1968-1974) (arranged chronologically)

Frederick Feied. "Steinbeck's Depression Novels: The Ecological Basis." Ph.D., Columbia University, 1968.

Richard Astro. "Into the Cornucopia: Steinbeck's Vision of
Nature and the Ideal Man." Ph.D., University of Washington, 1969.

Gary Bleeker. "Setting and Animal Tropes in the Fiction of
John Steinbeck." Ph.D., University of Nebraska, 1969.

Charles Mansfield McLain. "A Syntactic Study of Four Non-
Fiction Books by John Steinbeck." Ed.D., University of
Colorado, 1970.

Raymond Joel Silverman. "The Short Story Composite:
Forms, Functions, and Applications." Ph.D., University of
Michigan, 1970.

Sheldon S. Kagan. " 'Goin' Down the Road Feelin' Bad' ...
John Steinbeck's The Grapes of Wrath and Migrant Folklore."
Ph.D., University of Pennsylvania, 1971.

Joyce Diann Compton Brown. "Animal Symbolism and Imagery in John Steinbeck's Fiction from 1929 through 1939."
Ph.D., University of Southern Mississippi, 1972.

Raymond L. Griffith. "Dissonant Symphony: Multilevel
Duality in the Fiction of John Steinbeck." Ph.D., Loyola
University of Chicago, 1972.

Sunita Goel Jain. "John Steinbeck's Concept of Man." Ph.D.,
University of Nebraska, 1972.

Clifford L. Lewis. "John Steinbeck: Architect of the Unconscious." Ph.D., University of Texas, Austin, 1972.

Betty L. Perez. "The Collaborative Role of John Steinbeck
and Edward F. Ricketts in the Narrative Section of Sea of
Cortez." Ph.D., University of Florida, 1972.

Mimi Reisel Gladstein. "The Indestructible Woman in the
Works of Faulkner, Hemingway, and Steinbeck." Ph.D.,
University of New Mexico, 1973.

Steve Serota. "The Function of the Grotesque in the Works
of John Steinbeck." Ph.D., Oklahoma State University,
1973.

George H. Spies, III. "John Steinbeck's The Grapes of
Wrath and Frederick Manfred's The Golden Bowl: A Comparative Study." Ed.D., Ball State University, 1973.

Harry Stuurmans. "John Steinbeck's Lover's Quarrel with
America." Ed.D., University of Chicago, 1973.

Frederick Joseph Koloc. "John Steinbeck's In Dubious Battle: Background, Reputation and Artistry." Ph.D., University of Pittsburgh, 1974.

Barbara A. McDaniel. "Self-Alienating Characters in the
Fiction of John Steinbeck." Ph.D., North Texas State University, 1974.

Angela Patterson. "The Women of John Steinbeck's Novels
in the Light of Humanistic Psychology." Ph.D., United
States International University, 1974.

Kenneth D. Swan. "Perspectives of the Fiction of John
Steinbeck." Ed.D., Ball State University, 1974.

cf. Tetsumaro Hayashi, ed. John Steinbeck: A Guide to the
Doctoral Dissertations (1946-1969) (SMS, No. 1). Steinbeck
Society, Ball State University, 1971.   Hayashi plans to publish a sequel to the 1971 monograph in the near future; it
will be John Steinbeck: Research Opportunities and Disser-
tation Abstracts (1968-1978).

APPENDIX III

CONTRIBUTORS*

ASTRO, RICHARD

Chairman and Professor of English and Assistant to the Vice
President for Research, Oregon State University; member
and former Chairman of the Editorial Board of the Steinbeck
Quarterly; director of the Steinbeck Conference held in 1970
at Oregon State University; co-director, with Joel Hedgpeth,
of a conference called "Steinbeck and the Sea," held in 1974
at the Marine Research Center of the Oregon State University; author/editor of such books as Steinbeck: The Man
and His Work, with Tetsumaro Hayashi (Oregon State University Press, 1971); John Steinbeck and Edward F. Ricketts:
The Shaping of a Novelist (University of Minnesota Press,
1973); and Hemingway in Our Time, with Jackson Benson
(Oregon State University Press, 1974). [BB, CG, CR]

BENTON, ROBERT M.

Associate Professor of English, Central Washington State
College; keynote speaker at the Second MLA Steinbeck Society
Meeting held in New York City in 1973; published articles in
such journals as American Literature, Bulletin of the New
York Public Library, Early American Literature, and Stein-
beck Quarterly; published essays in such books as Steinbeck:
The Man and His Work, edited by Astro and Hayashi (1971)
and A Study Guide to Steinbeck: A Handbook to His Major
Works, edited by Hayashi (Scarecrow Press, 1974). [IDB,
LV, MID]

---

*At the end of each contributor's biographical sketch, the
symbols indicate the novels each covered in producing the
entries for this volume.

COURT, FRANKLIN E.

Assistant Professor of English, Northern Illinois University; published articles in such journals as English Literature in Transition, Modern Fiction Studies, and Steinbeck Quarterly; published an essay in a book, A Study Guide to Steinbeck: A Handbook to His Major Works, edited by Hayashi (1974). [OMM, P, PH]

HAYASHI, TETSUMARO (EDITOR)

Associate Professor of English, Ball State University; Folger Shakespeare Library Fellow, 1972; founder/director of the John Steinbeck Society of America; founder/editor of the Steinbeck Quarterly; general editor/project director of the Steinbeck Monograph Series; author/editor of twelve books including Steinbeck's Literary Dimension (Scarecrow Press, 1973); Steinbeck: The Man and His Work, with Richard Astro (Oregon State University Press, 1971); and A Study Guide to Steinbeck: A Handbook to His Major Works (Scarecrow Press, 1974); author/editor of seven monographs including John Steinbeck: A Guide to the Doctoral Dissertations (Steinbeck Society, 1971); Steinbeck Criticism: A Review of Book-Length Studies (1939-1973) (Steinbeck Society, 1974); Steinbeck and the Arthurian Theme (Steinbeck Society, 1975); author of over 40 articles which were published in such journals as East-West Review, Forum, Serif, Shakespeare Newsletter, Shakespeare Quarterly, and Steinbeck Quarterly; author of twelve short stories, three of which won literary prizes in New York City.

MORSBERGER, ROBERT E.

Professor of English and Chairman of the Department of English and Modern Languages, California State Polytechnic University; author/editor of numerous books and over 30 articles which were published in such journals as American Literature, New England Quarterly, Shakespeare Quarterly, Steinbeck Quarterly, and Western American Literature; published an essay, "Steinbeck's Zapata," in Steinbeck: The Man and His Work, edited by Astro and Hayashi (1971), and another essay, "Steinbeck on Screen," in A Study Guide to Steinbeck: A Handbook to His Major Works, edited by Hayashi (1974); more recently edited Steinbeck's Viva Zapata! published by the Viking Press in 1975; Michigan State University/USAID advisor in English, University of Nigeria, 1964-66; President of the Southern California Chapter of the American Studies Association. [EE, GW]

PETERSON, RICHARD F.

Associate Professor of English at Southern Illinois University; published articles in Expositor, Forum (Ball State University) ICarbS, and Steinbeck Quarterly; published essays in Steinbeck's Literary Dimension, edited by Hayashi (1973) and A Study Guide to Steinbeck: A Handbook to His Major Works, edited by Hayashi (1974); member of the Editorial Board of the Steinbeck Quarterly. [SRP, ST, TGU]

SLATER, JOHN F.

Associate Professor of English, University of Wyoming; published articles in Papers on Language and Literature and Steinbeck Quarterly; published an essay in A Study Guide to Steinbeck: A Handbook to His Major Works, edited by Hayashi (1974). [TF, WB, WOD]